LIBRARY OF NEW TESTAMENT STUDIES

655

formerly the Journal for the Study of the New Testament Supplement series

Editor
Chris Keith

Editorial Board
Dale C. Allison, Lynn H. Cohick, R. Alan Culpepper, Craig A. Evans, Robert Fowler, Simon J. Gathercole, Juan Hernández Jr., John S. Kloppenborg, Michael Labahn, Matthew V. Novenson, Love L. Sechrest, Robert Wall, Catrin H. Williams, Brittany E. Wilson

The Impact of Bodily Experience on Paul's Resurrection Theology

Kai-Hsuan Chang

LONDON • NEW YORK • OXFORD • NEW DELHI • SYDNEY

T&T CLARK

Bloomsbury Publishing Plc

50 Bedford Square, London, WC1B 3DP, UK

1385 Broadway, New York, NY 10018, USA

29 Earlsfort Terrace, Dublin 2, Ireland

BLOOMSBURY, T&T CLARK and the T&T Clark logo are trademarks of
Bloomsbury Publishing Plc

First published in Great Britain 2022
This paperback edition published 2023

Copyright © Kai-Hsuan Chang, 2022

Kai-Hsuan Chang has asserted his right under the Copyright, Designs and Patents Act, 1988,
to be identified as Author of this work.

For legal purposes the Acknowledgments on p. ix constitute an
extension of this copyright page.

Cover design: Charlotte James

All rights reserved. No part of this publication may be reproduced or transmitted
in any form or by any means, electronic or mechanical, including photocopying,
recording, or any information storage or retrieval system, without prior permission
in writing from the publishers.

Bloomsbury Publishing Plc does not have any control over, or responsibility for, any
third-party websites referred to or in this book. All internet addresses given in this
book were correct at the time of going to press. The author and publisher regret any
inconvenience caused if addresses have changed or sites have ceased to exist, but
can accept no responsibility for any such changes.

A catalogue record for this book is available from the British Library.

Library of Congress Cataloging-in-Publication Data
Names: Chang, Kai-Hsuan, author.
Title: The impact of bodily experience on Paul's resurrection theology / Kai-Hsuan Chang.
Description: London, UK ; New York, NY, USA : T&T Clark/Bloomsbury Publishing Plc, 2021. |
Series: The library of new testament studies, 2513–8790 ; volume 655 |
Includes bibliographical references and index. |
Summary: "This volume argues that bodily experience contributed significantly to the
development of Paul's ideas about resurrection, as seen in his extant
letters"– Provided by publisher.
Identifiers: LCCN 2021009031 (print) | LCCN 2021009032 (ebook) |
ISBN 9780567700919 (hb) | ISBN 9780567700926 (epdf) |
ISBN 9780567700940 (ebook)
Subjects: LCSH: Bible. Epistles of Paul–Theology. | Resurrection–Biblical teaching. |
Paul, the Apostle, Saint. | Human body–Religious aspects–hristianity.
Classification: LCC BS2655.R35 C43 2021 (print) | LCC BS2655.R35 (ebook) |
DDC 232.9/7–dc23
LC record available at https://lccn.loc.gov/2021009031
LC ebook record available at https://lccn.loc.gov/2021009032

ISBN: HB: 978-0-5677-0091-9
PB: 978-0-5677-0095-7
ePDF: 978-0-5677-0092-6
ePUB: 978-0-5677-0094-0

Series: Library of New Testament Studies, volume 655
ISSN 2513–8790

Typeset by Newgen KnowledgeWorks Pvt. Ltd., Chennai, India

To find out more about our authors and books visit www.bloomsbury.com
and sign up for our newsletters.

Contents

List of Figures			viii
Acknowledgments			ix
1	Introduction: Thinking within the Body		1
	1.1	Embodied: The Way the Human Mind Works	2
	1.2	Paul's Embodiment: A Fuller Range of Contextual Influence	5
	1.3	Toward an Embodied Approach to Paul's Development	11
2	A Seed of Paul's Development: The Reversal Schema		15
	2.1	The Experiential Patterns of Complex Thinking	17
		2.1.1 The Verticality Schema and the Life/Death Contrast	17
		2.1.2 The Container Schema and Cosmic Polarity	20
	2.2	The Traditional Experiential Patterns of Heavenly Ascent and Resurrection	23
		2.2.1 Heavenly Ascent, Resurrection, and the Path Schema	23
		2.2.2 The Relation between Resurrection and Ascent: A Schematic Analysis	27
	2.3	Paul's Alternative Experiential Pattern	31
	2.4	Conceptual Blending Theory: An Analytic Tool for Development	34
		2.4.1 The Single-Scope Network for Explaining Metaphorical Expressions	36
		2.4.2 The More Complex Blends and Their Meaning Constructions	38
	2.5	Conclusion	39
3	"We Will All Be Transformed": Transformation at Resurrection		41
	3.1	Experiential Context: Death Rites and the Corpse	42
		3.1.1 The Practice of Death Rites as an Important Context	43
		3.1.2 The Decomposition of the Body in Death Rites	47
	3.2	Intellectual Context: Cosmology and Afterlife—in Light of the Experiential Context	48

	3.3		The Seed-Sowing Metaphor and the Argument of Reversal	53
	3.4		"What You Sow Is Not the Body That Is to Be": A Conceptual Blending Analysis	58
		3.4.1	The First Blend: Resurrection and the Metaphor of Seed Sowing and Growing	59
		3.4.2	The Second Blend: The Reversal Resurrection and Cosmic Polarity	62
		3.4.3	The Ψυχικός-Πνευματικός Opposition and the Third Blend	67
	3.5		Conclusion	69
4	"We All Are Being Transformed": Experienced Transformation			71
	4.1		Intellectual Context: The Concept of the Body	72
	4.2		Experiential Context: The Perception of the Body in Pneumatic Experience	76
		4.2.1	The Ecstatic Experience of the Spirit Shared by Paul and His Congregations	77
		4.2.2	The Disturbance of Body Perception and Its Cultural Interpretations	82
	4.3		"The Body of Christ": Re-Picturing Pneumatic Experience with Ritual Experience	86
		4.3.1	The First Input: The Body Metaphor	87
		4.3.2	The Second Input (1): Applying Conceptual Blending Theory to Baptism	89
		4.3.3	The Second Input (2): Baptized in the Spirit	92
		4.3.4	The Third Input: Receiving the Spirit Conceptualized as Drinking Water	98
		4.3.5	The Overall Conceptual Blend and Its Effects	101
	4.4		Conclusion	106
5	"Baptized into His Death": The Convergence of Two Aspects of Transformation			107
	5.1		Paul's Two Aspects of Bodily Transformation	107
		5.1.1	Intellectual Context: A Blend of Intellectual Traditions and Paul's Suffering	109
		5.1.2	Experiential Context: Mortality and Paul's Clarification of Experienced Transformation	115
		5.1.3	Still in the Future	118

	5.2	An Unexpected Convergence Here and Now in Baptism	123
		5.2.1 The Conceptual Blend in Romans 6:3–4: Paul's Previous Teachings and His Argument	124
		5.2.2 "You Were Also Raised with Him": An Unexpected Convergence in Baptism	129
	5.3	Conclusion	135
6	Conclusion		137

Bibliography	143
Ancient Source Index	153
Author Index	158
Subject Index	160

Figures

2.1	The Verticality Schema	18
2.2	The Container Schema	21
2.3	The Hellenistic Conceptualization of the Heavenly and the Earthly Realms	22
2.4	The Path Schema	24
2.5	The Jewish Conceptualization of Heavenly Ascent	25
2.6	The Jewish Conceptualization of Resurrection as Restoration	25
2.7	The Jewish Conceptualization of Divine Judgment and Exaltation/Condemnation	28
2.8	Later Jewish Conceptualization of General Resurrection and Judgment	30
2.9	The Reversal Schema	32
2.10	Structuring and Compressing the Focus Input	37
3.1	Paul's Conceptualization of Resurrection through the Reversal Schema	54
3.2	The Resurrected Body and the Sowing Metaphor	60
3.3	Reversal Pattern of Resurrection and Heaven-Earth Polarity	64
3.4	Temporal Polarity from Transformation and the Adam-Christ Typology	68
4.1	The Cosmo-Somatic Hierarchy	74
4.2	The First Input of the Overall Blend in 1 Cor 12:13	89
4.3	The Second Input of the Overall Blend in 1 Cor 12:13	93
4.4	The Third Input of the Overall Blend in 1 Cor 12:13	100
4.5	The Conceptual Blend between the Reception of the Spirit and Baptism in 1 Cor 12:13	102
5.1	The Conceptual Blend Triggered by the Metaphor of Treasure	111
5.2	The Conceptual Blend Triggered by the Metaphors of Dwellings and Clothing	119
5.3	The Conceptual Blend between the Christ Event and Baptism	125

Acknowledgments

This work began as a doctoral dissertation at the Toronto School of Theology in the University of Toronto, and I would like to thank those who generously helped, in a variety of ways, to bring it to completion.

Thanks, first of all, are due to my supervisor, Professor Colleen Shantz, for her consistent support, warm encouragement, thought-provoking discussion, and wise advice at different stages of the project. Thank you to my external examiner, Professor Richard DeMaris, for offering extremely helpful feedback and continually caring about the publication of this work. Thanks to members of my committee, Professor John Kloppenborg, Professor Terence Donaldson, and Professor Judith Newman, for their careful reading, encouragement, and insightful comments. Thanks also to the University of Toronto for their incredible academic resources.

I am extremely grateful to China Evangelical Seminary and the Cherith Foundation for their trust in me and their financial support that made this work possible. Thanks also to the LNTS series of Bloomsbury, particularly the series editor, Professor Chris Keith, for this opportunity to publish with the series and to Sarah Blake for her tireless assistance. Thank you to Charles Meeks for proofreading my dissertation and the revised form as now presented, and Gregory Fewster and Warren Campbell for making suggestions during the proposal stage.

I am also extremely grateful that I made some best friends who made my journey of doctoral study enjoyable and memorable. Thanks to Bruce, Greg, Warren, and Ethan for forming a very fun, open-minded, and ambitious group that fully engaged in academic conferences and various other adventures. Thanks to Jeehoon, Jin, and Heejun for maintaining my mental health with happiness and thoughtful care. Thanks also to Corina, Brigidda, Sherin, Mari, Carolyn, and Jason for playing a significant part of this wonderful journey.

With the utmost gratitude, I wish to thank my parents for their consistent support throughout the decades. You provided me resources and shaped my personality to enjoy academic endeavors. Thanks also to my sister for understanding and caring.

Finally, thanks to the lovely ladies in my family, Shalom and Lucy, for their unconditional love, full sincerity and acceptance, unceasing laughter, and our numerous joyful and memorable moments. I hope this work may somehow reflect the enduring love and hope that you have been sharing with me, and it is to you that this work is dedicated.

1

Introduction: Thinking within the Body

Paul struggled with the hope of resurrection in Christ, and he struggled physically. It was difficult for Paul and his communities to conceive and articulate this hope in detail because the idea of resurrection was contradictory to the nature of the human body—everyone could see that the body wore away daily and that it would eventually decompose into dust. The Corinthians asked, "How are the dead raised? With what kind of body do they come?" (1 Cor 15:35 NRSV). However, Paul also articulates a theology that demonstrates that his view of resurrection changed and developed throughout his ministry, prompted by the interplay between his physical struggles and his theological reflection on resurrection. Paul was inspired by a variety of physical experiences in religious activities, such as the ritual experience in baptism (e.g., 1 Cor 12:13; Gal 27–28; Rom 6:3–4) and the ecstatic experience of the Spirit (e.g., 1 Cor 14:14–15; 2 Cor 12:1–4), in addition to the daily experience of mortality. At times, these religious activities provided Paul with alternative experiences of the body and, consequently, an alternative physical basis for conceptualizing the hope of resurrection. This development resulted in the diverse articulations about resurrection throughout his corpus of writings.

In this book, we will explore and explain the development of Paul's resurrection theology by looking at the correlation between his bodily experiences and his diverse articulations about resurrection. Faced with puzzling variations in Paul's claims, including those that he makes about resurrection, the law, Jews and Gentiles, and eschatology, scholars have long wondered whether, how, and to what extent Paul's thought might have changed or developed during the extent of time within which he composed his extant letters. While some variations can be explained as contingent expressions addressing different contextual issues, this explanation does not logically exclude the possibility that, in some cases, Paul had actually developed his ideas through his interactions with these contexts. Resurrection, among other topics, is a focal point of the modern scholarly discussion about Paul's development. Thus, by emphasizing the bodily aspect, this study is an exploration of the way that Paul's resurrection thought might have developed through contextual interactions. It argues that his thought about resurrection might be influenced not only by ideas available in his intellectual interaction with cultural backgrounds but also by a fuller range of his contextual experience. Specifically, it demonstrates that the bodily experience in some religious activities in Paul's time—death rites, spirit possession, and baptism—contributed significantly to the formation and development of his resurrection theology.

Such an exploration of the influence of experience on thought requires a methodological link between Paul's intellect and his bodily experience. Colleen Shantz has posed this methodological question in her book *Paul in Ecstasy*: how should we consider the emergence and formation of Paul's ideas while recognizing that he is "a full-blooded human agent" who does more than think and write?[1] Indeed, the demand for an embodied understanding of Paul and his mind is pressing and justified since it is generally agreed in New Testament studies that Paul should not be considered as a systematic theologian and that his letters are occasional products emergent from his contextual interactions with particular communities. However, as Shantz observes, in spite of more and more exceptions, a mind-body dualism is still lurking behind New Testament studies, and the body tends to remain peripheral in scholarly understandings of Paul.[2] The rather disembodied portraits of Paul's mind, as Shantz indicates, are partly due to the methodological difficulty of analyzing texts in terms of the body. After all, our most reliable access to Paul is through the texts that he produced or interacted with, and the one thing that we can directly identify in the texts that might have interacted with Paul's ideas are also ideas.[3] There exists a methodological gap between the body, on the one hand, and texts and articulated ideas, on the other. Thus, much attention has been paid to discursive and literary evidence, and the categorization of Paul's interactions with his environment that have contributed to the formation of his ideas has been largely limited to intellectual activities: borrowing or synthesizing ideas, accommodating various worldviews or values, and arguing with purported opponents who advocated different ideas. The absence of the body in our understanding of Paul is particularly problematic when dealing with the formation of Paul's resurrection-related ideas. Resurrection is itself a hope about the body and is naturally conceptualized in relation to the body, either in accordance with or in tension with the experience of the body.

1.1 Embodied: The Way the Human Mind Works

The concept of embodiment provides the theoretical basis for this study's methodology to explore the interaction between the body and text. In opposition to the body-mind dualism, embodied cognition studies and many cognitive linguists claim that our cognition is "embodied" in the sense that our somatic experience provides us the basis for the formation of many concepts that are most fundamental to our thinking and, in this sense, directly influences our conceptualization, the construction of meaning, and

---

[1] C. Shantz, *Paul in Ecstasy: The Neurobiology of the Apostle's Life and Thought* (Cambridge: Cambridge University Press, 2009), 2–6.
[2] Ibid., 3, 27–33.
[3] Ibid., 3–6.

language.⁴ According to the concept of embodiment, Paul's somatic experience had direct impact on his ideas and linguistic articulations.

Our experience and construal of reality is largely mediated through the sensory-motor systems of our physical bodies. Thus, because of the very nature of our bodies, we experience the world differently from other species and accordingly have a unique perception of the world.⁵ In other words, our experience and perception are embodied—they are bodily shaped and conditioned. For example, since the human visual system has three kinds of color channels, we have a specific experience of color that differs from that of rabbits, who have two color channels. Consequently, as Vyvyan Evans and Melanie Green indicate, our cognition is also embodied because "we can only talk about what we can perceive and conceive, and the things that we can perceive and conceive derive from embodied experience."⁶ Edward Slingerland also indicates that there is "a growing consensus in the fields of neuroscience and cognitive science" that human thought is largely derived from recurrent patterns of bodily experience.⁷ Thus, it is not possible to investigate the human mind—and so language—independently from the body. As psychologist Arthur M. Glenberg and his collaborators state, "the fundamental tenet of embodied cognition research is that thinking is not something that is divorced from the body; instead, thinking is an activity strongly influenced by the body and the brain interacting with the environment."⁸

That our mind and language are both somatically grounded is particularly observable in our metaphorical thinking and expressions. As George Lakoff and Mark Johnson indicate, a more concrete conceptual domain can function as a (usually somatic) basis from which a "conceptual metaphor" emerges that allows a more abstract domain to be understood.⁹ For example, a metaphorical expression "we have a long way to go before this project is done" is structured in relation to a concrete, recurrent bodily experience of walking on a journey, which functions as a somatic basis allowing us to understand the expression itself.¹⁰ Other metaphorical expressions that describe being in states like love or depression, such as "I am in love" or "she is out of her depression," further illustrate this point. In these expressions, abstract concepts like love and depression are metaphorically conceptualized through our repeated somatic experience of containment and containers. As Evans and Green indicate, due to the nature of our physical body, we experience an enclosed region in space (such as a room, a house, or an elevator) as a container that can constrain our activity,

---

⁴ V. Evans and M. Green, *Cognitive Linguistics: An Introduction* (Edinburgh: Edinburgh University, 2006), 46–7.
⁵ See ibid., 45.
⁶ Ibid., 46.
⁷ E. Slingerland, *What Science Offers the Humanities: Integrating Body and Culture* (Cambridge: Cambridge University Press, 2008), 56. On pages 56–9 and 162–3, Slingerland lists many works that provide empirical evidence to support this claim. See also the summary of evidence in Evans and Green, *Cognitive Linguistics*, 240–3.
⁸ A. M. Glenberg, J. K. Witt, and J. Metcalfe, "From the Revolution to Embodiment: 25 Years of Cognitive Psychology," *Perspectives on Psychological Science* 8 no. 5 (2013): 573.
⁹ G. Lakoff and M. Johnson, *Metaphors We Live By* (Chicago, IL: University of Chicago Press, 1980). M. Johnson, *The Meaning of the Body: Aesthetics of Human Understanding* (Chicago, IL: University of Chicago Press, 2007).
¹⁰ Johnson, *The Meaning of the Body*, 177.

and this sort of embodied experience allows us to conceptualize states such as love or depression in which we usually feel unable to escape the situation or change our mood or behavior.[11] By utilizing such metaphorical projections, recurrent patterns of somatic experience are an integral part of the functioning of human cognition and directly form our perception, conceptualization, and linguistic construction and articulation of the world.[12] Thus, our recurrent embodied experience not only shapes the way we perceive and make sense of the world but also fundamentally influence the way we conceptualize more complex and abstract ideas. In this sense, Paul, and everyone else, had to think within the body.

This kind of impact of recurrent experience on human cognition and, consequently, on the construction of complex ideas is also a prominent phenomenon in ritual and religious experience in addition to experience in daily life. As a kind of bodily practice, ritual and religious activities create repeated patterns of bodily experience. Thus, religious activities not only express or symbolize ideas but also provide recurrent experiential patterns that generate ideas and linguistic expressions, a process that participants in religious activities might not be consciously aware of.[13] Based on the concept of embodiment, the interface between bodily experience in religious activities and ideas articulated in texts is considered in this study as reciprocal and interactive. In other words, while practice and experience in religious activities reflect the theological ideas of Paul and his communities, these activities might also contribute to the development of ideas through experiential patterns.

Recently, based upon embodied cognition theory, Frederick S. Tappenden applied cognitive linguistic tools to the resurrection-related ideas in Paul and in Jewish traditions. In so doing, he breaks down resurrection ideas into experiential patterns. As I will introduce in Chapter 2, he demonstrates that these complex ideas about resurrection are fundamentally grounded in recurrent patterns of somatic experience and are imagined and expressed through conceptual metaphors. For example, through our repeated experience of verticality, such as perceiving a tree or climbing ladders, resurrection is usually conceptualized through metaphors like "resurrection is being awake" (e.g., Dan 12:1–3) and "resurrection is being raised up" (e.g., 1 Thess 4:13–18).[14] Tappenden's application of cognitive linguistic tools to Paul thus provides a methodological link between somatic experience and Paul's thinking about resurrection. As he concludes, Paul's "expectations are somatically oriented, his thinking corporally grounded."[15] Thus, Tappenden's work opens the door for this study to explore a fuller range of contextual influence on Paul's resurrection ideas, especially the contextual influence from somatic experience.

---

[11] Evans and Green, *Cognitive Linguistics*, 158.
[12] M. Johnson, *The Body in the Mind: The Bodily Basis of Meaning, Imagination, and Reason* (Chicago, IL: University of Chicago Press, 1987), xix.
[13] R. Uro, *Ritual and Christian Beginnings: A Socio-Cognitive Analysis* (Oxford: Oxford University Press, 2016), 156.
[14] F. S. Tappenden, *Resurrection in Paul: Cognition, Metaphor, and Transformation* (Atlanta: Society of Biblical Literature, 2016), 46–54.
[15] Ibid., 1.

1.2 Paul's Embodiment: A Fuller Range of Contextual Influence

While New Testament scholars agree that Paul was a situational thinker, and his letters were contextual products, unfortunately the insight of embodied cognition studies and the tools of cognitive linguistics have not been applied to the way Paul's thought might have been influenced by his context. Consequently, the impact of Paul's embodied experience in his context has been largely neglected by previous works on both sides of the long-standing debate concerning Paul's thought-development. On the one hand, those who reject developmental perspectives on Paul dismiss the essential influence of context on his thought altogether; on the other hand, those who propose developmental hypotheses of Paul only focus on the influence of his intellectual context and neglect his experiential context.

Scholars who reject developmental hypotheses typically explain Paul's diverse statements in his letters as contingent expressions that he produced simply in response to different contextual issues. This contextual explanation of Paul's variations is largely driven by discussion about Paul's diverse claims about the law, an issue that has gained much attention because it challenges the long-standing consensus regarding the law/gospel or work/faith contrast as the organizing center in Paul's thought-system.[16] As Jouette M. Bassler indicates, during the past few decades, Paul's diverse claims about the law, together with the nuanced depictions of Judaism in Pauline studies, have caused the "collapse of the traditional models" for understanding Paul.[17] Responding to the collapse, many scholars have tried to defend the coherence of Paul's thought system with another set of central ideas (such as Christology, reconciliation, eschatology, death and resurrection, and mystical participation in Christ) that is more consistent than the ideas about the law and explain Paul's differences with contextual reasons. This contextual approach to Paul with an assumption of unchanging central convictions has also been applied to the variations in Paul's resurrection thought.[18]

---

[16] For the traditional consensus regarding this contrast and the new paradigms, see T. L. Donaldson, *Paul and the Gentiles: Remapping the Apostle's Convictional World* (Minneapolis, MN: Fortress Press, 1997), 3–27. For the issue about Paul's attitude toward the law, see E. P. Sanders, *Paul and Palestinian Judaism: A Comparison of Patterns of Religion* (Philadelphia: Fortress Press, 1977); J. D. G. Dunn, "The New Perspective on Paul: Paul and the Law," in *The New Perspective on Paul: Collected Essays* (ed. J. D. G. Dunn; Tübingen: Mohr Siebeck, 2005), 131–42. S. Westerholm, *Perspectives Old and New on Paul: The "Lutheran" Paul and His Critics* (Grand Rapids, MI: W. B. Eerdmans, 2004). T. L. Donaldson, "Zealot and Convert: The Origin of Paul's Christ-Torah Antithesis," *CBQ* 51 no. 4 (1989): 655–82.

[17] J. M. Bassler, "Preface," in *Pauline Theology Volume 1: Thessalonians, Philippians, Galatians, Philemon* (ed. Jouette M. Bassler; Minneapolis, MN: Fortress Press, 1991), ix.

[18] E.g., G. Vos, "Alleged Development in Paul's Teaching on the Resurrection," *Princeton Theological Review* 27 (1929): 193–226; J. Weiss, *The History of Primitive Christianity* (trans. and ed. F. C. Grant; New York: Wilson-Erickson, 1937); J. Lowe, "An Examination of Attempts to Detect Developments in St. Paul's Theology," *Journal of Theological Studies* 42 (1941): 129–42; V. P. Furnish, "Development in Paul's Thought," *JAAR* 38 (1970): 289–303; J. Gillman, "Signals of Transformation in 1 Thessalonians 4:13–18," in *CBQ* 47 no. 2 (1985): 263–81; and B. F. Meyer, "Did Paul's View of the Resurrection of the Dead Undergo Development?" *Theological Studies* 47 no. 3 (1986): 363–87. See also Tappenden, *Resurrection in Paul*, 77 (footnote 72).

However, the contextual explanation and the developmental explanation of Paul's variations are not mutually exclusive. In fact, the developmental approach to Paul relies on the scholarship of the contextual approach because Paul's development emerged from his context. This interactive relationship between Paul's context and thought is already recognized in one of the most influential models of the contextual approach to Paul: J. Christiaan Beker's model of "coherence and contingency." With this model, Beker tries to consider the reciprocal, dialogical interaction between the coherence conviction in Paul's thought and the contingent expression addressing a particular context.[19] For Beker, the coherence of Paul's gospel is not one specific idea or center of Paul's thought but "constituted by the apocalyptic interpretation of the death and resurrection of Christ."[20] In other words, the coherence "does not become a static, unalterable structure of thought" but is interpreted through a "fluid relation" to the various contingent situations, a "hermeneutical process" in which there is always a possibility of "compromise or accommodation" of the coherence.[21] As Paul J. Achtemeier indicates, Beker's model does not logically exclude the possibility that a "new coherence" could emerge at some point from some debates or other contingent situations that demand theological breakthrough.[22]

Following Beker, the four volumes of *Pauline Theology* edited by Jouette M. Bassler, David M. Hay, and E. Elizabeth Johnson (1991–1997) represent a comprehensive effort from scholars treating Paul as a situational thinker and redescribing the nature of Paul's thought-system. In these four volumes, scholars examine Paul's thought letter by letter, and Beker's contextual model of "coherence and contingency" is taken as a leading approach. For example, modifying Beker's work, Bassler's contextual model makes the role of experience more explicit by suggesting that "the raw material of Paul's theology (the kerygmatic story, scripture, traditions, etc.) passed through the lens of Paul's experience (his common Christian experience as well as his unique experience as one 'set apart by God for the gospel') and generated a coherent (and characteristic) set of convictions."[23] These convictions, Bassler argues, were then interpreted into specific expressions in the contingent situation of each letter.[24] What is missing here, however, is a rigorous way to identify in Paul's letters the impact of experience on his convictions and expressions. More recently, Alan Segal and Shantz

---

[19] J. C. Beker, "Recasting Pauline Theology: The Coherence-Contingency Schema as Interpretive Model," in *Pauline Theology Volume 1: Thessalonians, Philippians, Galatians, Philemon* (ed. Jouette M. Bassler; Minneapolis, MN: Fortress Press, 1991), 17–21. See also J. C. Beker, *Paul the Apostle: The Triumph of God in Life and Thought* (Philadelphia: Fortress Press, 1980).

[20] Beker, "Recasting Pauline Theology," 18.

[21] Ibid., 19.

[22] P. J. Achtemeier, "Finding the Way to Paul's Theology: A Response to J. Christiaan Beker and J. Paul Sampley," in *Pauline Theology Volume 1: Thessalonians, Philippians, Galatians, Philemon* (ed. Jouette M. Bassler; Minneapolis, MN: Fortress Press, 1991), 28. However, Beker rejects the developmental character of Paul's thought. He treats Paul in a rather disembodied way when he describes that Paul's coherence of the gospel "incarnates" itself into the contingencies, and so understands the coherence as unchanging and its relationship to the contingency as unidirectional. See Beker, "Recasting Pauline Theology," 21–2.

[23] J. M. Bassler, "Paul's Theology: Whence and Whither?" in *Pauline Theology Volume II: 1 & 2 Corinthians* (ed. David M. Hay; Minneapolis, MN: Fortress Press, 1991), 11.

[24] Ibid.

have appealed to neurobiological studies in their treatments of some of Paul's somatic-oriented ideas. They argue that somatic experiences, especially ecstatic experiences, might have contributed to Paul's ideas of participation in Christ, resurrection, and bodily transformation.[25] In this way, instead of simply explaining Paul's differences as contingent expressions, contextual elements may also be regarded as generating Paul's embodied experience and so contributing to his differences in ideas. Thus, like embodied cognition studies, these kinds of arguments on the basis of somatic experience, including neurobiological mechanisms, would also provide theoretical grounds for developmental interpretations of Paul's resurrection thought.

However, like the scholars who argue against developmental interpretations of Paul, most scholars who propose such interpretations have also suffered from neglecting the experiential aspect of Paul's context. Ironically, as early as the late nineteenth century, consideration of the influence of contextual experience on Paul's thought was one of the triggers for the emergence of the first developmental hypothesis of Paul's ideas. In 1870, emphasizing the apostle's experiences of conversion and moral crisis, Auguste Sabatier argued that Paul's doctrine "is always the outgrowth of his experience" and so "must have had a history."[26] Sabatier is thus the first to propose a developmental understanding of Paul by considering the influence of contextual experience on a person's thought.[27] However, Sabatier only focuses on Paul's intellectual development without dealing with his embodied experience. Sabatier attempts to trace out what he calls the "progressive character of Paulism" and to write "a biography of his mind and a history of his thought."[28]

Later developmental hypotheses of Paul largely continue to treat his thought-development as a fundamentally intellectual process, and his somatic experience has not received enough attention.[29] As Jeffery R. Asher summarizes, during the second half of the nineteenth century and the first half of the twentieth, based on "the presupposition that there existed an intellectual conflict in Paul's mind between Jewish and Hellenistic modes of thought," a number of scholars have followed Sabatier and hypothesized about the development in Paul's idea of resurrection and in his eschatology in general.[30] The assumed intellectual conflict is regarded as the main factor that propelled Paul's development from Jewish eschatology to Hellenistic immortality. For example, following Sabatier and influenced by Hermann Lüdemann's work on Pauline anthropology, Otto Pfleiderer argues that Paul's Jewish and Hellenistic modes of thought "met in one bed

---

[25] A. Segal, *Life after Death: A History of the Afterlife in Western Religion* (New York: Doubleday, 2004), 322–50. Shantz, *Paul in Ecstasy*, 93–108, 110–44.
[26] A. Sabatier, *The Apostle Paul: A Sketch of the Development of His Doctrine* (trans. George G. Findlay; New York: Pott, 1891), ix. Several eminent works advocating a developmental understanding of Christian doctrine were published during this time, such as Adolf Harnack's *History of Dogma* (1886) and James Orr's *The Progress of Dogma* (1901).
[27] Ibid., 1.
[28] Ibid., ix, 1.
[29] Shantz spends a whole chapter arguing that this is a tendency of Pauline studies in general. She then concludes that chapter by indicating that it is worth exploring what kind of Paul's thought might arise from (bodily) experience. See Shantz, *Paul in Ecstasy*, 20–66.
[30] J. R. Asher, *Polarity and Change in 1 Corinthians 15: A Study of Metaphysics, Rhetoric, and Resurrection* (Tübingen: Mohr Siebeck, 2000), 17.

without really coalescing."³¹ Meanwhile, the Jewish eschatological framework and the hope of somatic resurrection that Paul had before conversion turned out to be unable to accommodate the issues arising from his new faith in Christ, especially the problem of the delayed Parousia and the death of believers.³² Thus, although the risen life was supposed to be eschatological and supernatural, Paul had to claim in later letters that believers could participate in it here and now through baptism, which served as the imitation of Christ's death, and this life could be revealed in communal interactions. The "transcendent eschatological idea" of life then inevitably became an "immanent ethical one" in order to be meaningful before the Parousia.³³ Similarly, Ernst G. G. Teichmann also observes a growing emphasis on the idea of the indwelling Spirit. He considers the death of believers before the Parousia as a contextual reason for Paul's adoption of Hellenistic idea of the immortal soul, an idea that seemed to be more in line with the idea of the indwelling Spirit than the Jewish idea of bodily resurrection.³⁴ In sum, it is argued in the Pleiderer-Teichmann line of developmental interpretation that, facing the reality of death, Paul had to "spiritualize" and moralize his somatic hope and lean toward the Hellenistic idea of the immortal soul, and the conviction of the indwelling Spirit legitimized this shift toward Hellenistic thought.³⁵

These early developmental theories suffer from two related weaknesses. First, they falsely assume a sharp dichotomy between Paul's Jewish and Hellenistic modes of thought, and so depict Paul as having to gradually change from one mode to another. However, since the Second World War, most New Testament scholars have come to recognize that it is misleading to categorize an idea strictly as either Jewish or Hellenistic since the two did not stand in isolation but interacted extensively.³⁶ As Dale B. Martin indicates, "all Judaism of the ancient world that would have had anything to do with early Christianity was already Hellenized, and ... all forms of Greek culture in the same period had been influenced by 'oriental' cultures."³⁷ It is too simplistic, as seen in the Pleiderer-Teichmann line, to regard Paul's growing emphasis on the mystical reception and possession of the indwelling Spirit as an indication of Paul's personal Hellenization and as a gradual replacement of the Jewish somatic expectations. Indeed, Paul evidently understands resurrection as a somatic issue even in his later letters. He never stops being concerned with the body; he expects the "redemption of bodies" (Rom 8:23) and a time when our "body of humiliation" will be transformed into "the

---

[31] O. Pfleiderer, *Paulinism: A Contribution to the History of Primitive Christian Theology* (trans. Edward Peters; London: Williams and Norgate, 1891). Cf. H. Lüdemann, *Die Anthropologie des Apostels Paulus und ihre Stellung innerhalb seiner Heilslehre: nach den vier Hauptbriefen* (Kiel: Universitätsbuchhandlung, 1872); Meyer, "Paul's View of the Resurrection," 364; and A. Schweitzer, *Paul and His Interpreters: A Critical History* (trans. W. Montgomery; New York: Schocken Books, 1964), 67.
[32] Pfleiderer, *Paulinism*, 259–76. Schweitzer, *Paul and His Interpreters*, 67.
[33] Pfleiderer, *Paulinism*, 19.
[34] E. Teichmann, *Die paulinische Vorstellungen von Auferstehung und Gericht und ihre Beziehungen zur jüdischen Apokalyptic* (Freiburg: Akademische Verlagsbuchhandlung, 1896), 33–67.
[35] Meyer, "Paul's View of the Resurrection," 366.
[36] D. B. Martin, "Paul and the Judaism/Hellenism Dichotomy: Toward a Social History of the Question," in *Paul Beyond the Judaism/Hellenism Divide* (ed. T. Engberg-Pedersen; Louisville, KY: Westminster John Knox Press, 2000), 30.
[37] Ibid.

likeliness of the body of his (Christ's) glory" (Phil 3:21). Emphasizing the somatic aspect of Paul's thought, Tappenden also indicates that the sharp dichotomy between Jewish and Hellenistic ideas is a "problematic assumption" in many developmental theories of Paul.[38]

This leads to the second weakness of the early developmental theories. While scholars who advocate contextual explanations of Paul's variations usually dismiss the contextual influence on his thought, the early stage of developmental theories of Paul emphasizes his intellectual activities and only considers his somatic experience as confirmation of ideas or as the motivation to borrow or combine ideas. The ideas that are confirmed, borrowed, adopted, or (more creatively) synthesized and adjusted are typically ready-made and current in Paul's cultural backgrounds. Thus, by falsely assuming a sharp dichotomy between Paul's Jewish and Hellenistic modes of thought, the Pleiderer-Teichmann line of interpretation depicts Paul as having to gradually change from one to another ready-made system of thought. In other words, somatic experience is taken as subsidiary to intellectual activity in the formation process of Paul's resurrection theology. Thus, as we have seen, although it has been noticed in this line of interpretation that both the death of some believers before the Parousia and the pneumatic experience of the indwelling Spirit in the Christian communities somehow directed Paul's resurrection thinking, these two experiences are considered as merely providing the impetus to adopt Hellenistic ideas about resurrection. The contribution of these experiences to Paul's ideas, however, has not been fully explored. As I will discuss in Chapters 3 and 4, both the observation of body-decomposition in death (and death rites) and the phenomenon of body bewilderment in pneumatic ecstasy contribute significantly to Paul's idea of *bodily transformation*—an important element in Paul's resurrection thought and a debated issue in the topic of Paul's development.[39]

In the early twentieth century, the Pfleiderer-Teichmann line of developmental understandings of Paul was challenged. In this period, Paul is usually considered as a mature theologian who applied his well-developed doctrinal system in various circumstances, albeit with different emphases or rhetorical purposes. By assuming his maturity, Paul is depicted in these contextual approaches as having a disembodied mind in relation to his circumstances. Although his mind addressed a particular context in which his body was located, that context did not have an impact on his thinking. Thus, apart from a dramatic and comprehensive reorientation of value in Paul's conversion experience, only a very limited role is assigned to experience in the formation of Paul's thought since the relationship between his mind and occasional circumstance is considered unidirectional rather than reciprocal.[40]

However, again, contingency and development are by no means mutually exclusive, and contingent, practical situations are contributors to thought-development. In

---

[38] Tappenden, *Resurrection in Paul*, 77 (footnote 72).
[39] Shantz has suggested the influence of ecstatic experience on Paul's idea of transformation. See her *Paul in Ecstasy*, 136–40.
[40] As Shantz notes, the approach that "grounds Paul's theology unmitigatedly in a [single] moment of revelation" depicts Paul as reflecting upon his one and only initiatory religious experience in the rest of his life. Thus, it is in fact another way to uphold the mind-body dualism and would leave the influence of Paul's subsequent experience unexplored. Ibid., 46, 55.

addition, the challenges and struggles of Paul's intense missionary work seems to be underestimated in the contextual approaches used to argue against developmental understandings. As Charles H. Dodd observes, Paul had to go through an intense experience of "bitter humiliation," as reflected in 2 Cor 10–13, and a grave illness that almost caused his death, as mentioned in 2 Cor 1:8–10.[41] Dodd further suggests that these contextual experiences forced Paul to "outgrow" his immaturity and significantly changed his mindset from a "world-renouncing attitude" to a "world-affirming attitude."[42] Dodd's psychological analysis has called the image of a fully mature Paul (during the period of time of his extant letters) into question and led to a second wave of developmental approaches to Paul.[43] Indeed, although Paul may craft contingent expressions when he interacts with different circumstances, with embodied theoretical basis and a proper approach, it is also worth looking for "discernible shifts" in his ideas that might have been caused by contextual experiences. Particularly, as we have seen, experiences of facing believers' death (and his own near-death illness) and receiving the Spirit had significant impacts on Paul's thought.[44]

Moreover, the ritual practice of baptism is another somatic experience that has not been fully treated in light of embodiment. In the debate concerning Paul's resurrection thought, baptism is usually treated as an enactment of the idea of realized or experienced resurrection (either literally or metaphorically), even though, as A. J. M. Wedderburn points out, there is no evidence indicating any understanding of baptism as such before Col 2:12 (an idea that might have been developed from Rom 6:3–4).[45] Elsewhere, this notion of baptismal resurrection is found only in some

---

[41] C. H. Dodd, "The Mind of St. Paul: A Psychological Approach," *Bulletin of the John Rylands Library* 17 no. 1 (1933): 103–4. Dodd emphasizes Paul's use of the words ταπεινόω and ταπεινός in 2 Cor 10:1; 11:7; 12:21. He argues that ταπεινός originally means an insult in Greek and that it was Christianity that "made 'humility' a virtue." At any rate, a bitter conflict regarding Paul's authority and his frustration is clear in this passage.

[42] Ibid., 91–105. C. H. Dodd, "The Mind of St. Paul: Change and Development," *Bulletin of the John Rylands Library* 18 no. 1 (1934): 110. Richard N. Longenecker's wordings in R. N. Longenecker, "Is There Development in Paul's Resurrection Thought?" in *Life in the Face of Death: The Resurrection Message of the New Testament* (ed. R. N. Longenecker; Grand Rapids, MI: W. B. Eerdmans, 1998), 176.

[43] As Longenecker summarizes, many scholars, including J. A. T. Robinson, F. F. Bruce, W. D. Davies, and W. L. Knox, have followed Dodd in tracing Paul's developments, especially the developments in resurrection thought between 1 Cor 15 and 2 Cor 5, but also developments in other Pauline themes (Longenecker, "Development," 177). Moreover, influenced by Dodd, Charles H. Buck, Greer M. Taylor, and John C. Hurd try to incorporate Dodd's developmental theory of Paul into Paul's biographical chronology (C. Buck and G. Taylor, *Saint Paul: A Study of the Development of His Thought* [New York: Scribner, 1969]; John C. Hurd Jr. *The Origin of 1 Corinthians* [London: S.P.C.K., 1965]). For further discussion on Pauline chronologies, see J. Knox, *Chapters in a Life of Paul* (rev. John Knox; ed. Douglas R. A. Hare; Macon: Mercer University Press, 1987); R. Jewett, *A Chronology of Paul's Life* (Philadelphia: Fortress Press, 1979); G. Lüdemann, *Paul, Apostle to the Gentiles: Studies in Chronology* (trans. F. Stanley Jones; Philadelphia: Fortress Press, 1984); J. Knox, "On the Pauline Chronology: Buck-Taylor-Hurd Revisited," in *The Conversation Continues: Studies in Paul & John: In Honor of J. Louis Martyn* (ed. R. T. Fortna and B. R. Gaventa; Nashville: Abingdon Press, 1990), 258–74.

[44] Longenecker argues that the idea of bodily transformation occurring at resurrection in 1 Cor 15 is one of the "discernible shifts" in Paul's extant letters (Longenecker, "Development," 190–1).

[45] A. J. M. Wedderburn, *Baptism and Resurrection: Studies in Pauline Theology against Its Greco-Roman Background* (Wissenschafliche Untersuchungen zum Neuen Testament 44; Tübingen: Mohr, 1987), 211–32, 393. As I will indicate in this study, I agree with Wedderburn that there is only co-burial in Romans, no co-resurrection.

other Christian writings from the late first century CE.[46] The symbolic approach to ritual, which regards ritual merely as the enactment of ideas, has anachronistically interpreted early Christian rites according to a well-developed theological framework of later times.[47] At the same time, it rules out the generative role of ritual experience in a process of thought-development. However, applying cognitive linguistic tools, I will focus on the recurrent experiential pattern of the baptismal rite itself and the early Christian perceptions of this pattern. In so doing, I will argue that baptism appears to provide a crucial experiential pattern that allows the idea of experienced resurrection to emerge in Colossians.

1.3 Toward an Embodied Approach to Paul's Development

Building on Tappenden's analysis of resurrection ideas, I will apply cognitive linguistic tools to explore the formation, maturation, and articulation of Paul's resurrection theology. Two particular issues on this topic have gained considerable attention from scholars: (1) whether or not the idea of bodily transformation at resurrection is absent in 1 Thess 4 and is Paul's innovation in 1 Cor 15, and (2) whether or not the idea of experienced resurrection occurring at baptism can be found in undisputed Pauline letters.

As I will further discuss in Chapter 3, Asher has paved the way for my treatment of the first issue.[48] By illustrating the philosophical backgrounds and the rhetorical function of the idea of bodily transformation in 1 Cor 15, Asher explores Paul's contextual reason for introducing this very idea to the Corinthians. By comparing Paul's statements to Hellenistic cosmology, Asher shows that Paul's argument of transformation in 1 Cor 15 was dependent on Greek philosophical systems because both Paul in this passage and the philosophers perceived transformation as substantive, materialistic, and as involving cosmic polarities with opposite qualities (cf. 1 Cor 15:42–44).[49] However, Hellenistic philosophers did not apply the idea of transformation to human body. Rather, based on their hierarchical cosmology, the philosophers believed that it is

---

[46] See the evidences offered in C. L. Mearns, "Early Christian Eschatological Development in Paul: The Evidence of 1 Corinthians," *JSNT* 22 (1984): 19–35 (esp. 34). Cf. C. L. Mearns, "Early Christian Eschatological Development in Paul: The Evidence of I and II Thessalonians," *New Testament Studies* 27 (1980–1): 137–57.

[47] Embodied cognition theory has had a great impact on recent ritual theories. One of the most significant developments recently made by ritual theorists is the critique of much functionalism and symbolic analysis that merely "regard rites as enactments of myths, theological ideas, or moral principles." See R. L. Grimes, *Beginnings in Ritual Studies* (Studies in Comparative Religion, rev. ed.; Columbia: University of South Carolina Press, 1995), 66. Nevertheless, recently some functionalist theories have also focused on the role of ritual in generating social groups, such as Richard Sosis and Candace Alcorta's "commitment signaling theory" and Harvey Whitehouse's "modes of religiosity theory."

[48] Asher, *Polarity and Change*, 21.

[49] For example, the layer of air is cold in contrast to the layer of fire, and is thin in contrast to the layer of earth. Ibid., 176–7.

"metaphysically impossible for a terrestrial body to ascend to a celestial realm."[50] For most philosophers, such as the Stoics, the soul is separated from the body at death, and the soul of the virtuous goes "up to the dissolution of everything into fire."[51] Asher thus convincingly argues that Paul's idea of substantive transformation (1 Cor 15:35–50) and his expressions of opposite qualities—ἐν φθορᾷ and ἐν ἀφθαρσίᾳ, ἐν ἀτιμίᾳ and ἐν δόξῃ, ἐν ἀσθενείᾳ and ἐν δυνάμει, and σῶμα ψυχικόν and σῶμα πνευματικόν (15:42–44)—show that he is responding to a common criticism of resurrection from philosophical schools.

Asher then applies rhetorical analysis to this passage and demonstrates how Paul carefully conveys the idea of "substantive transformation of human body" within the framework of Hellenistic philosophy and cosmology, and, in so doing, he responds to the Corinthians' denial of resurrection on the very basis of this framework.[52] In other words, the idea of transformation as it is presented in 1 Cor 15 is Paul's answer to the challenge against resurrection arising from a specific contextual situation and so is very likely an innovation crafted for this situation. Paul has a clear contextual reason to introduce this idea. Moreover, in addition to identifying contextual a reason for Paul's innovation, Asher further indicates that transformation later becomes an important element in Paul's teaching (2 Cor 3:18; Rom 12:2; Phil 3:20–21).[53] Thus, the idea of transformation seems not just a contingent strategy for the argument in 1 Cor 15 but an indication of Paul's development.

In terms of methodology, I will follow Asher in identifying Paul's development by considering (1) whether Paul has contextual reasons to generate a specific innovation and (2) whether the innovation recurred or had continual effects in Christian groups. However, by applying cognitive linguistic tools to these two considerations, I will demonstrate that Paul's fundamental development as it appears in 1 Cor 15 is a change in the experiential pattern on which his transformation idea is constructed. In other words, it is a change in what cognitive linguists call "image schema." This change is crucial for Paul's contextual rhetorical purpose and is one that cannot be accounted for by the Hellenistic philosophical backgrounds. Rather, this innovation in schema directly addresses an experiential issue of body-decomposition that is regularly observed in death and death rites. Addressing this issue, Paul introduces an alternative experiential pattern of the sowing and growing of a seed—a V-patterned schema of reversal—to emphasize that God can reverse the body's destined pattern of going down into the earth and instead transform the body into a heavenly form. I will also argue that this new image schema of reversal explains a significant innovation in 1 Cor 15 that Asher's analysis does not recognize and explain: the timing of transformation as occurring at resurrection.

Moreover, this new schema of reversal is different from the existing schemas for imagining resurrection in Jewish traditions (and 1 Thess 4) and exerts a continuing

---

[50] Ibid., 82.
[51] T. Engberg-Pedersen, *Cosmology & Self in the Apostle Paul: The Material Spirit* (Oxford: Oxford University Press, 2010), 21. SVF 2.809/LS 53W (Arius Didymus; LS tr.).
[52] Asher, *Polarity and Change*, 82.
[53] Ibid., 3, 205, 207.

effect on Paul's later thought. Thus, it appears that the reversal schema of resurrection and bodily transformation is not only a contingency responding to the situation in Corinth but also indicates a significant development in Paul. This leads to the second issue of Paul's development: the experienced resurrection. In Chapter 5, I will argue that the reversal schema for imagining transformation and resurrection accords with the physical pattern of being immersed into water and being raised up in baptism—a V-patterned movement. Thus, bodily practice in baptism provides a recurrent, experiential pattern for what is expected in resurrection. Applying the cognitive linguistic tool of conceptual blending theory, I will suggest that, for specific contextual reasons, Paul enacts conceptual blends in 1 Cor 12 and Rom 6 that might respectively account for the emergences of the ideas of experienced transformation in 2 Cor 3:18 and conjoined resurrection in Col 2:12.

In the following chapters, I will analyze several key passages from Paul's letters about resurrection and transformation using cognitive linguistic tools: 1 Thess 4 (Chapter 2); 1 Cor 15 (Chapters 2 and 3); 1 Cor 12 (Chapter 4); 2 Cor 3–5 and Rom 6 (Chapter 5). Unlike many other Pauline topics, the authenticity and chronological order of these passages about resurrection is commonly affirmed. Chapter 2 begins by introducing three cognitive linguistic tools—image schema, conceptual metaphor, and conceptual blending—in order to overcome the methodological gap between texts/ideas and the body. By using these tools to analyze resurrection thought in terms of the recurrent patterns of physical experience, I will demonstrate that Paul imagines resurrection and transformation in 1 Cor 15:35–58 using an image schema (the reversal schema) unlike typical Jewish conceptions. It also differs from his description in 1 Thess 4, and even 1 Cor 15:1–34. Chapter 3 will then be devoted to analyzing the rhetorical function and the conceptual effects of this alternative image schema. Considering the experiential backgrounds of contemporary death rites in addition to the intellectual backgrounds of philosophy and cosmology, I will argue that Paul's new reversal schema directly addresses the most fundamental challenge to resurrection usually raised by the Gentiles: the mortality of the body observed in the decomposition of the corpse. Also, applying conceptual blending theory, I will indicate that the reversal schema generates important ideas of resurrection and transformation that continually occur in Paul's later writings.

In Chapter 4, I will consider the emergence of another aspect of transformation in Paul: the experienced transformation evident in 2 Cor 3:18. Conceptual blending analysis will help us to explain the way in which this idea might have emerged from the experiences of both spirit possession and baptismal practice. In Chapter 5, I will deal with the interplay between the two aspects of bodily transformation in Paul, the eschatological transformation and the experienced transformation. While Paul clearly distinguishes the two aspects and enacts distinct sets of conceptual blends to expound each aspect in 2 Cor 3–5, the ritual experience of baptism and its physical pattern of reversal appear to function in Rom 6:3–4 as the convergence point of the two transformations. Again, blending analysis helps to account for this convergence in baptism and to explore its conceptual effects on Paul's resurrection thought.

This study demonstrates a promising approach to analyze ancient texts in terms of somatic experience. Specifically, by applying this embodied cognitive approach to the two methodological considerations summarized above—the contextual reason for an innovation and the recurrence of an innovation—this study contributes to the scholarly debate about the nature of Paul's thinking. While leaning toward developmental hypotheses about Paul's thought, I emphasize the experiential aspect of Paul's thought-development and particularly the role of ritual experience in the process. Paul's thinking, as reflected in his extant texts, is an integral part of his "full-blooded" interaction with his world. In other words, this study helps to appreciate Pauline letters as witnesses of an ongoing progress of the early Christian movement, in which Paul's ideas also developed through contextual interactions. By situating Paul somatically and more fully in his context, this study catches a glimpse of the formation and development of early Christian communities. While scholars who apply social scientific approaches to early Christianity have considered the development of religious ideas as responses to social formation, my study explores the role of the interplay between ideas and ritual/experience in such a formation process. Therefore, this study will contribute to a fuller picture of early Christianity by identifying and analyzing this interplay.

In addition, my study also helps faith communities to reflect on the way that Paul the apostle received divine revelation and the way that he articulated the gospel of Christ. Instead of a wooden understanding of the reception of revelation, my study portrays a dynamic process in which Paul's mind, body, communities, and contemporaries were all involved and integrated. By exploring this process, my study can improve our knowledge of God, especially God as the Creator of human beings and the whole universe and as the Lord acting among his people.

2

A Seed of Paul's Development: The Reversal Schema

Paul struggled with the hope of physical resurrection. He struggled to an extent that he had to rely on an alternative pattern of physical experience to re-picture the traditional scenario of resurrection. This new experiential pattern, which was distinct from the experiential patterns used in Jewish traditions of resurrection, emerged from a common experience of observing the growth of a sown seed (1 Cor 15:36–38) and generated an innovative idea of bodily transformation occurring at resurrection (15:52–54). The alternative experiential pattern and the generation of the new idea constituted a significant development in Paul's thought that would exert a continuing impact on Paul's resurrection theology. In other words, the developmental process of Paul's resurrection theology was fundamentally fueled by a change in the experiential pattern behind his thinking. Thus, the first goal of this chapter is to consider resurrection thought in terms of experiential patterns: how do experiential patterns fundamentally shape a person's complex thinking and, specifically, resurrection ideas? What was the mechanism of such cognitive effects? To answer these questions, I will largely rely on Frederick S. Tappenden's work to introduce the way that complex imaginations and abstract ideas about resurrection in both Paul and Second Temple Judaism were constructed on the basis of recurrent patterns of embodied experiences.[1]

Based on the experiential patterns behind resurrection ideas analyzed in this chapter, my second goal is to explain Paul's innovative idea of the timing of transformation as occurring at resurrection. I will diverge from Tappenden's analysis here and, instead, lean toward scholars who advocate developmental understandings of Paul's thought, such as Richard N. Longenecker. Following Joachim Jeremias, Longenecker has argued that the idea that resurrection consists of not only revivification of the corpse but also its transformation is first introduced in 1 Cor 15 and is not seen in either 1 Thess 4:13–18 or Jewish apocalyptic writings.[2] As Longenecker quotes Jeremias,

---

[1] F. S. Tappenden, *Resurrection in Paul: Cognition, Metaphor, and Transformation* (Atlanta: Society of Biblical Literature, 2016).
[2] R. N. Longenecker, "Is There Development in Paul's Resurrection Thought?" in *Life in the Face of Death: The Resurrection Message of the New Testament* (ed. R. N. Longenecker; Grand Rapids, MI: W. B. Eerdmans, 1998), 190.

There [Jewish apocalyptic literature], the concept is—as may be seen for example from the Syriac Apoc. of Baruch xlix-li—that the dead are raised in their earthly state. Literally, Syr. Bar. 1, 2 says "nothing being changed in their appearance." This is, as Syriac Baruch continues, to secure their identity (1.3f.). Only after the judgment the righteous are changed.[3]

Thus, Longenecker convincingly indicates that Paul had a "discernable shift" when he wrote 1 Corinthians and depicted an idea of resurrection distinct from what is reflected in Jewish traditions and 1 Thessalonians.[4] For example, unlike the timing in 1 Corinthians, it is explicitly stated in Dan 12:1–3 that the resurrected are transformed only later when they are elevated after the judgment.

This change of the timing of transformation demands an explanation. As we have seen in Chapter 1, Jeffery R. Asher's method of identifying Paul's innovation requires contextual reasons to explain the generation of a new idea. Addressing 1 Cor 15, Asher argues that the idea of "substantive transformation of the body" (15:42–44) indicates Paul's innovation responding to the Hellenistic rejection of resurrection on the basis of philosophy and cosmology. According to Hellenistic philosophers, matter must undergo a substantive transformation with corresponding change in quality in order to traverse cosmological realms. Thus, a resurrected body must be transformed substantively to inherit the kingdom of God (15:50).[5] However, Asher's analysis of contextual reasons is limited to those of intellectual interactions. Thus, he does not fully explain the experiential reason that prompted Paul to seriously deal with the concept of cosmological polarity at length. This may also be why he neither recognizes Paul's innovation of the timing of transformation as occurring at resurrection, nor explains the contextual reason for this innovation of timing. According to Asher's survey of the philosophical backgrounds of resurrection thought, the Jewish idea of "transformation after heavenly ascent" (instead of the new idea of "transformation at resurrection"), wherein it is articulated in terms of substantive and qualitative change and within the worldview of polarity, could have met the requirement of the Hellenistic philosophy that Paul was addressing. The contextual reasons for Paul's innovation of timing is still missing.

Thus, in this chapter, by first breaking down resurrection thought into recurrent patterns of physical experience, I will demonstrate that the fundamental change in Paul's resurrection thinking as reflected in 1 Cor 15 was a new experiential pattern that generated his innovation of the timing of transformation. That is, applying cognitive linguistic tools to compare Paul with Jewish resurrection texts, I will show that Paul's argument for resurrection and transformation in 1 Cor 15 reveals an alternative conceptual structure that coordinates with different embodied experiences. Thus, the cognitive linguistic tools introduced and applied in this chapter, image schema

---

[3] J. Jeremias, "Flesh and Blood Cannot Inherit the Kingdom of God (1 Cor. XV.50)," in *NTS* 2 no. 3 (1956): 159.
[4] Longenecker, "Development," 190–1.
[5] J. R. Asher, *Polarity and Change in 1 Corinthians 15: A Study of Metaphysics, Rhetoric, and Resurrection* (Tübingen: Mohr Siebeck, 2000), 82, 172–201.

and conceptual metaphor, will not only ground the general ideas in Paul's time about resurrection in human embodied experiences but will also help to indicate a significant change in Paul's conceptual structure for imagining resurrection. Moreover, the theory of conceptual blending will also be introduced in order to further explore the function and influence of Paul's new conceptual structures for imagining resurrection. Based on the schematic analysis and conceptual blending theory introduced in this chapter, in Chapter 3 I will further elucidate Paul's experiential context for utilizing his new experiential pattern and conceiving a new timing for transformation.

2.1 The Experiential Patterns of Complex Thinking

The image schematic analysis in this section draws significantly on the cognitive linguistic works of George Lakoff, Mark Johnson, and Mark Turner.[6] Their works have explored how abstract and complex ideas might have been constructed according to our image schematic and bodily grounded cognition and conceptualization. Johnson considers image schemas arising from embodied experience and metaphorical projections of image schemas as the central means for the creation of complex meanings.[7] Lakoff and Johnson then further investigate the mechanism of these projections in detail by exploring what they call "conceptual metaphors," which are constructed on the basis of image schemas and so grounded in recurrent embodied experience. They thus argue that metaphor is central to human conceptualization and that the nature of human thought and language is by and large metaphorical. According to Lakoff, "as soon as one gets away from concrete physical experiences and starts talking about abstractions or emotions, metaphorical understanding is the norm."[8] As we will see, this is exactly the case in the human abstract ideas about life, death, and resurrection or afterlife.

2.1.1 The Verticality Schema and the Life/Death Contrast

Johnson defines an image schema as "a dynamic pattern that functions somewhat like the abstract structure of an image, and thereby connects up a vast range of different experiences that manifest this same recurring structure."[9] In other words, an image schema is not a rich mental image but rather a schematic, skeletal structure that

---

[6] See esp. M. Johnson, *The Body in the Mind: The Bodily Basis of Meaning, Imagination, and Reason* (Chicago, IL: University of Chicago Press, 1987); *The Meaning of the Body: Aesthetics of Human Understanding* (Chicago, IL: University of Chicago Press, 2007); G. Lakoff, *Women, Fire, and Dangerous Things: What Categories Reveal about the Mind* (Chicago, IL: University of Chicago Press, 1987); G. Lakoff and M. Johnson, *Philosophy in the Flesh: The Embodied Mind and Its Challenge to Western Thought* (New York: Basic Books, 1999); *Metaphors We Live By* (Chicago, IL: University of Chicago Press, 2003); G. Lakoff and M. Turner, *More than Cool Reason: A Field Guide to Poetic Metaphor* (Chicago, IL: University of Chicago Press, 1989).
[7] Johnson, *The Meaning of the Body*, xiv-xv, 173–4.
[8] G. Lakoff, "The Contemporary Theory of Metaphor," in *Metaphor and Thought* (2nd ed.; ed. A. Ortony; Cambridge: Cambridge University Press, 1993), 205.
[9] Johnson, *The Body in the Mind*, 2.

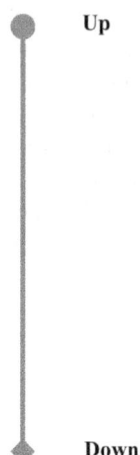

Figure 2.1 The Verticality Schema.

summarizes some of our complex experiences into a simple pattern.[10] Thus, image schema is a tool that can reveal our conceptual structures arising from recurrent patterns of experiences. For example, the image schema "verticality" (or "up-down" schema, see Figure 2.1) emerges from our repeated experiences of up-down orientation from both perceptions and motor activities, such as perceiving a tree, looking at the sky and the ground in different directions, looking at the level of water rising in a container, standing erect, walking upstairs or downstairs, and stooping to pick fallen things.[11] The verticality schema, then, is the structure that we learn from these experiences and by which we comprehend and explain these experiences. While this structure has very limited content in itself, it functions with an inherent logic since our embodied experiences of verticality have a recurrent pattern that is predictable due to the nature of the body and the nature of the physical world.[12] For example, as Vyvyan Evans and Melanie Green observe, while we have symmetrical organs on the horizontal axis such as eyes and ears on the both sides, we generally perceive the vertical axis of our bodies in a different way because it is a head on the top and feet on the opposite end. And because we walk erect and experience gravity that attracts everything downwards, the vertical axis of human body is "functionally asymmetrical." Accordingly, we tend to perceive the verticality schema as unbalanced due to the pattern of our embodied experience.[13]

Based on the conceptual schemas and their correlations with our somatic experiences, Johnson further argues that the recurrent patterns of our experiences

---

[10] Ibid., 2, 28–9, 208. See also the introduction in V. Evans and M. Green, *Cognitive Linguistics: An Introduction* (Edinburgh: Edinburgh University, 2006), 176–205.
[11] Examples are taken from Johnson, *The Body in the Mind*, xiv–xv. See also Tappenden, *Resurrection in Paul*, 34.
[12] Johnson, *The Meaning of the Body*, 139.
[13] Evans and Green, *Cognitive Linguistics*, 178.

can be extended to create and organize more abstract concepts through various metaphorical projections—one of which he calls "conceptual metaphors." According to him, a more concrete conceptual domain usually supplies the image schema by which a conceptual metaphor emerges that allows a more abstract domain to be understood on the grounds of experience.[14] For example, based on our interaction with the environment, we expect the level of water to go up when there is more water in a container. With this recurrent pattern, the metaphor "more is up; less is down" arises and allows us to understand more abstract ideas such as "his income is rising" and "he is underage for drinking."[15] Similarly, in a fight, the victor is typically standing on the top while the loser may lie down or prostrate oneself in a lower position. Physical size and height usually indicate a person's strength and predict the outcome of a fight. Also, it is more difficult to move or stand up when one is carrying a heavy weight. Thus, having force or control over others is metaphorically conceived as being relatively up, and lacking force or being subject to control is conceived of as being down.[16] We therefore have expressions such as "the king's power rose," "she has control over me," and "I am under the yoke of that oppressive regime." Moreover, Lakoff and Johnson also indicate that the metaphor "conscious is up; unconscious is down" arises from the up-down schema and our correlated experiences. We repeatedly observe and experience that humans generally lie down when they sleep and stand up when they are awake. Thus, we have metaphorical expressions such "get up," "wake up," "she fell asleep," and "he sank into a coma."[17] Additionally, we expect people with serious illness or who are dying to physically lie down instead of standing up like a healthy/living person.[18] Thus, the metaphor "health/life is up; sickness/death is down" also arises and generates expressions such as "she is at the peak of health" and "Lazarus rose from the dead."[19]

Accordingly, as Lakoff and Turner observe, mortality is usually conceived metaphorically in religious ideas as being down and immortality/divine as being up.[20] Thus, for example, Hellenistic philosophers usually imagined the soul as immortal and ascending to higher strata of cosmos at the moment of death while the corpse descends into the grave and the earth. As Johnson concludes, "metaphor is not merely a linguistic mode of expression but one of the chief cognitive structures" by which we can project the embodied patterns that we learn through our recurrent experiences in order to generate and organize our more abstract concepts and complex reasoning.[21]

As with Hellenistic philosophy, Tappenden indicates that Second Temple Jewish conceptualizations of life and death are also largely structured according to the up-down schema.[22] For example, in Ps 22:30, those who "go down to the dust" are

---

[14] Johnson, *The Body in the Mind*, xv. See also Tappenden, *Resurrection in Paul*, 35.
[15] Lakoff and Johnson, *Metaphors We Live By*, 15–16.
[16] Lakoff and Turner, *More than Cool Reason*, 149.
[17] Lakoff and Johnson, *Metaphors We Live By*, 15.
[18] Ibid., 15–16.
[19] Ibid., 15.
[20] Lakoff and Turner, *More than Cool Reason*, 150.
[21] Johnson, *The Body in the Mind*, xv.
[22] Tappenden, *Resurrection in Paul*, 46–54.

those who "cannot preserve their lives." In Job 14:10–12, a person's death is described as lying down without rising again. Similarly, Tappenden also notes that death is usually conceptualized as going down into the earth (Gen 37:35; Ps 55:15; Prov 9:18; Isa 14:15) and Sheol is understood in Jewish cosmology as the lower stratum of the world (Job 11:8; Ps 139:8; Amos 9:2). Consequently, escape from Sheol would require ascent (Ps 30:4).[23] Furthermore, we have seen that "conscious is up; unconscious is down" is another metaphor built upon our physical experience of verticality.[24] Thus, a more complex metaphor that "life is being awake/conscious; death is sleeping/unconscious" arises from the verticality schema that is shared by the recurrent patterns of both experiences: both sleeping people and dead corpses are lying down in an inattentive and inactive state, and so are not able to wake up.[25] This kind of up-down organization of life and death by analogy to awaken and sleeping is indeed seen in Hebrew traditions. For example, in Job 14:12, "sleep" (בכש) is used to describe a man's death since he is not going to "awake" (ץיק) from his sleep. In Dan 12:2, death is described as "sleeping in the dust of the ground" and, accordingly, resurrection is described as "awake." Similarly, in his earliest extant letter, Paul also describes death as sleeping (1 Thess 4:13–15) and resurrection as arising up (ἀνίστημι) from sleep (4:14, 16).

2.1.2 The Container Schema and Cosmic Polarity

Another important image schema that greatly influences human conceptualizations of life, death, body, and afterlife is the "container" schema (or "in-out" schema), which we have briefly mentioned. Johnson indicates that the container schema arises from our physical experience of containment and containers: "From the beginning, we experience constant physical containment in our surroundings (those things that envelop us). We move in and out of rooms, clothes, vehicles, and numerous kinds of bounded spaces. We manipulate objects, placing them in containers (cups, boxes, cans, bags, etc.)."[26] Thus, the container schema denotes an enclosed region in space and consists of at least three structural elements: the interior, the boundary, and the exterior (see Figure 2.2).[27] The in-out structure of the schema marked by the boundary implies "separation, differentiation, restriction, and limitation."[28] Thus, an inherent logic of the container schema, particularly important for this study, is that the properties or states of the interior are different from those of the exterior. As we repeatedly experience and perceive with various physical containments, we begin to conceive of some properties or states as restricted in a bounded region and only shared among the things interior, which are separated from the exterior. For example, hot water is contained in a cup. Warmer air or a certain smell is restricted in a room. People are surrounded and protected by walls, and so are relatively safe in a city.

---

[23] Ibid., 49.
[24] Lakoff and Johnson, *Metaphors We Live By*, 15.
[25] See the same argument in Tappenden, *Resurrection in Paul*, 36–9.
[26] Johnson, *The Body in the Mind*, 21.
[27] Lakoff and Johnson, *Philosophy in the Flesh*, 31.
[28] Johnson, *The Body in the Mind*, 22.

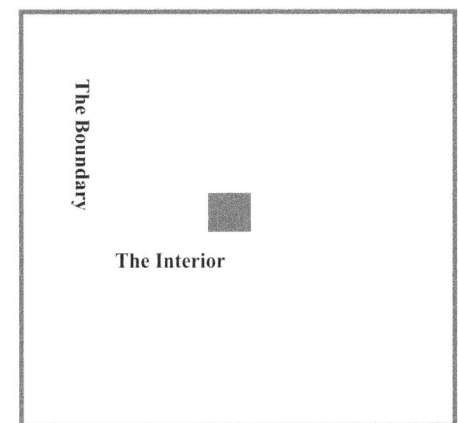

Figure 2.2 The Container Schema.

The container schema is pervasive in Paul's expressions. The most famous and complex example would be Paul's peculiar expression "in Christ" (ἐν Χριστῷ). Through this phrase, Paul metaphorically conceptualizes Christ as a container in which a believer is in a new state different from the exterior. Being in Christ, one is a new creature (2 Cor 5:17) and is justified (Gal 2:17), living (Rom 6:11), no longer condemned (8:1), and free from the law of sin and death (8:2). As Tappenden argues, the container schema connotes multiple grammatical categories of the sense of preposition ἐν, including locative and spherical senses.[29] That is, based on the container schema, the imagination of being in the new state under Christ's "influence, control, or domain" (the spherical sense of ἐν) might also involve being inside his very body (the locative sense).[30] In fact, in 2 Cor 5:1–8, Paul describes our human bodies also as containers and as analogical to a tent and a house. People will be in a different state when they depart their present bodies and live in the heavenly house. This example represents a very locative sense of human bodies as containers. I will return to the issue of the human body as a locative container (including Christ's body) in Chapter 4 when dealing with Paul's famous metaphorical expression of "being baptized into the body of Christ" (1 Cor 12:13).

As mentioned, based upon the inherent logic of the container schema concerning the interior state, a conceptual metaphor that "states are containers" emerges to allow us to conceptualize various states, such as "I am in love" or "she is out of her depression."[31] In this way, Paul metaphorically depicts the different states of the earthly body and heavenly body through the container schema. As Tappenden observes, Paul says that "it is sown in (ἐν) destruction, it is raised up in immortality; it is sown in dishonor, it is

---

[29] See the grammatical categorization in S. E. Porter, *Idioms of the Greek New Testament* (2nd ed.; Sheffield: JSOT Press, 1996), 156–7.
[30] Tappenden, *Resurrection in Paul*, 180–3.
[31] Lakoff and Johnson term this conceptual metaphor "states are locations," but they explain that "by 'locations,' we mean bounded regions in space. Each bounded region has an interior, an exterior, and a boundary." See their *Philosophy in the Flesh*, 180.

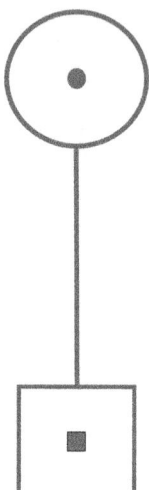

Figure 2.3 The Hellenistic Conceptualization of the Heavenly and the Earthly Realms.

raised up in glory; it is sown in weakness, it is raised up in power" (1 Cor 15:42b–43). In the same passage, when Paul writes that there are "heavenly bodies and earthly bodies" (15:40), he appears to conceptualize both heaven and earth as cosmological locations in the form of bounded regions, in which things are supposed to be in corresponding states and possess corresponding properties. That is, heaven and earth are portrayed as two opposite containers.[32] Thus, the first man is "out of earth" (ἐκ γῆς), earthly; the second man is "out of heaven" (ἐξ οὐρανοῦ) and is heavenly (15:47–49). It is immortal, glorious, and powerful in heaven, and destructive, dishonorable, and weak in the earthly realm. That is why "the glory of the heavenly [body] is one, and the glory of the earthly is another" (15:40). Again, as Asher observes, in this passage Paul seems to be appropriating the Hellenistic idea of hierarchical cosmos that locates different elements in different cosmic strata.[33]

As shown in Figure 2.3, the conceptualization of the hierarchical cosmos in Hellenistic philosophy can be simplified and diagramed through an integration of the verticality and container schemas.[34] According to the schematic logic of this figure, the up-down axis is asymmetrical. Heaven and earth are imagined as different containers in which things are in different states respectively. It would require substantive/qualitative transformations for things to go across the terrestrial and the celestial realms. However, the Greek philosophers did not apply such transformation in substance to human bodies and did not consider human bodies capable of traversing different realms. Thus,

---

[32] For a similar analysis see Tappenden, *Resurrection in Paul*, 114–16.
[33] Asher, *Polarity and Change*, 78–89, 176–205.
[34] This is a much-simplified diagram since in Hellenistic cosmology there are at least four basic elements arranged hierarchically on the vertical axis. My point here, however, is to address the different states and qualities in the celestial and the terrestrial realms, respectively, and thus the transformation needed for traversing them.

Asher argues that the cosmological polarity depicted in Figure 2.3 appears to be an important reason for the Corinthians' rejection of bodily resurrection.[35] As will be shown below, this denial presumes that the resurrected are supposed to go through divine judgment and eventually exist in divine sovereignty.

The understanding of the celestial and the terrestrial realms as seen in the Jewish ascent accounts also involves cosmological polarity and can be diagramed as the image schema in Figure 2.3. This does not mean that the understandings of cosmological polarity are exactly the same in Hellenistic philosophies and in the ascent tradition, because an image schema only provides the skeletal conceptual structure that has very limited content in itself. Nevertheless, they do reflect very similar conceptual structures and experiential grounds for their conceptualizations. For example, the hymnist in the Hodayot states that, although he was once limited in a "wicked boundary" (גבול רשע), God has lifted him up to an "eternal height" (רום עולם) where he can enjoy the "eternal lot" and can participate in the "eternal council" (1QH^a xi 21–25). Heaven and earth are conceptualized as two different containers located on an asymmetrical, vertical axis. The interior properties in these two containers are those of eternity and wickedness, respectively. However, in the ascent tradition, human beings are allowed to traverse these two different realms with their bodies by God's supernatural aid. Thus, as we have seen in 1 En. 71:11, the Self-Glorification Hymn (4Q491), and Dan 12:3, a sort of bodily transformation is usually correlated with heavenly ascent, though the emphasis is usually on glory or morality rather than the substantive transformation seen in Hellenistic philosophies. Regarding the conceptualization of ascent, we need to introduce another image schema, the path schema, because the static schemas introduced so far are not enough for the imagination of a transformation process.

2.2 The Traditional Experiential Patterns of Heavenly Ascent and Resurrection

In this section, I will first introduce the path image schema. Then, integrating and applying the image schemas of verticality, container, and path, I will analyze concepts of heavenly ascent (which usually involves transformation) and resurrection (which is usually related to heavenly ascent) in the Second Temple Jewish traditions. While still drawing upon Tappenden's work, my analysis will differ from his by clearly distinguishing heavenly ascent and resurrection.

2.2.1 Heavenly Ascent, Resurrection, and the Path Schema

The path schema is pervasive in our daily experience. As Johnson states, "our lives are filled with paths that connect up our spatial world."[36] He indicates that a path consists of a route in space for moving from one position to another position, such as the path

---

[35] Asher, *Polarity and Change*, 82.
[36] Johnson, *The Body in the Mind*, 113.

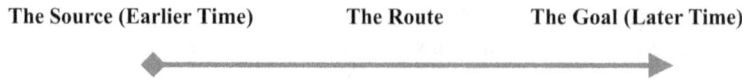

Figure 2.4 The Path Schema.

from one's house to where one works, or the path of an arrow from a bow to an animal or a target.[37] Human beings "tend to experience paths as directional" because they have purposes (such as going home, taking a fruit, or hitting an animal with an arrow) when they traverse paths or make objects traverse paths. That is, they experience paths as moving along a route from a source toward a goal.[38] The source-route-goal structure of the path schema (see Figure 2.4) is commonly used in human language to conceptualize various activities with certain processes in which certain purposes might be achieved or certain changes might be involved. For example, emerging from the image schema of path, a metaphor such as "purposeful activities are journeys" allows us to understand a professor's expression when a student's thesis proposal was just approved (a source): "We have a long way to go (a route) before this dissertation is done (a goal)."[39] Moreover, since our experience of moving from one point to another is a process that takes time, a temporal dimension is evident in the path schema. As Johnson indicates, a "time line" is usually mapped onto the conceptual path.[40] Thus, in Figure 2.4, the time at the goal is usually conceptualized as later than the time at the source. Yet it is not necessary that the earlier time at the source is on the left and the later time at the goal on the right.

We are now ready to look at the ascent tradition. As shown in the integrated diagram in Figure 2.5, the path schema creates a horizontal axis to the previous schema that is vertically oriented (Figure 2.3) for imagining heavenly ascent. The horizontal axis allows the temporal dimension of an ascent process to be diagramed. It is a concrete, literal process with an actual path from earth up to heaven. When one goes through the ascent process, that person's state at the source (the earthly container) is supposed to be different from the state at the goal (the heavenly container), and the latter state is considered to be temporally later according to the horizontal time line. Since it is the difference between the source and goal locations/containers that suggest different states, respectively, transformation would be imagined as temporally later in the image schema and most likely completed at the goal. After all, the transformation in this diagram depends on the goal because it is the goal that requires the object to be transformed. In most ascent traditions, transformation is depicted as the last part of the whole process. For example, according to the Similitudes, Enoch says that "all my flesh melted" and "[my] spirit was changed" (1 En. 71:11) after "the Spirit moved Enoch to the heaven of heavens" (71:5).[41]

---

[37] Ibid.
[38] Ibid., 114.
[39] Johnson, *The Meaning of the Body*, 177.
[40] Johnson, *The Body in the Mind*, 114.
[41] George W. E. Nickelsburg and James C. VanderKam indicate that, in 1 En. 71:11, the whole being of Enoch (face, flesh, spirit, voice) is transformed in the presence of God in heaven. See G. W. E. Nickelsburg and J. C. VanderKam, *1 Enoch 2: A Commentary on the Book of 1 Enoch Chapters 37–82* (Minneapolis, MN: Fortress, 2012), 327.

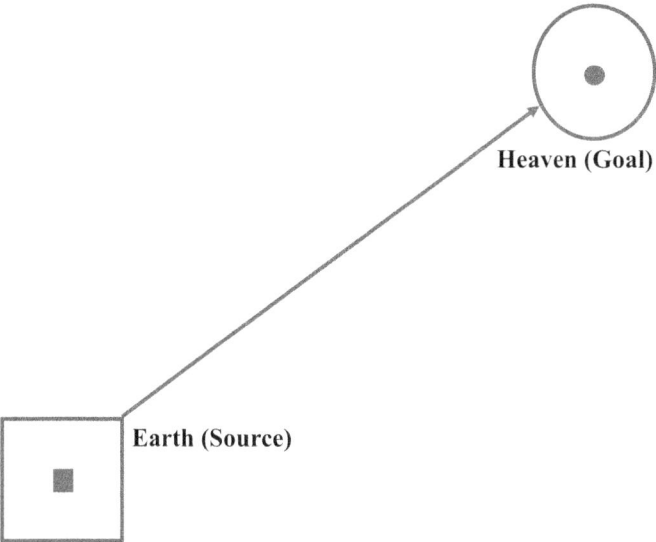

Figure 2.5 The Jewish Conceptualization of Heavenly Ascent.

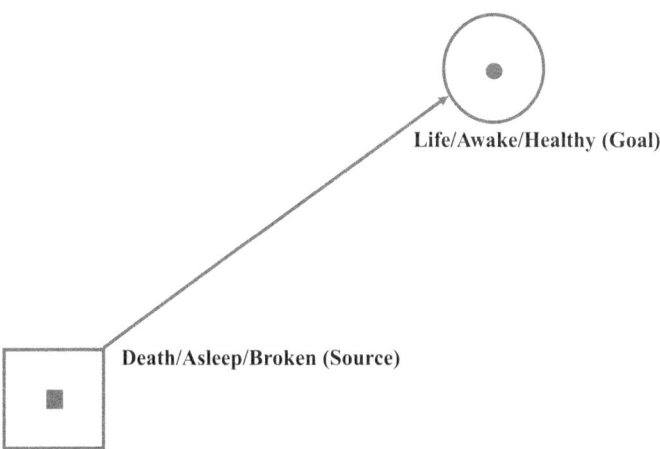

Figure 2.6 The Jewish Conceptualization of Resurrection as Restoration.

Similarly, as shown in Figure 2.6, Jewish conceptualizations of resurrection can also be diagramed (in a more metaphorical sense) through the conceptual structure that integrates the verticality schema, the container schema, and the path schema. As we have seen, life and death are metaphorically depicted in Jewish traditions as awake and asleep through the up-down structure. Accordingly, resurrection is depicted as a process of changing (or moving) vertically from the asleep/down state to the awake/up state (Dan 12:2; 1 Thess 4:14, 16) and so reveals a conceptual structure of movement along a route from a lower container to a higher container. Since resurrection is a futuristic hope, there is a clear temporal interval between the source and the goal.

However, there are important differences between Figures 2.5 and 2.6. First, while the ascent path in Figure 2.5 represents an actual upward movement, the upward path of resurrection diagramed in Figure 2.6 is a metaphorical one in which life and death are conceptualized through the up-down orientation. Second, and more importantly, the metaphorical path in Figure 2.6 does not traverse strata in a hierarchical cosmos. Thus, the Jewish idea of resurrection itself does not suggest bodily transformation into a heavenly or glorious form (as the ascent tradition would suggest due to the traversing of realms).[42] Rather, resurrection is consistently conceived as the restoration of the life before death. This distinction between resurrection and ascent is explicitly described in 2 Bar 49–51, where it is stated that the dead will rise in their earthly state and that only after judgment and exaltation will they be transformed into "the splendor of the angels" (51:4–6). Regarding resurrection itself, what happens to the dead at the "goal" is the restoration of their consciousness and body, not the change of their body. It is also based on this restoring nature that resurrection serves as "a remedy for bodily tortures" in 2 Macc 7, where seven brothers and their mother are put to death for observing the Torah.[43] It is said that the brothers' rescue from death is their resurrection to life, and that God will heal their bodily tortures (7:10–11). As the third brother says about resurrection, "I know God will give them [his tongue and hands] back to me again" (7:11).

It would therefore be a mistake to confuse the ideas of resurrection and ascent simply because they are imagined and expressed through very similar conceptual structures. As Lakoff indicates, based on their inherent logics, image schemas can "motivate" our metaphorical expressions. However, they do not "predict" our metaphorical expressions.[44] Thus, we can explain the emergence of a metaphor and its somatic anchor through schematic analysis, but we cannot predict an emergence of a metaphorical expression on the basis of schematic structures or patterns of somatic experiences. For example, although "more," "strong/powerful," "healthy," and "life" are all frequently conceptualized as "up" through the up-down schema, we do not communicate efficiently by saying "my income became strong/powerful/alive last year." Instead, we say "my income rose last year." Some expressions simply did not

---

[42] Tappenden, *Resurrection in Paul*, 54–55. As mentioned, in addition to my focus on ritual practice and experience, this study differs from Tappenden (2016) by treating resurrection and ascent as closely related yet distinguished ideas. Tappenden's analysis of "resurrection ideals" actually includes the idea of heavenly ascent. I agree with Tappenden that resurrection *per se* is also imagined through the integration of verticality, container, and path schemas, and so can be illustrated through a schematic structure that is very similar to the conceptual structure of ascent. Nevertheless, as I will briefly argue below, conceptual structures are skeletal in nature and do not predict the concepts infilled in the structures. Moreover, it is the idea of divine judgment that correlates resurrection with ascent in Jewish traditions.

[43] G. W. E. Nickelsburg, *Resurrection, Immortality, and Eternal Life in Intertestamental Judaism and Early Christianity* (Cambridge, MA: Harvard University Press for Harvard Theological Studies, 2006), 121.

[44] Lakoff, *Dangerous Things*, 438.

emerge and become well received in English. In the same way, the hope for resurrection emerged in Jewish traditions as concerning the restoration of life and the body, not the change of the body. This linguistic phenomenon is actually explicable by means of our schematic analysis. According to the logic inherent in the path schema, the final state of the traversing object depends on the goal of the path. Thus, since the diagram of resurrection in Figure 2.6 does not involve a cosmological gap between earth and heaven, it is reasonable that the idea of bodily transformation needed for traversing the cosmological realms did not emerge together with the idea of resurrection itself. In sum, resurrection is never configured as identical with heavenly ascent in spite of the similar conceptual structures and the close correlation between them in Jewish eschatology.

2.2.2 The Relation between Resurrection and Ascent: A Schematic Analysis

In Second Temple Jewish eschatology, the concepts of divine judgment and rule link resurrection and ascent or exaltation in a sequential and consequential way. That is, the hope for either bodily resurrection or an immortal soul usually functions to make divine judgment and reward possible for the deceased, and the reward typically includes ascent/exaltation and participation in divine rule.[45] George W. E. Nickelsburg indicates that, in the earliest intertestamental texts, the persecution descriptions usually culminate with the judgment scene, and the hope for resurrection arose as an answer to a specific problem of vindication for the righteous who were killed unjustly during the persecution of Antiochus IV Epiphanes—the righteous who were not able to see judgment if there was no resurrection.[46] As Nickelsburg demonstrates with Dan 12 (which Nickelsburg identifies as the earliest datable intertestamental reference to resurrection) and its contemporary parallels (Jub. 23, T. Mos. 10, and T. Jud. 25), resurrection is the means by which the righteous who died for the sake of their piety are able to receive vindication before God, and by which the apostates and oppressors who died without being punished are able to receive their condemnation.[47] In some

---

[45] Nevertheless, in some cases such as 2 Maccabees and Psalms of Solomon, resurrection is not a prerequisite for God's judgment but is itself a consequence of judgment. People are raised and their lives and bodies are restored because they are vindicated by God. Thus, resurrection itself (and eternal life as in Psalms of Solomon) is the reward for the righteous and destruction is the condemnation for sinners. It is noteworthy that, in these cases, the idea of transformation is not involved in resurrection. Although in Psalms of Solomon the eternal life of the resurrected is described with the imagery of light, it is clearly, as Nickelsburg observes, "the theophanic glory" rather than the "angel-like splendor" of the resurrected. See Nickelsburg, *Resurrection*, 164.

[46] Ibid., 32, 213.

[47] In some cases, resurrection is itself the vindication for the righteous (e.g., Isa 26:14–21), and the idea of transformation is not present. Nevertheless, in many other cases, resurrection is how both the righteous and the oppressors are brought to face divine judgment. Thus, "resurrection to life, on the one hand, and to punishment, on the other, was an answer" to the unjust death of the righteous. In these latter cases, ascent and transformation for the righteous is usually expected after judgment. Ibid., 32, 23–59. Similarly, N. T. Wright indicates that the emergence of the hope of resurrection "is what sometimes happens when the hope of ancient Israel meets a new challenge," such as the threat

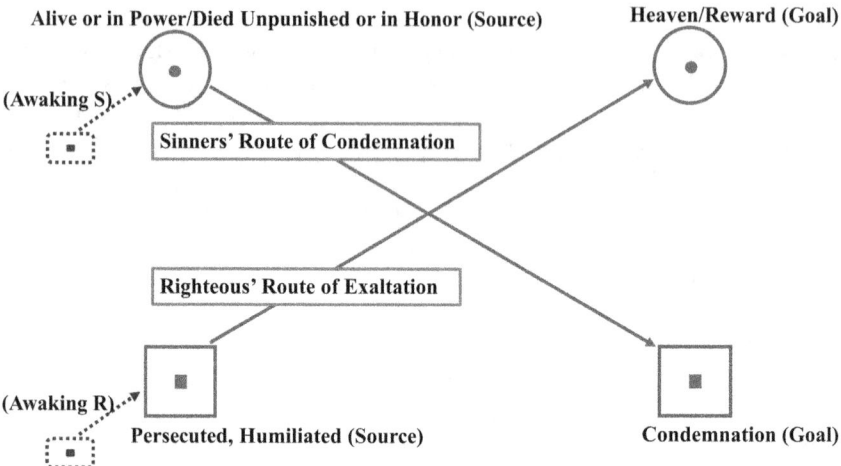

Figure 2.7 The Jewish Conceptualization of Divine Judgment and Exaltation/Condemnation.

other texts, instead of resurrection, immortality of the soul serves to enable divine judgment. For example, in the Wisdom of Solomon, the souls of the righteous are in God's hand and are kept from any torment (3:1). Similarly, the author of 1 En. 102–104 does not say that God will give new life to our bodies. Rather, it is the spirits of the righteous that will descend into Sheol at death (102:5) and later will ascend to heaven and receive good things (104:1–6), and the spirits of the sinners that will descend into Sheol with great agony without later ascent (103:4–8). Thus, in 1 En. 102–104, the soul continues to exist and can be judged, rewarded, and exalted despite the destruction of the body.

I rely on Tappenden's analysis to diagram the "Jewish conceptualization of divine judgment and exaltation/condemnation (enabled by resurrection or immortality)" in Figure 2.7.[48] It is to be noted that, while the diagram in Figure 2.7 is largely taken from Tappenden's work and is based on his analysis, I maintain that it illustrates the idea of divine judgment and that the role of resurrection is not central in this diagram. As shown in Figure 2.7, the hope for divine judgment is the overturning of a situation in which the righteous are under the control of the persecutors and are persecuted and humiliated.[49] The source location of the righteous is conceived as low and the source location of the persecutors or the apostates as high. Again, this image of high

---

of judgment for Hosea and Isaiah 24 and the fact of exile for Ezekiel 37 and Isaiah 53. See N. T. Wright, *The Resurrection of the Son of God* (Minneapolis, MN: Fortress Press, 2003), 122.

[48] Since Tappenden's "resurrection ideals" actually include exaltation and heavenly ascent, his analysis of "resurrection gestalt" is largely about the overturning structure of divine judgment and the following exaltation and condemnation for the persecuted righteous and the unpunished sinners, respectively. See Tappenden, *Resurrection in Paul*, 58–69, 85. See also footnote 37.

[49] Tappenden calls this concept "reversal" in ibid., 58. In §3.1.4, I will use the term "reversal" to describe another important concept of Paul; here I call the concept that Tappenden observes and diagrams as "overturning."

and low positions is a common metaphor based upon our repeated patterns of bodily experiences: having control is being up, and being subject to control is being down. Thus, in the Jewish hope for divine judgment, it is expected that an overturning of the current, unjust situation will happen: the low-standing righteous will be freed from oppression, rewarded, and raised high (either in status or further physically to heaven, or both) after the judgment, and, on the contrary, the persecutors and apostates who are currently standing high will be punished and humbled or brought down. As Tappenden shows with intertestamental texts, such an overturning schema (Figure 2.7) of two contrasting up-down movements is characteristic of the hope for divine judgment and rule (cf. 1 En. 99:11–102:3; Dan 12:1–3; Jub. 23:27–31).[50] It is noteworthy that, in Figure 2.7, what constitutes the overturning schema is the contrast of reward/exaltation versus punishment/descent.

However, resurrection (or immortality of the soul) does not serve to effect the overturning but to provide the condition in which the overturning might take place. That is, since some righteous were already put to death during the persecution, either resurrection (as shown in the "Awaking R" and "Awaking S" routes in Figure 2.7) or immortality of the soul would be required for the judgment. In both cases, a temporary upward movement of awaking and/or ascending to judgment is necessary for both the righteous and the unpunished sinners. This temporary upward movement is not an outcome of divine judgment but a precondition for the judgment and therefore does not include the glorious transformation. As we have seen, the requirement of resurrection for judgment is presumed in Dan 12:2–3, where both those who will receive everlasting life and shine like the stars and those who will receive everlasting disgrace first need to "awake from the dust." Instead of resurrection, the author of 1 En. 22 seems to hold the idea of immortality and claim that both the spirits of the righteous and of the sinners who died unpunished will be raised for judgment. The spirits of the sinners who were judged and punished already before they died will not be raised for judgment (1 En. 22:1–13).[51]

In 1 Thessalonians, Paul's description of resurrection (4:16) and ascent that follows resurrection (4:17) also reflects the conceptual structure in Figure 2.7. The contrast between the righteous and the persecutors is clear throughout the whole letter (e.g., 1:6; 2:2; 3:3–4; 4:16–18; 5:2–9), and the Parousia of the Lord is expected to overturn the current persecution of the righteous (1:6–10; 5:2–9), presumably through divine judgment (1:10). Like in 1 En. 102–104, Paul does not mention the temporary upward movement of the sinners. Nevertheless, like in Dan 12:2–3, Paul explicitly distinguishes resurrection (the "Awaking R" route) and exaltation (the "Righteous Route of Exaltation") with temporal adverbs. The resurrection of the dead will happen first (ἀναστήσονται πρῶτον; 1 Thess 4:16), and then (ἔπειτα …; 4:17) the living will be seized up together with the resurrected (4:17). Paul's description coincides with the structure in Figure 2.7 in which resurrection and the ultimate ascent are

---

[50] Ibid.
[51] Nickelsburg, *Resurrection*, 168–71. In some texts, such as 1 En. 102–104, only the spirit of the righteous is described as ascending from Sheol for judgment while the ascent of the sinners for judgment (the "Awaking S" route) is not mentioned.

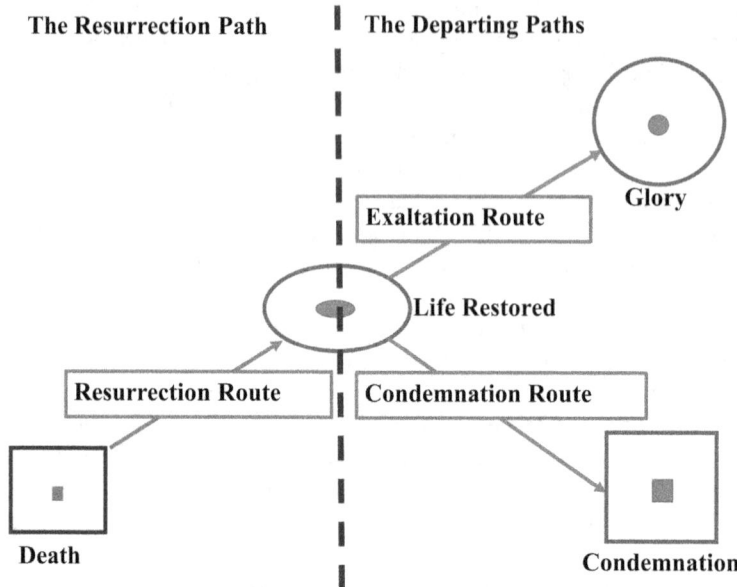

Figure 2.8 Later Jewish Conceptualization of General Resurrection and Judgment.

distinguishable; they are two distinct stages of the eschatological event. Throughout the whole letter, the expectation for divine judgment and rule is conceptualized as a schematic overturning that involves the ultimate upward movement of the righteous and the ultimate downward movement of the persecutors (cf. 1:10; 2:16–19; 5:3, 9). Resurrection provides the necessary condition for this expectation to be fulfilled for the deceased—that is why they do not need to grieve for the deceased (4:13). Thus, similar to Jewish traditions, resurrection is introduced in 1 Thessalonians as a means by which the deceased might be rewarded together with the living.

Such a distinction is clear in Jewish traditions even when "resurrection became a formalized topos" within the descriptions of eschatological judgment.[52] As Nickelsburg demonstrates with 4 Ezra 7, by the second half of the first century CE, the judgment scene is no longer the overturning of a specific unjust situation (like the persecution of Antiochus in Dan 12); it has become a general scene and a traditional way of describing eschatological events. Accordingly, resurrection also gradually became general for all the dead. In 4 Ezra 7, 2 Bar 49–51, Sib. Or. 4, and T. Benj. 10, "*all* humans are raised" or restored to life in order to face divine judgment for what they did in life.[53] Thus, as shown in Figure 2.8, what is imagined in these texts about judgment is no longer an overturning but two departing paths from one equal source location (the restored life). After resurrection and after judgment, the righteous will be transformed into a glorious form, shining like the light, stars, or angels (e.g., 4 Ezra 7:97, 125), and the

---

[52] Ibid., 214.
[53] Ibid., 175 (original emphasis), 171–7.

wicked will be condemned. As we can see in Figure 2.8, the resurrection path and the ascent path are clearly considered as two distinguishable processes, and the bodily transformation is imagined as completed at the goal of the path for the righteous. It is unreasonable to consider that sinners might also be transformed into a glorious state through the resurrection route, which is for all people. Thus, this schematic diagram of the later texts further confirms that resurrection itself does not involves glorious transformation. In the same way, it appears that Paul's conceptual structure in 1 Thess 4, as shown in Figure 2.7, also temporally distinguishes resurrection and the ultimate ascent as two distinct events, and only the latter might suggest a kind of bodily transformation.

In sum, although both resurrection and ascent/exaltation are conceptualized in Second Temple Jewish traditions through the basic structure as shown in Figures 2.5 and 2.6, they are clearly understood as two distinct events. While resurrection enables all human beings or the righteous (and sometimes the sinners) to stand judgment, ascent/exaltation is the reward for the righteous through God's rule after judgment, a reward that may involve transformation. They are distinct yet closely correlated as sequential and consequential in the imagination of divine judgment and rule in the eschatological end. If, as Asher argues, the Corinthians' denial of resurrection was based on their conviction of cosmic polarity (the incompatibility between the "Life Restored" and the "Glory" containers in Figure 2.8), their denial might have assumed the whole sequential and consequential process: the resurrected righteous are supposed to go through divine judgment and ascend into divine sovereignty to receive good things. The assumption of ascent is evident in Asher's own statement about the problem of resurrection for the Corinthians: "it is metaphysically impossible for a terrestrial body to *ascend* to a celestial realm."[54]

2.3 Paul's Alternative Experiential Pattern

It is noteworthy that Paul's argument for resurrection in 1 Cor 15 appears to mark the beginning of his thought-development diverging from the Second Temple Jewish traditions analyzed above. In this passage, Paul reveals two distinct conceptual structures in his imagination of resurrection. In the first part of the chapter (1 Cor 15:12–34), like in 1 Thessalonians, Paul's argument fits the Jewish traditions and reflects the conceptual structure diagramed in Figure 2.8. He understands resurrection as necessary for "those who have fallen asleep in Christ" (1 Cor 15:18) before they can face the end (cf. "εἶτα τὸ τέλος" in 15:24), that is, before they can stand Christ's judgment and ultimate rule (15:24–25). Without resurrection, Paul, like the deceased in the traditions that we analyzed above, could not partake in the divine sovereignty that would defeat every authority and power (15:24–25), and so would have been persecuted in vain (15:30–32). Paul uses this traditional logic to indicate that his message about resurrection must be true; otherwise, he would not risk his life for it. In the second half of this chapter

---

[54] Asher, *Polarity and Change*, 82 (my emphasis).

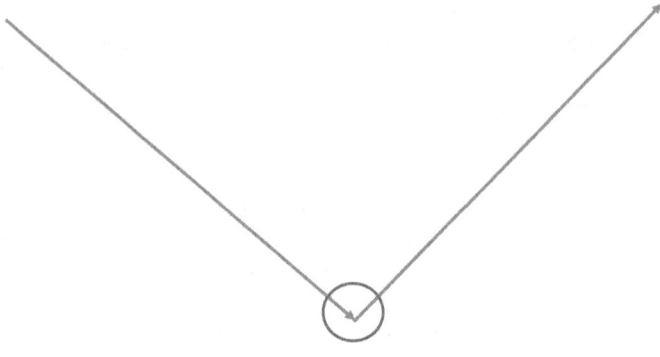

The Turning Point

Figure 2.9 The Reversal Schema.

(1 Cor 15:35–58), however, the metaphor of "sowing" (15:36–38) appears to offer an alternative image schema—the reversal schema—for readers to imagine resurrection and to conceptualize the innovative idea of bodily-transformation-at-resurrection.[55]

The "sowing" (σπείρω; 15:36) action is a common human experience that suggests a downward movement of the seed into the earth, and the growth of a plant (15:37) is typically perceived as an upward movement. When this metaphor is further developed in 15:42–44, Paul uses the verb σπείρεται as in opposition to ἐγείρεται (to be raised up) and so provides an image of two opposite movements. Thus, as shown in Figure 2.9, this metaphor shows a reversal schema consisting of a downward movement, an upward movement, and, most importantly, a turning point. As Lakoff and Johnson indicate, in addition to the journey metaphor, the "changing is turning" metaphor is another common conceptualization of events of change. That is, "remaining in a state is [imagined or expressed as] going in the same direction" and "changing is turning." For examples, "he went on talking" and "the milk turned sour."[56] Our repeated experience of reversing our moving direction also suggests an inherent logic for the schema that a sort of change and a decision (likely together with a change in emotion, environment, physical condition, etc.) occurs right at the turning point. Thus, unlike the traditions framed in the container and path schemas, the transformation in the reversal schema does not depend on the difference between the source and the goal. That is, the transformation conceptualized in this schema is not suggested by ascending to a different realm and is not based on the idea of cosmological polarity. Rather, like our common experience of changing direction and of seed sowing, a radical and fundamental transformation is understood to occur at the turning point

---

[55] What is innovative in the traditional scenario before 15:35 is that the wicked powers that will be destroyed by Christ includes "death" (15:26). As I will demonstrate in §3.2.2 and in Chapter 4, Paul builds up his alternative imagination of resurrection and bodily transformation in 15:35–54 within the reversal schema, and echoes the idea of death (and so mortality) as an enemy to be destroyed in time (15:54).

[56] Lakoff and Johnson, *Philosophy in the Flesh*, 207.

(or underneath the earth), and the upward movement represents rather the further continual advancement of that fundamental transformation.

This is a transformation of the body. As I will show in the analysis of Paul's rhetorical strategy and structure in the next chapter, the sowing metaphor introduced in 15:36–38 is meant to answer Paul's rhetorical question, "with what kind of body do they [the dead] come?" (15:35).[57] While everyone knows that the plant was the seed, as Paul describes, the body of the plant will be visibly different from the body of the seed that was sown (15:37). Thus, this sowing metaphor conveys both the continuity of identity and the discontinuity of the bodily form. Through this metaphor, Paul intends to introduce the new idea that the body of the dead person who is buried will be transformed into a new form when it is raised up. In 15:42–44, Paul delineates the resurrection of the dead by repeating the pair of verbs denoting two opposite movements—σπείρεται and ἐγείρεται—and emphasizes that what is raised up has become different from what is sown/buried (cf. John 12:24, where a sown seed is also metaphorically depicted as dying in the earth). In other words, Paul applies the sowing metaphor as analogical to death and resurrection, and, in so doing, integrates the idea of bodily transformation into his imagination of resurrection within the reversal schema. In this schema, the transformation is conceived as occurring at the turning point. The idea of transformation-at-resurrection is thus generated from such an integration.

Unlike the examples we have been considering so far, this integration of ideas is not accomplished only by metaphorical projections but also by the operation of conceptual blending (also called conceptual integration). While the sowing metaphor offers the reversal schema in which a visible transformation occurs, a seed is not transformed into an "imperishable body" in the way that Paul asserts about the transformation at resurrection (15:42). In fact, a plant is precisely an "earthly body" and would never show "the glory of the heavenly body" (15:40). In Paul's imagination, however, this kind of cosmological polarity between heaven and earth is no longer a spatial one but is accounted for by the consequential and temporally successive relation between what was sown/buried and what will be raised up.[58] In other words, in addition to what the sowing metaphor offers through metaphorical projection, there are new meanings generated in Paul's use of this metaphor and in Paul's imagination of resurrection through the reversal schema. As we will see shortly, this kind of generation of new

---

[57] As I will explain in greater detail in Chapter 3, Asher indicates that Paul's argument about the inconsistency of the Corinthians' denial of resurrection concludes in 15:34 and that his argument of "accommodation and correction" starts in 15:35. According to Asher's analysis, in 15:35–57, Paul attempts to accommodate the Hellenistic cosmology and to demonstrate that resurrection is totally compatible with that cosmology. Thus, Asher further points out that this question in 15:35b is a "leading question." This question suggests the possibility of a different kind of body and redirects the discussion to the kind of body that might be compatible with the idea of resurrection. Paul then begins his answer of this leading question with the seed-sowing metaphor. See Asher, *Polarity and Change*, 63, 77.

[58] Asher rejects this interpretation and argues that Paul is not emphasizing "temporal succession" at all in 1 Cor 15:42–44. See ibid., 98, 106–16. However, by using the verb σπείρεται, Paul is still working with the sowing metaphor. Thus, the successive relation and the continuity of identity are still in effect. I will further argue this point in Chapter 4.

meanings is characteristic of human conceptual blending. Thus, a methodological introduction of the conceptual blending theory is needed before analyzing 1 Cor 15:35–54 in the next chapter in order to explore the full function of the reversal schema in Paul's argument.

2.4 Conceptual Blending Theory: An Analytic Tool for Development

My introduction and application of conceptual blending theory (blending theory) draws upon Gilles Fauconnier and Mark Turner's classic work, as well as Evans and Green's excellent introduction to the theory.[59] Blending theory is partly built upon conceptual metaphor theory and can deal with linguistic and conceptual phenomena that conceptual metaphor theory (metaphor theory) cannot fully explain.[60] As Evans and Green indicate, while metaphor theory helps us ground human conceptualization and linguistic meaning in bodily experience, the crucial insight of blending theory is that our meaning construction usually involves an "emergent conceptual structure" that gives rise to what is "more than the sum of its parts."[61] That is, human thought and meaning construction is not simply the summation of compositional elements and cannot rely solely upon a unidirectional projection that conceptualizes one conceptual domain according to another. Evans and Green offer as an example the expression "that surgeon is a butcher," which includes two conceptual domains according to metaphor theory: that of surgery and that of butchery.[62] This expression apparently conveys a negative assessment. By conceptualizing a surgeon as a butcher, we evaluate the surgeon

---

[59] G. Fauconnier and M. Turner, *The Way We Think: Conceptual Blending and the Mind's Hidden Complexities* (New York: Basic Books, 2002); Evans and Green, *Cognitive Linguistics*, 400–44. Moreover, for uses of conceptual blending theory in New Testament studies, see B. Howe, *Because You Bear This Name: Conceptual Metaphor and the Moral Meaning of 1 Peter* (BibInt 81; Leiden: Brill, 2006); V. K. Robbins, "Conceptual Blending and Early Christian Imagination," in *Explaining Christian Origins and Early Judaism: Contributions from Cognitive and Social Science* (ed. P. Luomanen, I. Pyysiäinen, and R. Uro; Leiden: Brill, 2007), 161–95; H. Lundhaug, "Conceptual Blending in the *Exegesis* of the Soul," in *Explaining Christian Origins and Early Judaism: Contributions from Cognitive and Social Science* (ed. P. Luomanen, I. Pyysiäinen, and R. Uro; Leiden: Brill, 2007), 141–60; *Images of Rebirth: Cognitive Poetics and Transformational Soteriology in the Gospel of Philip and the Exegesis on the Soul* (NHMS73; Leiden: Brill, 2010); F. S. Tappenden, "Aural-Performance, Conceptual Blending, and Intertextuality: The (Non-)Use of Scripture in Luke 24.45–48," in *The Gospel of Luke* (ed. T. R. Hatina; London: T&T Clark, 2010), 180–200; "Luke and Paul in Dialogue: Ritual Meals and Risen Bodies as Instances of Conceptual Blending," in *Resurrection of the Dead: Biblical Traditions in Dialogue* (ed. G. van Oyen and T. Shepherd; Leuven: Peeters, 2012), 203–28; *Resurrection in Paul*, 2016; R. Roitto, *Behaving as a Christ-Believer: A Cognitive Perspective on Identity and Behavior Norms in Ephesians* (Winona Lake, IN: Eisenbrauns, 2011); R. H. von Thaden Jr., *Sex, Christ, and Embodied Cognition: Paul's Wisdom for Corinth* (Dorset, UK: Deo., 2012); T. Kazen, "The Role of Disgust in Priestly Purity Law: Insights from Conceptual Metaphor and Blending Theories," *Journal of Law, Religion and State* 3 no. 1 (2014): 62–92.

[60] Evans and Green, *Cognitive Linguistics*, 400.

[61] Ibid., 400, 437–9.

[62] J. Grady, T. Oakley, and S. Coulson, "Blending and Metaphor," in *Metaphor in Cognitive Linguistics: Selected Papers from the Fifth International Cognitive Linguistics Conference, Amsterdam, July 1997* (ed. R. W. Gibbs and G. Steen; Amsterdam: John Benjamins, 1999), 101–24.

as incompetent even if we consider both butchery and surgery as skilled professions. This negative assessment does not derive from either the conceptual domain of butchery or the domain of surgery but from a particular kind of combination of the two. Thus, metaphor theory cannot fully explain this negative assessment through the unidirectional metaphorical projection. In order to explain the conceptual effect of such an expression, we need a model that is more complex than the metaphorical projection from the source domain to the target domain. Blending theory accounts for new meanings like this negative assessment as deriving from the emergent conceptual structure that arises from a general cognitive operation called conceptual blending.

The basic units of a conceptual blending operation are called mental spaces.[63] As Fauconnier and Turner indicate, mental spaces are "small conceptual packets constructed as we think and talk, for purposes of local understanding and action."[64] They are temporary packets that are constructed "on-line" and operate within working memory.[65] A mental space includes elements and relations between those elements. For example, "Mark buys coffee in Starbucks" constitutes a mental space that has individual elements (Mark, coffee, Starbucks) and relations between them (buying, in). Moreover, Fauconnier and Turner further indicate that, while a mental space operates in working memory, it is built in part by recruiting structures preexisting in long-term memory. The space of "Mark buying coffee" also recruits preexisting structures such as "eating and drinking, buying and selling, social conversation in public places." These structures are relatively stable patterns. In this way, a mental space can contain embodied conceptual structures arising from our long-term memory of recurrent patterns of experiences.

A conceptual blending network consists of at least four mental spaces: a minimum of two input spaces are to be linked by means of a generic space that contains the relation structure common to the input spaces, and a blended space consisting of elements and structure selectively projected from the input spaces together with the elements and structure emerging from the blending operation.[66] For example, in the expression "that surgeon is a butcher," there is one input space for a surgeon working on a patient who is alive and another input space for a butcher working on a dead animal. The generic space then contains a highly schematic structure shared by both inputs: a skilled agent working with a certain technique, instrument (a sort of knife), and purpose on an object. This generic space appears to effectively link the two inputs on a conceptual level. In the blended space, there is an agent who does not exist in either of the input spaces—a surgeon who performs an operation on a living patient with the skill or even the purpose of a butcher. While a surgeon performs reconstruction in order to save the patient's life and to repair the functioning of the patient's body, a butcher

---

[63] Thus, in addition to conceptual metaphor theory, blending theory is built upon mental space theory and so inherits its focus on local meaning constructions that happen "dynamically as thought and discourse unfold." See Fauconnier and Turner, *The Way We Think*, 102; Evans and Green, *Cognitive Linguistics*, 369.
[64] Fauconnier and Turner, *The Way We Think*, 102.
[65] Evans and Green, *Cognitive Linguistics*, 369. Fauconnier and Turner, *The Way We Think*, 103.
[66] Fauconnier and Turner, *The Way We Think*, 39–57. See also Lundhaug's description in "Conceptual Blending in the *Exegesis* of the Soul," 143.

dismembers the object. The new meaning of incompetence derives from the emergent structure in which a surgeon possesses improper skills that would lead to an opposite purpose—dismembering the patient and destroying the life and bodily functioning of the patient.[67]

Moreover, according to blending theory, the inputs are still conceptually linked (online) with the blended space and are informed by this blended, tragic scenario in which a butcher's skills are fatal to a patient. Thus, instead of the unidirectional projection in metaphor theory, blending theory recognizes a significant cognitive operation called backward projection.[68] Through backward projection, a strong contrast between the two inputs is strengthened in the whole blending network. This contrast makes the surgeon appear to be ridiculously incompetent. This kind of strengthening or enriching effect can be very meaningful when one of the inputs is a ritual practice. Ritual practice provides repeated embodied basis that conveys meaning and so the meaning of the ritual might be developed through the constant enriching effect. Thus, backward projection is also helpful in explaining the emergence of new meanings. We will see this effect in the conceptual blends enacted in baptism.

In sum, blending theory is a robust tool for analyzing the conceptual mechanism of the emergence of new meanings—the emergent structure in the blended space and the backward projection of the emergent structure to the inputs that in turn enriches the inputs. The effectiveness of a conceptual blend, however, is largely determined by the principle of "human scale."[69] An effective blend generates new meanings on the basis of human experience.[70] Below, two brief examples of different types of conceptual blends taken from Paul's letters will illustrate how conceptual blending theory can account for the emergence of new meanings with the principle of human scale, the mechanism of emergent structure, and backward projection.

2.4.1 The Single-Scope Network for Explaining Metaphorical Expressions

The first example (1 Cor 15:25–26) shows that blending theory can complement metaphor theory by considering a typical metaphorical expression as a single-scope blending network. As shown in Figure 2.10 (diagramed by Fauconnier and Turner), a single-scope network has two input spaces with distinct organizing structures, and only one of the structures is projected to organize the elements in the blended space. Thus, one of the inputs (the "framing input") offers the structure to compress the diffuse elements and structures in another input (the "focus input").[71] This network is very similar to metaphorical projection. Fauconnier and Turner indicate that the

---

[67] Evans and Green, *Cognitive Linguistics*, 405.
[68] Fauconnier and Turner, *The Way We Think*, 18–20.
[69] Ibid., 312.
[70] On this point, Evans and Green offer an example of a professor who lectures on the topic of evolution, saying, "The dinosaurs appeared at 10 pm, and humans only showed up on the stroke of twelve." In this case, by blending the long evolutionary time with the time period of a 24-hour day, the professor tries to achieve human scale in order to make evolution more imaginable for us. Evans and Green, *Cognitive Linguistics*, 418–19.
[71] Fauconnier and Turner, *The Way We Think*, 130.

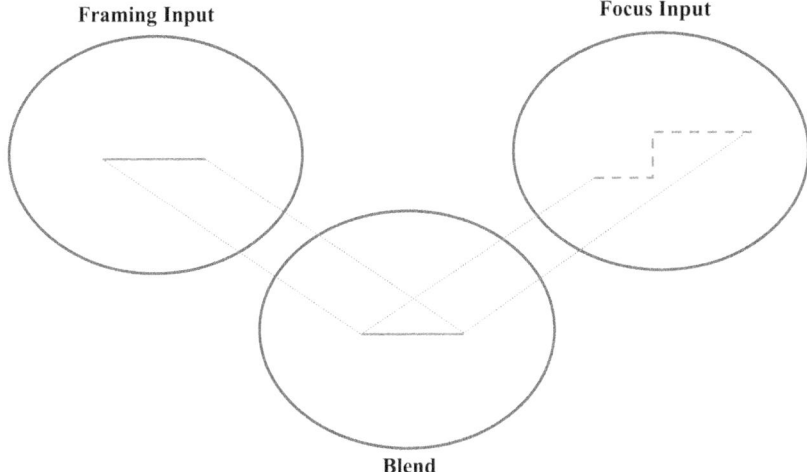

Figure 2.10 Structuring and Compressing the Focus Input (adapted from Fauconnier and Turner, *The Way We Think*, 130).

single-scope network is the "prototype" of source-target metaphors and makes us feel that "one thing (usually more concrete) is giving us insight into another thing (usually more abstract)."[72] This is also the way that a conceptual blend functions to provide "global insight" by compressing diffuse structures to more compact and concrete structures offered by the framing input that can achieve "human scale."[73]

Paul's metaphor of death as enemy in 1 Cor 15:25–26 can be considered as a single-scope network of conceptual blend: "For he [Christ] must reign until he has put all his enemies under his feet. The last enemy to be destroyed is death." Here the focus input is the imagination of general resurrection as an eschatological event occurring during Christ's ultimate rule. In context, Paul tries to argue that general resurrection for all people will surely occur because Christ is the first fruits, whose resurrection has guaranteed our resurrection in the future (15:20, 23). In 15:25–26, Paul builds his argument by organizing the eschatological imagination with a structure of a war between two reigns—the framing input. This framing input itself has pre-compressed the complexity of wars into a scenario with a simple outcome: one reign defeats another, destroys the dominion of another, and rules according to its own will.[74] Thus, this framing input provides a human scale for imagining the eschatological events, including the event of general resurrection. In the blended space, Christ and "Death" are two powers in conflict, and Christ will destroy Death since he has already defeated Death: he himself has been raised from the dead.[75]

---

[72] Ibid., 127, 129.
[73] Ibid., 312.
[74] Fauconnier and Turner observe that "the most obvious kind of compression in single-scope networks is the use of preexisting compressions from the framing input." See ibid., 129.
[75] According to the context in the previous verse, the present tense of the verb καταργεῖται in 15:26 should be understood as referring to what occurs "when the end comes" after Christ's Parousia

Although Paul's imagination of resurrection in 1 Cor 15 before 15:35 is a traditional scenario that fits the conceptual structure diagramed in Figure 2.7, this metaphor of death as an enemy to be destroyed by Christ appears to be new. As I will demonstrate in Chapter 3, this understanding of death (as a temporary power or enemy) helps Paul to further blend (in 15:35–54) the Corinthians' idea of spatial polarity of the bodies in cosmos into a temporal schema of resurrection and bodily transformation: in time, death will be swallowed up in victory, and the dead and the mortal will be changed to be immortal (15:52–54).

2.4.2 The More Complex Blends and Their Meaning Constructions

It is to be noted that not all conceptual blends are metaphorical, and some conceptual blends are more complex than framing one thing according to another (like in a metaphor).[76] These more complex blends are called double-scope or multiple-scope networks, in which more than one input contributes to the organizing structure in the blended space. These networks of blends are particularly relevant to the study of Paul's thought-development because new meanings frequently emerge from such blends. In a double-scope network, the two input spaces have distinct (and sometimes incompatible) organizing structures, and the structure of the blended space includes parts of each of those input structures as well as the new structure emerging from the blending operation.[77] Since both inputs contribute significantly to the structure of the blended space, sometimes their incompatible structures may "clash." According to Fauconnier and Turner, such clashes do not prevent the blending operations but lead to highly innovative blends.[78] We have seen this kind of clash in the tragic incompatibility between a surgeon and a butcher. A new meaning of negativity emerges through the blend of these two input spaces that could both be positive.

Romans 6:3–4 is a clear example of a double-scope network of conceptual blending, where Paul says,

> Or do you not know that as many as were baptized into Christ Jesus were baptized into his death? Therefore, we have been co-buried (συνετάφημεν) with him

---

(15:23–24). See G. D. Fee, *The First Epistle to the Corinthians* (rev. ed.; Grand Rapids, MI: W. B. Eerdmans, 2014), 838.

[76] For example, in the 1990s, some responded to the view that the United States needed a leader like Margaret Thatcher by saying, "But Margaret Thatcher would never get elected here because the labor unions cannot stand her." This expression is a conceptual blend in which Thatcher runs for president in the United States and fails. This new, emergent scenario is not metaphorical but is generated through the blend between the real characters of Thatcher in the real Britain, on the one hand, and the real United States on the other hand. Moreover, as Fauconnier and Turner indicate, the purpose of this blend is to highlight the difference between the United States and Britain, and this purpose is achieved by the *backward projection* of the blended scenario to the two inputs of reality. In other words, the inputs are still linked with the blended space and are informed by this blended scenario in which Thatcher is defeated. A powerful contrast between the two inputs, American and British political contexts, is thus established. Fauconnier and Turner, *The Way We Think*, 18–20.

[77] Ibid., 131.

[78] Ibid.

through baptism into [his] death, so that, just as Christ was raised from the dead by the glory of the Father, so we too might walk in newness of life.

As many have noted, the expression "co-buried" (συνετάφημεν) and the reference to Christ's death echoes 1 Cor 15:3–4 where Christ is described as dead and buried (ἐτάφη).[79] Paul considers a believer's somatic experience in baptism as participation in Christ's death and burial. Moreover, in Rom 6:4, Paul also considers a believer's new life after baptism an analogy to Christ being raised up from the dead. Thus, the first input in this blending network is Christ's reversal pattern of died-buried-raised up as delineated in 1 Cor 15:3–4. The second input is a believer's experience in baptism, which shows a similar reversal pattern of being immersed into water and then raised up from water. The repeated practice of baptism in Christian groups provides a human scale for imagining the eschatological event in Christ's pattern. The most striking phenomenon in this conceptual blending is that a believer is co-buried with Christ into Christ's death in the blended space. The idea of being united with Christ in his death and burial is a significant development in Paul's thought and would in turn generate further developments. This idea of co-burial does not exist either in Christ's reversal pattern of death and resurrection (where only Christ is buried) or in baptismal practice (where a believer is baptized/immersed rather than buried). That is, the emergent structure of co-burial in the blended space is created by the structures of both inputs and is more than their sum. Through backward projection, this new idea would also enrich the meaning of the baptismal rite itself. Here, the blended space and both inputs are not metaphors, and Paul indeed intends to conceptualize a kind of participation in death that is more than a metaphorical death, as his argument about the law requires (cf. 1 Cor 7:1–6). The emergence of the innovative idea of participating in Christ's death through a double-scope conceptual blend will be fully discussed in Chapter 5 because both inputs are pre-blended and require more blending analysis in Chapters 3 (the reversal structure of burial and resurrection) and 4 (the way that baptismal practice is related to the idea of union with Christ), respectively.

2.5 Conclusion

Applying cognitive linguistic tools (image schema and conceptual metaphor) to Paul's writings, I have demonstrated in this chapter that complex imaginations and abstract ideas about life, death, and resurrection or afterlife in both Hellenistic and Second Temple Jewish traditions were fundamentally constructed on the basis of recurrent patterns of human embodiment. Indeed, though it is logical and implicit that cognition only occurs while embodied, the relationship between this embodiment and thinking specifically about resurrection has not been fully explored by scholars. Thus, I have also indicated Paul's innovative conceptual structure of reversal in his imagination of resurrection, a conceptual structure that emerged from an alternative experiential

---

[79] E.g., see J. Kloppenborg, "An Analysis of the Pre-Pauline Formula 1 Cor 15:3b-5 in Light of Some Recent Literature," *CBQ* 40 no. 3 (1978): 351–67.

pattern to that of the existing traditions, which implied a different timing of bodily transformation. In the next chapter, I will apply conceptual blending theory to further explore the complex interactions and conceptual blends between this reversal structure and various ritual activities in Pauline communities. In so doing, I will explain the contextual reason for Paul to introduce the experiential pattern of reversal and to accordingly generate the idea of a different timing of transformation.

3

"We Will All Be Transformed": Transformation at Resurrection

Paul's argument for resurrection and transformation in 1 Cor 15:35–57 marks a milestone in his thought-development. In this passage, addressing a particular issue in the Corinthian community, a creative image of resurrection occurring simultaneously with bodily transformation was generated and carefully expounded. This image then exerted a continuing influence on the later thoughts of Paul and Pauline communities. I have mentioned that there are two aspects of innovation in this passage: the substantive transformation of the human body and the timing of transformation as occurring at resurrection. Regarding the former, Jeffery R. Asher has demonstrated that the idea of substantive transformation in this passage was Paul's strategical use of Hellenistic philosophies in order to accommodate the cosmology held by the Corinthians. He thus convincingly suggests that this idea in 1 Corinthians reveals Paul's thought-development. However, Paul's innovation on the timing of transformation cannot be adequately accounted for by simply considering this intellectual context. Rather, we have to further look at the experiential context. I suggest that the most fundamental target issue that Paul's argument in this passage addresses is not philosophical cosmology but a very common human experience and observation—the decomposition of the corpse, especially observable in death rites. I will argue that, due to this vivid and powerful embodied experience, Paul had to provide an alternative image schema of reversal for imagining resurrection, an alternative schema that generated the idea of simultaneous transformation.

Thus, this chapter will show how the experiential context of ancient death rites and the related intellectual context of philosophical cosmology might have influenced the formation and articulation of Paul's resurrection ideas. First, I will explore how death rites were practiced (the experiential context) and conceptualized in Greco-Roman societies (the related intellectual context). As we will see, Paul's argument in 1 Cor 15 is largely concerned with both the practices of ancient death rites and the ideas about cosmology and afterlife conveyed in those practices. Second, building upon the studies of Normand Bonneau and Asher on Paul's rhetorical style and structure in 1 Cor 15, I will analyze this passage by applying cognitive linguistic tools—image schema, conceptual metaphor, and conceptual blending.[1] In so doing, I will demonstrate the change in Paul's image schemas for imagining resurrection and explain the specific rhetorical function of this schematic change. It will become clear that Paul's arguments in 1 Cor 15:35–57 are primarily driven by the seed-sowing metaphor (15:36–38), which changes his image schema for resurrection, and is crafted to enact a set of conceptual blends that respond to some Corinthian dissenters' rejection of bodily resurrection. Their rejection is based upon their embodied experience in death rites and their cosmology and imagination of afterlife that is related to and coherent with their experience in death rites. Thus, there is a clear correlation between Paul's use of metaphor and image schema on the one hand and the Corinthians' embodied experience on the other.

Specifically, as revealed in 15:35, the Corinthian dissenters' rejection is concerned with the body. I will indicate that the decomposition of the body was a central element in ancient death rites and was a clear indication of the mortality of the body. This undeniable mortality observed in decomposition has strengthened the Hellenistic idea of afterlife based on the cosmic polarity that Paul is dealing with: that the mortal, earthly body cannot participate in the heavenly realm (cf. 15:50). Thus, bodily resurrection is either impossible or at least not relevant to the ascent of the immortal soul. Nevertheless, Paul does not negate the Corinthians' experience and cosmology. Instead, Paul tries to persuade the dissenters by introducing a new idea that is compatible with their experience and cosmology. This new concept is the transformation that results in the temporal polarity of the body (15:42–44a). Technically, Paul introduces and defends his new idea by triggering three conceptual blends: the blend between resurrection and the reversal pattern of seed sowing and growing (15:36–38), and two further blends between the (new) reversal pattern of resurrection first with cosmic polarity (15:39–41) and then with the Adam-Christ typology (15:44b–49). Before turning to the three conceptual blends themselves, it is necessary to consider the context of the problem that these blends address and to locate these blends within the rhetorical strategy and structure of Paul's whole argument in 1 Cor 15.

3.1 Experiential Context: Death Rites and the Corpse

In this section, we will first look at the pervasiveness and social function of death rites in the Greco-Roman world in order to recognize that the practice and experience of death rites were important backgrounds for understanding Paul's argument about resurrection in 1 Cor 15. Second, I will indicate that the observation of body-decomposition was a crucial experience that not only directed the practices in ancient death rites but also influenced ancient ideas about the afterlife. Specifically, I will point out the significance of the downward movement of the mortal body and the verticality schema in imagining the afterlife. By understanding better the experiential context of death rites and body-decomposition, we will improve our understanding of the intellectual context surrounding conceptions of cosmology and the afterlife.

---

[1] N. Bonneau, "The Logic of Paul's Argument on the Resurrection Body in 1 Cor 15:35-44a," *Science et Esprit* XL V/1 (1993): 79–92; Jeffrey R. Asher, *Polarity and Change in 1 Corinthians 15: A Study of Metaphysics, Rhetoric, and Resurrection* (Tübingen: Mohr Siebeck, 2000).

3.1.1 The Practice of Death Rites as an Important Context

Death rites, including funerals and the commemoration of the dead, played an important role in the social maintenance of both Hellenistic and Roman societies. As Richard E. DeMaris summarizes, the concept of the deceased going through a long and difficult journey to the world of the dead, and that death is only the beginning of such a transition, was widespread in antiquity.[2] Significantly, the living considered themselves responsible for helping the deceased go through this transition. A great amount of resources were spent on elaborate death rites because of the responsibility of the living to help the dead and the fear associated with failing in these duties.[3] As social anthropologist Edmund R. Leach indicates, human rites facilitate and manage boundary-crossings such as transitions between different social statuses.[4] In this way, death rites in ancient Greek and Roman societies functioned to facilitate and manage the long and dangerous process of boundary-crossing caused by death. The deceased only just began at the moment of death to leave the society of the living and had not yet been properly situated in the world of the dead. Through death rites, the living could settle the deceased in their world and resolve the uncertainties of the status and transitional process of the deceased. At the same time, the living could restabilize the social order of the living world disrupted by death.[5] The denial of a funeral would not only cause the dead to suffer infinitely but also jeopardize the living since the dead were considered vindictive.[6] Thus, a vicarious funeral might be carried out in some cases when the body of the deceased was not available (Dio Cass. 75.4.2-3 [Cary, LCL]).

In both Hellenistic and imperial periods, proper mourning and burial were the first obligation to help the transition of the dead. The funeral would be immediately carried out on the day of death. As Everett Ferguson summarizes, before disposal (either cremation or inhumation), the body should be "washed, anointed, clothed, and crowned with flowers." These activities were followed by lamentations, a funeral speech, breast-beating, hair-pulling, and a certain period of mourning (nine, thirty, or forty days).[7] These were also common to early Christian funerals.[8] Moreover, Franz

---

[2] R. E. DeMaris, "Corinthian Religion and Baptism for the Dead (1 Corinthians 15:29): Insights from Archaeology and Anthropology," *JBL* 114 no. 4 (1995): 663.
[3] Ibid.
[4] E. R. Leach, *Culture and Communication: The Logic by Which Symbols Are Connected: An Introduction to the Use of Structuralist Analysis in Social Anthropology* (Themes in the Social Sciences; New York: Cambridge University Press, 1976), 34–35. See also R. L. Grimes, "Defining Nascent Ritual," *JAAR* 50 no. 4 (1982): 550.
[5] M. C. Kearl, *Endings: A Sociology of Death and Dying* (New York: Oxford University Press, 1989), 95–106. See also DeMaris, "Corinthian Religion," 675.
[6] F. Cumont, *After Life in Roman Paganism: Lectures Delivered at Yale University on the Silliman Foundation* (New Haven, CT: Yale University Press, 1922), 47, 64.
[7] E. Ferguson, *Backgrounds of Early Christianity* 3rd ed. (Grand Rapids, MI: W. B. Eerdmans, 2003), 244; J. M. G. Barclay, "'That you may not grieve, like the rest who have no hope' (1 Thess 4.13): Death and Early Christian Identity," in *Pauline Churches and Diaspora Jews* (ed. J. M. G. Barclay; Tübingen: Mohr Siebeck, 2011), 231. For a detailed introduction of the Greek funeral, see R. Garland, *The Greek Way of Death* (London: Duckworth, 1985), 21–37; for the imperial funeral, see J. M. C. Toynbee, *Death and Burial in the Roman World* (Aspects of Greek and Roman Life; London: Thames & Hudson, 1971), 43–55.
[8] Barclay, "Death and Early Christian Identity," 231.

Cumont indicates that the deceased would inhabit the tomb as their "eternal house" (*domus aeterna*), a phrase that is frequently seen in funeral inscriptions of the Romans. In other words, the tomb was not only the passage through which the soul could traverse to another world, but also a lasting residence.[9] If a corpse was not properly disposed, the soul was thought to be wandering around without a dwelling place.[10] Thus, for example, the soul of Polydorus in the Aeneid was "installed" by a funeral ceremony in a cenotaph that was raised for him even though his body was already lost (Virgil, Aeneid, III, 67).[11] This belief of the tomb as the permanent house of the dead is evident in the ways that the tomb was built to be like a home, and in the ritual activities of offering food and drink in the tomb.[12] In the imperial period, usually a circular cavity was formed in a grave with a pierced hole in the bottom that was connected with a tube to an urn that held the remains of the dead. Through the holes and tubes, the living could send down food and drink directly to the buried remains.[13] It was believed that the dead, like the human bodies that they used to have, still needed nourishment for subsistence and refreshment. Thus, regular sacrifices and meals for the dead were offered by both the Greeks (on the third, seventh or ninth, and thirtieth day after the burial) and the Romans (on the day of burial, the ninth day, and the birthday of the deceased annually). Annual commemorations and sacrifices were also held by the Romans at festivals of Parentalia and Lemuria for all the deceased.[14]

Thus, as Cumont concludes, the deceased "were not cut off from the society of the living" but rather "remained in communication with their friends and their kin, who met together at their new dwellings."[15] Through the burial, the mourning, the libation, and the commemorations, the deceased were recognized as still dwelling among and participating in the social networks as they did when they were alive. Onno M. Van Nijif also observes that funerary monuments "seem to speak the language of belonging."[16] By the same token, as Richard S. Ascough argues, funerary practices show a "strategy of social differentiation" in the sense that those practices and those who participated in the practices would reflect the social position of the deceased, as well as the position

---

[9] Cumont, *After Life*, 48. Regarding this idea of lasting residence, Robert Garland indicates that "the Greeks saw nothing inconsistent in cherishing a belief in the dead living in Hades alongside the more straight-forward idea of their continued existence within or in the vicinity of the tomb." See Garland, *The Greek Way of Death*, 76, 119.

[10] S. I. Johnston, *Restless Dead: Encounters between the Living and the Dead in Ancient Greece* (Berkeley: University of California Press, 1999), 9–14; Toynbee, *Death and Burial in the Roman World*, 43, 54.

[11] Cumont, *After Life*, 48.

[12] Ferguson, *Backgrounds*, 249. For the coexistence of the tomb as the residence of the dead and other views of afterlife abodes (such as Hades or Heaven), see Toynbee, *Death and Burial in the Roman World*, 37.

[13] Garland, *The Greek Way of Death*, 110–15; Toynbee, *Death and Burial in the Roman World*, 37; K. Hopkins, *Death and Renewal* (Sociological Studies in Roman History 2; Cambridge: Cambridge University Press, 1983), 233–4.

[14] Ferguson, *Backgrounds*, 244.

[15] Cumont, *After Life*, 57–8.

[16] O. M. van Nijif, *The Civic World of Professional Associations in the Roman East* (Amsterdam: J.C. Gieben, 1997), 38.

of the participants, in a larger social context.¹⁷ The social position might include not only one's kin or ethnic identity but also one's broader social connections such as one's cult, religion, or occupation. This social phenomenon is evident in the operation of the Greco-Roman associations since, as Éric Rebillard indicates, "funerary activity is the most documented aspect of the life of the associations in the epigraphic evidence."¹⁸ By holding funerals, monuments, and inscriptions, an association proclaimed not only the identity of the deceased within the group but also the identity and position of the group as a whole in the imperial and hierarchical society.¹⁹ A significantly increasing phenomenon of death practices during the imperial period was that more and more funerary epitaphs identified the occupation of the deceased. This also indicates a trend of using death rites to locate a person not only within their kin but also within the group of persons who shared the same occupation—one of the major forms of associations.²⁰ As Ascough states, in the first century CE, "burial became an important aspect of social construction" and an important aspect for private groups, including the Christian groups.²¹

Ramsay MacMullen indicates that, emerging from within preexisting social connections, Christian communities appeared as newcomers to the social and cultural systems already established around them.²² Thus, it was inconceivable for Christians to displace all practices of pagan funerary customs even though these practices were largely intertwined with non-Christian cults and religious beliefs (cf. 1 Cor 5:10). Many funerary activities remained common to early Christians and non-Christians for a very long time.²³ For example, MacMullen indicates that Christians in the imperial period were often buried in common cemeteries with non-Christians, and that in such cases no criteria are really effective for scholars to distinguish between Christian or non-Christian burials, including "the orientation, position of arms, or even the coin in the mouth" that apparently reflects a non-Christian perspective of afterlife.²⁴ Richmond Lattimore also demonstrates the continuation of "pagan elements in Christian epitaphs,"

---

[17] R. S. Ascough, "Paul's 'Apocalypticism' and the Jesus Associations at Thessalonica and Corinth," in *Redescribing Paul and the Corinthians* (ed. R. Cameron and M. P. Miller; Atlanta: Society of Biblical Literature, 2011), 168.

[18] É. Rebillard, *The Care of the Dead in Late Antiquity* (trans. E. T. Rawlings and J. Routier-Pucci; Ithaca: Cornell University Press, 2009), 37. According to Ramsay MacMullen, by the second century CE, about "a third of the urban male population" of Rome were members of one or more associations, which could be formed on the basis of family connections, neighborhood connections, common cults, common ethnic identities, or common occupations (R. MacMullen, *Enemies of the Roman Order: Treason, Unrest, and Alienation in the Empire* [Cambridge, MA: Harvard University Press, 1966], 174); cf. P. A. Harland, *Associations, Synagogues, and Congregations: Claiming a Place in Ancient Mediterranean Society* (Minneapolis, MN: Fortress, 2003).

[19] Hopkins, *Death and Renewal*, 211–16. Sometimes, however, associations might hold death rites for nonmembers. In such cases, an association also proclaimed its status in the social order. See Nijif, *Professional Associations*, 49.

[20] Ascough, "Paul's 'Apocalypticism,'" 168. Nijif, *Professional Associations*, 42.

[21] Ascough, "Paul's 'Apocalypticism,'" 167, 170.

[22] R. MacMullen, *Christianizing the Roman Empire: A.D. 100–400* (New Haven, CT: Yale University Press, 1984), 78.

[23] Ibid., 78–9.

[24] Ibid., 153. See also N. Hayward, "Early Christian Funerary Ritual," in *Early Christian Ritual Life* (ed. R. E. DeMaris, J. T. Lamoreaux, and S. C. Muir; New York: Routledge, 2018), 116–17.

such as references to Tartarus (Diehl 3453, 3454) and Styx (Diehl 1519).[25] However, early Christians still tried to make some "selective efforts" in death rites to claim their identity and distinctiveness. According to Justin Martyr, Christians were criticized for not offering the dead libations, fat, crowns, or other sacrifices (First Apology 24.2). As John M. G. Barclay suggests, this accusation appears to refer to memorial meals beside the grave.[26] It is hard to tell how common the omission of libations among Christians was. Later, in *De spectaculis*, Tertullian maintains that Christians should avoid two kinds of idolatry, the offerings and sacrifices both to pagan deities and to the dead, because "the dead and gods are one and the same thing" (13.3–4). Nevertheless, as Rebillard notes, Tertullian was not describing things that Christians were not actually doing but arguing and explaining why they should not do these things.[27]

Peter M. Fraser has emphasized the social function of such memorial meals and pointed out that "commemorative reunions at the tomb" were not only held for the memory of the deceased but also "in general to cement the bonds which linked the members of the koinon to each other."[28] Byron R. McCane also indicates that "the cult of the dead had the effect of preserving those relationships even beyond the boundary of death."[29] Thus, given the Romanization in Thessalonica, I agree with Ascough that one of the "idols" from which Paul made the Thessalonians turn away to "serve the living and true God" (1 Thess 1:9) could be the cult of their dead and their ancestors.[30] Barclay also suggests that the severe social tensions reflected in 1 Thessalonians might be related to the disruption of their normal process of funerary practices.[31] Nevertheless, the picture revealed in 1 Corinthians is significantly different. On the one hand, whereas the Thessalonians worried about their deceased, the Corinthians did not consider their dead members as lost. Instead, similar to the vicarious death rites among pagans, they had baptism for the sake of the dead (1 Cor 15:29). On the other hand, as Barclay notes, Paul did not regard "social alienation," characteristic of the Thessalonian Christians, as characteristic of the Corinthian community.[32] Rather, there is no indication of social conflicts between the Corinthian community and the outsiders. When Paul mentions his experience of being rejected and humiliated by the outsiders, he contrasts himself with the Corinthians with a bitter tone: we are fools, you are wise; we are weak, you are strong; we are dishonored, you are honored (4:9–14).[33] The reception of the Christian faith did not appear to upset the Corinthians' previous social connections (4:10). They invited people to their gatherings (14:24–25) and were

---

[25] R. Lattimore, *Themes in Greek and Latin Epitaphs* (Urbana: University of Illinois Press, 1962), 301–39.
[26] Barclay, "Death and Early Christian Identity," 232.
[27] Rebillard, *The Care of the Dead*, 143.
[28] P. M. Fraser, *Rhodian Funerary Monuments* (Oxford: Clarendon Press, 1977), 63.
[29] B. R. McCane, *Roll Back the Stone: Death and Burial in the World of Jesus* (Harrisburg, PA: Trinity Press International, 2003), 52.
[30] Ascough, "Paul's 'Apocalypticism,'" 176.
[31] Barclay, "Death and Early Christian Identity," 222.
[32] J. M. G. Barclay, "Thessalonica and Corinth: Social Contrasts in Pauline Christianity," in *Pauline Churches and Diaspora Jews* (ed. J. M. G. Barclay; Tübingen: Mohr Siebeck, 2011), 189.
[33] Barclay points out that, according to the context, the last pair of contrast in 1 Cor 4:10, ἔνδοξοι (honored) and ἄτιμοι (dishonored), refers to the Corinthians' public reputation (ibid., 189).

invited to the meals of the nonbelievers, even in the temples (8:10; 10:27). Consequently, the issue of "food offered to idols" (1 Cor 8, 10) was still controversial and needed to be addressed by Paul. Considering the social harmony that they enjoyed with larger society, it would be unrealistic to imagine that the Corinthian Christians were not involved at all in those funerary and social practices. In fact, as will be demonstrated in the next section, the Corinthians appear to be greatly influenced by the ideas of the body, afterlife, and the hierarchical cosmic divisions that were all related to their contemporary death rites.

3.1.2 The Decomposition of the Body in Death Rites

The decomposition of the body of the deceased was central to ancient death rites and imaginations about the afterlife. As Cumont indicates, the belief that the dead continue to live was always dominant, yet it had to be conceptualized in coherence with the common and undeniable experience that the body rapidly turns into dust. Thus, through experience, people came to believe that those who used to live among them and sometimes still showed up in their dreams had become different from the human beings of flesh and blood with whom they used to interact.[34] Instead, the soul detached itself from the corpse "with the final breath" and subsisted when the body decomposed to dust.[35] Homer, in one common depiction, associated the soul (ψυχή) with one's breath. A person would become inactive when it leaves (Iliad 23.62–107). Thus, in both Hellenistic and Roman societies, the idea that the separation of the body and the soul, or the shade (umbra), or some "light essence" that used to animate the body, occurred at death was widespread and was only the beginning of a complex transition process for the soul to go to its permanent residence.[36]

It is noteworthy that, as reflected in ritual practices, the transition process of the deceased was usually conceived as being in parallel with the decomposition of the body. For example, according to Servius (in Aeneid 3.68), the funeral fire would set free the soul and allow it to reunite with the universal soul immediately. As Donna C. Kurtz and John Boardman point out, the process of death appeared to be considered as not fully complete until the flesh had rotted away and only the bones remained, and cremation would accelerate the process (which could be considered either good or bad).[37] George E. Mylonas indicates that the burial practices of the Mycenaeans reflected this understanding of the significance of body-decomposition. Both the "psyche" of the Homeric heroes and the "spirit" of the Mycenaeans were thought to remain sentient and so the living had to treat the corpse well until the body was destroyed by fire or decayed in a grave. When the flesh was no longer extant, the practice of clearing the chamber for later burials was characterized by "complete indifference and disrespect for the bones." Mylonas concludes that "the moment the flesh was dissolved and the body was transformed into a pile of bones,

---

[34] Cumont, *After Life*, 46. See also Toynbee, *Death and Burial in the Roman World*, 34, 38.
[35] Toynbee, *Death and Burial in the Roman World*, 43–4.
[36] Ferguson, *Backgrounds*, 249; DeMaris, "Corinthian Religion," 675.
[37] D. C. Kurtz and J. Boardman, *Greek Burial Customs* (Ithaca: Cornell University Press, 1971), 330.

it was apparently believed that the spirit was released from this world, that it had descended into its final abode."[38]

The Jewish practice of "secondary burial" reflects a similar perspective on the decomposition of the body and the transition process in death. In this practice, after the flesh rotted away, the bones would be dug up for preservation—the secondary burial of the bones.[39] As Steven Fine indicates, many scholars believe that the decay of the flesh was thought to have a function of atoning, so that the bone was considered "spiritually pure" and the deceased could finally be at peace when the body decomposed completely.[40] The closest relatives of the deceased were considered "socially liminal" and were supposed to be mourning during the period of time between primary and secondary burial, that is, when the body is decaying. In this period, for example, it was believed that since a deceased husband was going through a transition to the world of the dead, the widow's social interactions might be unsafe for the husband's journey.[41] Thus, the burial of the bones marked the end of the mourning period and the whole transition process of the deceased. These kinds of significances of body-decomposition accord with the observations of Robert Hertz in the Melanesian Islands: "Death is fully consummated only when decomposition has ended; only then does the deceased cease to belong to this world so as to enter another life."[42] Thus, the completion of body-decomposition indicated the point where people had to extend their experience of the body and life to pure imagination of the afterlife. This is also the point where we have to bring our exploration of the experiential context into our refreshed understanding of the intellectual context to reconfigure how the afterlife was imagined on the basis of human experience.

3.2 Intellectual Context: Cosmology and Afterlife—in Light of the Experiential Context

We have seen that the decomposition of the body usually implied that the soul or anything that continued to live had to depart from the body and reside somewhere else in the cosmos. There were two strands of thought in Hellenistic-Roman societies regarding the destination of the soul of the deceased after it departs the body: the subterranean world and the celestial world. The former view is a more intuitive concept since the body also goes down into earth even though it apparently does not continue to live. Thus, the tomb was considered the "antechamber" of the actual dwelling of souls that had departed the body and gone down into the immense cavity under the earth, Hades.[43] As DeMaris summarizes, it would require divine or ritual assistance to

---

[38] G. E. Mylonas, *Mycenae and the Mycenaean Age* (Princeton, NJ: Princeton University Press, 1966), 113.
[39] E. M. Meyers, "Secondary Burial in Palestine," *BA* 33 no. 1 (1970): 2–29.
[40] S. Fine, "A Note on Ossuary Burial and the Resurrection of the Dead in the First Century Jerusalem," *JJS* 51 no. 1 (2000): 72.
[41] McCane, *Death and Burial*, 75.
[42] R. Hertz, *Death and the Right Hand* (trans. R. Needham and C. Needham; London: Cohen and West, 1960), 47.
[43] Cumont, *After Life*, 70

help the soul go through the difficult journey and safely arrive at the distant abode.[44] For example, in order to assist the decent of the soul, both the Greeks and Romans placed a coin in the mouth of the dead. This is their payment for crossing the boundary of the underworld because the figure of Charon would charge the dead for ferrying them across the river Styx.

The second strand of thought was the ascent of the soul. This strand was a combination of Hellenistic philosophies and astral religion, which became predominant in the Roman Empire. In this idea of ascent, the abode of the blessed souls was not the underworld but the celestial regions, where they could enjoy immortality with the heavenly bodies.[45] In this view, the soul was usually conceived as consisting of the same matter as the heavenly bodies and possessing different qualities from those of the human body (see further below about the hierarchical worldview). Thus, it might ascend while the body undoubtedly descended. Nevertheless, some means of assistance were also dedicated to help the ascent of the soul to heaven. For example, it was common to place a small ladder in tombs for the dead to ascend. In the mysteries of Mithras, the ladder was made of seven different metals symbolizing the substantive transformation of the soul when it went through the transition between the planetary spheres.[46]

The world of the afterlife, either the subterranean or the celestial, was conceived as consisting of divisions. As for the former, according to the description of Virgil's Aeneid (a developed form of Greek view that passed to the Romans), the souls or shades of the deceased would be judged when they cross the river Styx.[47] They would be either sent down through the left road to arrive at the place of punishment or led down through the road on the right to the blissful place. As for the ascent view, as Ferguson indicates, while philosophers were influenced by astral religions and thought the soul joined the stars, the idea of judgment, punishment, and the parting destinies of the virtuous and the wicked still persisted and led to the divisions of the cosmos into upper and lower hierarchical regions.[48] Thus, the former divisions in the underworld (with departing roads for the virtuous and the wicked) were relocated above the earth with a clear cosmic hierarchy and polarity between the celestial and the terrestrial realms. As we have seen in Figure 2.3, the verticality and container schemas are fundamental to this sort of imagination.

This hierarchical arrangement of cosmological spheres (as different containers on a vertical axis) required matter that traversed different spheres to undergo a substantive transformation with corresponding changes in quality.[49] For example,

---

[44] DeMaris, "Corinthian Religion," 675–6.
[45] The idea of the ascent of souls seems to have been introduced into Greece from the East since astrolatry was popular in the East. See Cumont, *After Life*, 95.
[46] R. L. Gordon, "Mithraism and Roman Society," *Religion* 2 no. 2 (1972): 97. See also O. Panagiotidou with Roger Beck, *The Roman Mithras Cult: A Cognitive Approach* (London: Bloomsbury, 2016), 105–13.
[47] Ferguson, *Backgrounds*, 249.
[48] Ibid., 250.
[49] D. B. Martin, *The Corinthian Body* (New Haven, CT: Yale University Press, 1995), 15. Martin has suggested a hierarchical model to illustrate the nature of the distinction between the celestial and the terrestrial realms understood in the popular philosophical schools. As he argues, "a 'one world'

as Dale B. Martin indicates, the most dominant philosophical tradition in the first century, Stoicism, understood the cosmos as constituted by a *scala naturae*, which was hierarchical and thoroughly materialistic. The kind of material element at the top of the *scala* is called *aether* in Cicero. Elsewhere, Cicero's *aether* is called "designing fire" (πῦρ τεχνικόν) or identified as *pneuma*.[50] For the Stoics, the matter in heaven and the heavenly bodies are constituted by *aether* or designing fire.[51] As Asher summarizes, in periodic conflagrations, the matter of the world is consumed into fire. In the subsequent cosmogony, through condensation, fire successively becomes air, water, and finally earth, and all these four basic elements are arranged hierarchically with fire at top in the celestial realm (Diog. Laert. 7.142). Each of the four basic elements has a quality opposite to that of a paired element. For example, air is cold in contrast to fire and thin in contrast to earth. The transformation of one element into another, then, occurs by means of the change of one quality into its opposite.[52] Asher also demonstrates that polarities or opposites defined the understanding of transformation of not only the Stoics but also Aristotle, the Peripatetics, Plato, and some later Platonists.[53]

For Hellenistic philosophers, such transformation did not apply to human bodies. Rather, the soul had to depart from the body. Considering the soul as of divine origin, Cicero claimed that the ultimate abode of the blessed souls is in the spheres of the constellations; thus, the soul would ascend if the person had allowed the soul to attain its true nature and possibility.[54] The body, however, turned into dust according to our undeniable common experience. In fact, the souls of those who had followed the passions of the fleshly body would find it very difficult to ascend through the hierarchical layers of the cosmos (Somn. 29). Similarly, according to the Pythagorean Numenius, a person's soul originally descended through the cosmic spheres from heaven to earth. Thus, after death, the soul went back to the heavenly abode through the same path and "divested itself of the dispositions and qualities" that it had acquired during the original descending path to earth.[55] Interpreting Pythagoreans and Posidonius, Virgil also mentioned that the soul had to purify itself from the pollutions that it acquired when it was dwelling in the fleshly body.[56] That

---

model is much closer to the ancient conception, and, instead of an ontological dualism, we should think of a hierarchy of essence."

[50] LS 46D (Stobaeus; LS tr.) and *Stoicorum Veterum Fragmenta* (SVF) 2.774 (Diogenes Laertius), respectively.

[51] *De Natura Deorum* 2.39–43. See also D. B. Martin, "Paul and the Judaism/Hellenism Dichotomy: Toward a Social History of the Question," in *Paul Beyond the Judaism/Hellenism Divide* (ed. T. Engberg-Pedersen; Louisville, KY: Westminster John Knox Press, 2000), 3–38; *The Corinthian Body*, 3–38; and the summary in Troels Engberg-Pedersen, *Cosmology & Self in the Apostle Paul: The Material Spirit* (Oxford: Oxford University Press, 2010), 19–22.

[52] Asher, *Polarity and Change*, 180–83. See also M. Pohlenz, *Die Stoa: Geschichte einer geistigen Bewegung* (Göttingen: Vandenhoeck [und] Ruprecht, 1948–1949), I:70–71.

[53] Asher, *Polarity and Change*, 177.

[54] G. Luck, "Studia Divina in Vita Humana: On Cicero's 'Dream of Scipio' and Its Place in Greco-Roman Philosophy," *HTR* 49 no. 4 (1956): 214.

[55] Cumont, *After Life*, 107.

[56] Ibid., 184–5. See also R. Beck, *The Religion of the Mithras Cult in the Roman Empire: Mysteries of the Unconquered Sun* (Oxford: Oxford University Press, 2006), 83–4.

the body went down after death and the (blessed) soul went above was clear in these ideas about the divisions of cosmos. Ferguson then indicates that a combined idea eventually coalesced between the two strands of views of the soul's ultimate abode. The celestial sphere above became the abode of the virtuous, and the underworld beneath the earth was for the wicked.[57]

Asher has noticed that these Hellenistic ideas of afterlife and a hierarchical cosmos are related to the resurrection issue in 1 Cor 15. He persuasively shows that Paul's antithetical expressions of cosmic polarity (1 Cor 15:39–41) and his idea of substantive transformation with corresponding qualities (15:42–44a) indicates that he was dealing with the hierarchical cosmology of Hellenistic philosophies. Indeed, it would not be surprising if some Corinthians were familiar with these philosophical thoughts and cosmology. First of all, the Gentile background of the Corinthian community is quite explicit in Paul's descriptions of the members' idolatrous way of life before their conversion (e.g., 6:9–11; 8:7, 10; 12:2). As Gordon D. Fee indicates, what is reflected in 1 Corinthians is a "predominantly Gentile community" in which most members were thoroughly Hellenized.[58] Moreover, although the wealthier (and likely more educated) members appeared to be the minority, they seemed to exert significant influence over the community since they patronized it by at least providing the locations and food for meeting together (11:17–26; cf. Rom 16:1–2, where Phoebe is described as a patron [προστάτις]).[59] As Asher argues, it is reasonable to suggest that persons of these wealthier households had received education in rhetoric and some basic principles of philosophical systems.[60] This suggestion could be confirmed by Paul's use of Stoic slogans in 1 Cor 8–9 for his argument about freedom, and other philosophical slogans in 4:8; 6:12, 13; 8:1, 4; and 10:23.[61]

However, Asher does not relate a philosophical cosmology and Paul's argument with the more fundamental experiences of death rites and the vivid observation of body-decomposition. In fact, as we have seen, the idea of cosmic polarity conceptualized through the verticality schema was closely connected to the downward movement of the body. The simple fact that the body reduces into dust and goes down into the earth suggests the body's necessary departure from the soul or whatever essence continues to live, if there is anything that continues to live. In addition, the procedures and various periods of death rites were usually carried out in accordance with the decomposition of the body. The common observations and ritual experiences of body-decomposition would be vivid and fundamental to all the Corinthian believers living in a Gentile environment, whether educated

---

[57] Ferguson, *Backgrounds*, 250.
[58] G. D. Fee, *The First Epistle to the Corinthians: Revised Edition* (rev. ed.; Grand Rapids, MI: W. B. Eerdmans, 2014), 4.
[59] G. Theissen, *The Social Setting of Pauline Christianity: Essays on Corinth* (trans. and ed. John H. Schütz; Philadelphia: Fortress Press, 1982), 98–9; J. K. Chow, "The Rich Patron," in *Christianity at Corinth: The Quest for the Pauline Church* (ed. E. Adams and D. G. Horrell; Louisville, KY: Westminster John Knox Press, 2004), 197–206. Martin suggests it was "the strong" (upper class) who rejected the idea of bodily transformation. See Martin, *The Corinthian Body*, 122.
[60] Asher, *Polarity and Change*, 127.
[61] D. B. Martin, *Slavery as Salvation: The Metaphor of Slavery in Pauline Christianity* (New Haven, CT: Yale University Press, 1990), 66.

or not. Indeed, the core message delivered in Paul's seed-sowing metaphor is God's creative power that can transform the body that dies beneath earth (15:36; see also John 12:24, where a sown seed is conceived as dying beneath earth) and can reverse its downward movement into earth into an upward movement. In other words, the message delivered in the seed-sowing metaphor is a reversal of body-decomposition.

Moreover, as will be demonstrated, the theme of cosmic polarity in Paul's argument serves to further exposit this very message of reversal. It is not the idea of vertical polarity but the reversal pattern of the sowing metaphor that provides the driving force for the whole argument in 1 Cor 15:35–57. In other words, according to Paul's rhetorical structure, the issue of body-decomposition seems to be more fundamental than cosmic polarity. Thus, the direct target of Paul's message of reversal appears to be the decomposition of the body, though undoubtedly the philosophical concept of cosmic polarity is closely connected and must be addressed. Indeed, the close combination of body-decomposition and soul-ascent in a hierarchical cosmos, a combination that was crucial to death rites, would make the traditional view of bodily resurrection—the restoration of the body—not convincing or appealing enough to the Gentiles. In this case, the experiential context strengthens the intellectual context and provides the fundamental contextual reason for Paul's innovation. The correlation between Paul's rhetorical structure and image schemas analyzed in the next section will affirm the essential role of the experiential context.

We should further note that, in the imperial period, Gentiles often connected the decomposition of the body with the Christian preference of inhumation and regarded it as their reason for rejecting the Christian belief of resurrection. This preference and the general shift from cremation toward inhumation was not distinctively Christian but a common phenomenon in the eastern Mediterranean, including the Roman colonies there. However, Rebillard indicates that some Gentiles still ridiculed Christians for preferring inhumation to cremation because they (falsely) attributed to Christians an unreasonable belief that the destruction of the corpse, including the destruction made by cremation or by any other reason, could prevent resurrection.[62] According to Octavius Januarius, Caecilius Natalis rejected resurrection and maintained that "but of course every body, withdrawn from the flame or not, is eventually reduced to earth" (Octavius, 11.4). However, Christians clearly stated that they refused cremation for the sake of their respect for the human body. They understood that all corpses would decompose anyway and rejected any idea that the preservation of the body by human effort was the prerequisite for resurrection.[63] As Paul also argues in 1 Cor 15, the body is not going to be preserved but to be transformed by God.

---

[62] Rebillard, *The Care of the Dead*, 82.
[63] Octavius explains the restoration of the body in a supernatural way: the elements of the body "are preserved in the safekeeping of God" no matter how it decomposed (34.10). See Rebillard, *The Care of the Dead*, 83–5.

3.3 The Seed-Sowing Metaphor and the Argument of Reversal

Drawing on Bonneau and Asher's work on Paul's rhetorical structure, the analysis of image schema and conceptual blending in the rest of this chapter will demonstrate that Paul's resurrection ideas in 1 Cor 15, which are different from the ideas in 1 Thess 4, are articulated specifically to respond to the circumstantial issues in Corinth. In other words, Paul has contextual reasons to introduce these distinct ideas in 1 Cor 15.

Paul reveals two distinct image schemas in his teaching about resurrection in 1 Cor 15, and these two schemas clearly correspond to his rhetorical structure. It appears that Paul has a specific rhetorical purpose to offer an alternative schema in the second half of this chapter. In the first half (15:1–34), Paul is defending the received traditions.[64] According to Asher, Paul employs a common didactic technique, "the theme of inconsistency," to show that the dissenters' rejection of resurrection is inconsistent with the received gospel tradition and with their own ritual practice.[65] Paul's image schema of resurrection reflected in 15:1–34 fits what is seen in the Second Temple Jewish traditions and in Paul's previous teaching in 1 Thess 4 (see Figure 2.7). At the heart of that traditional schema is an upward movement (of the righteous dead, the oppressed, and the persecuted). However, in the second half (15:35–58), where the alternative schema is introduced and expounded, Paul changes his didactic technique and begins to directly deal with the challenges raised by the dissenters against bodily resurrection. As Asher accurately indicates, here Paul starts to employ another didactic technique of "accommodation and correction," which was also a widely used pedagogical device in antiquity.[66] With this new technique, Paul attempts to correct the dissenters' denial of resurrection not by negating their experience but by accommodating it. As I will show below, Paul accomplishes this didactic goal by enacting a set of conceptual blends driven by the metaphors of seed sowing and growing (15:36–38). As illustrated in Figure 3.1, the sowing metaphor provides an alternative schema of reversal for imagining resurrection (see the contrast of σπείρεται and ἐγείρεται as two opposite movements in 15:42–44), a schema that is different from the schema in 15:1–34 (and in 1 Thess 4 and other Jewish resurrection traditions) and becomes dominant in the whole argument after 15:35. It is, then, reasonable to say that this reversal schema is

---

[64] Asher has indicated that Paul's "deliberative rhetoric" in the whole of 1 Cor 15 appeals to the "advantage of accepting the doctrine of resurrection." Paul claims that the stability of their faith (15:1–2) and their ultimate eschatological destiny (15:55–57) depend on this doctrine. As Asher indicates, Paul begins this chapter with the verb γνωρίζω (15:1) and so immediately reveals his instructional intent. This verb then refers to the gospel that Paul previously delivered to the Corinthians (15:2). Thus, with a didactic style, Paul defends what he delivered before in the first half of this chapter. In the second half, Paul addresses the challenge that the dissenters raised against what he delivered. See Asher, *Polarity and Change*, 47, 53–8.
[65] While the theme of inconsistency is also used in polemical contexts, other didactic features in 1 Cor 15 suggest that Paul's use of this theme here is didactic (e.g., the syllogistic arguments in 15:12–34, the appeal to his own experience as a model in 15:30–32, and, as will be demonstrated below, the metaphorical style in 15:35–44a). See Asher, *Polarity and Change*, 59–63.
[66] Ibid., 63, 83–7.

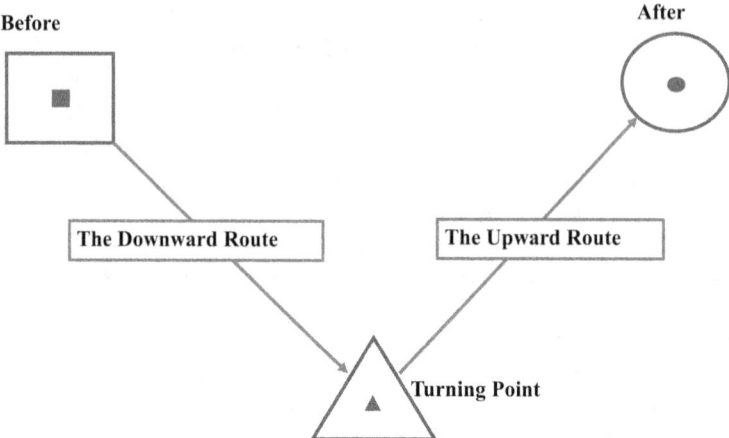

Figure 3.1 Paul's Conceptualization of Resurrection through the Reversal Schema.

introduced for the sake of the very issue that is dealt with in 15:35–58—the dissenters' denial of resurrection.

Based on Bonneau and Asher's analysis of Paul's rhetorical structure, I outline Paul's argument in 1 Cor 15:35–58 as below. Three conceptual blends are enacted in this passage and constitute the essence of the whole argument.

1. A leading question concerning the body in resurrection (15:35)
2. The argument of metaphor
   2.1. Resurrection framed by the metaphors of seed sowing and growing (15:36–38)—the First Blend that generates the reversal imagination of resurrection
   2.2. An exposition of the sowing metaphor with the idea of cosmic polarity (15:39–41)—a new input of cosmic polarity
   2.3. The application of the sowing metaphor (15:42–44a)—the Second Blend that corrects the denial of the Corinthians
3. The argument of scripture (15:44b–49)—another new input of Adam-Christ typology that enacts the Third Blend
4. The solution to the leading question (15:50–54) and the message (15:55–58)

According to this outline, Paul's strategy of responding to the dissenters is to ask a "leading question" and then answer this question.[67] His answer consists of two major arguments: an argument of metaphor and an argument of scripture. The argument of metaphor is built upon the sowing metaphor and contains two conceptual blends, and the argument of scripture further blends the reversal pattern offered by the metaphor with the Adam-Christ typology in the scripture. It is, then, reasonable to say that the reversal schema is introduced for the sake of the very issue that is dealt with in

---

[67] Ibid., 69.

15:35–58, the dissenters' denial of resurrection, and that this schema helps Paul to respond to the denial by enacting conceptual blends.

First, Paul defines the problem as about the body with two questions in 15:35: "How are the dead raised? With what kind of body do they come?" As Asher indicates, these two questions are not distinct because "the second question clearly amplifies the first."[68] This style is similar to Socrates' dialectical method of amplification. Socrates would begin with "a general, open-ended question" and immediately offers more questions, in which his intents of asking the general question would be revealed.[69] In Paul's case, the second question specifies the first by focusing the general question of resurrection on the body. The issue of resurrection that Paul intends to deal with in the following argument is about the body.

At the heart of the body issue is the fact that the Jewish hope of resurrection is a hope counting on God's power to reverse reality. The sowing metaphor that immediately follows the leading questions is intended to address this very issue arising from the nature of the hope and the nature of the body. As Bonneau notes, Paul attempts to defend "the reasonableness of what to common sense appears impossible—the existence of a resurrected body."[70] Indeed, the Jewish idea of bodily resurrection did not arise from reasonableness according to common sense. On the contrary, this hope arose in response to the irreversible death of the righteous in persecution and functioned to make it possible for those righteous to witness and participate in divine judgment and the consequent overturning of the unjust reality.[71] In other words, the hope of resurrection was a hope against perceivable reality, including the reality of body-decomposition and the unjust environment (even though it was also imagined through conceptual structures—the schemas of verticality, container, and path—that emerged from human experience). Of course, the conviction that the deceased continue to live in the form of soul or "light essence" is also a hope against reality. However, to imagine that the soul departs the body and still lives is to build the imagination upon what no one is able to see.[72] On the contrary, the idea of the restoration of destroyed bodies is an idea directly against observable and irreversible facts. Such a hope about the body could only rely on a belief in God's power to confront the irreversibility of reality.

Indeed, resorting to God's ability to reverse reality is what Paul tries to do. After the questions in 15:35, Paul quickly turns to God's creative power on various bodies in the universe. After introducing the sowing metaphor and the transformation of the seed, Paul attributes this transformation to God in 15:38 and then proceeds in 15:39–41 to describe various bodies in the universe that God has given.[73] Thus, as I have suggested, behind the issue raised by the dissenters about the body is the common (and usually ritual) experience that the bodies of the dead turn into dust and descend into the

---

[68] Ibid., 68.
[69] Ibid., 68–9.
[70] Bonneau, "Resurrection Body," 91.
[71] Nickelsburg, *Resurrection*, 32, 213.
[72] In fact, this imagination may be coherent with some forms of experiences in dreams or altered states of consciousness and so may be constructed upon those experiences.
[73] See Fee, *Corinthians*, 865; Asher, *Polarity and Change*, 79–80.

earth, and the cosmological concept related to this experience that such mortal bodies would never move upwards to partake in the afterlife in the heavenly realm (cf. 15:50). Strengthened by their ideas of afterlife and hierarchical cosmos, the impression that the body does not continue to live and can only move downwards is so powerful and vividly undeniable that Paul cannot simply refute or ignore it. Paul needs to take the decomposition of the body seriously and to persuade the Corinthians that God's creative power is able to reverse what is experienced as downwards and irreversible. This pressing need of accommodation appears to explain Paul's use of the seed-sowing metaphor (15:36–38), which offers an alternative image schema for Paul's imagination of resurrection.

Thus, I suggest that it is the decomposition of the body that prompts Paul's use of the sowing metaphor and so the change of his image schema for imagining resurrection. In order to accommodate the phenomenon of decomposition, Paul needs to directly address the downward movement of the body. In this regard, the alternative schema of reversal consists of a downward movement, an upward movement, and a turning point. Therefore, the reversal schema provides Paul's accommodating purpose the necessary elements to respond to the decomposition of the body and the closely connected idea that only the soul departs and ascends. In short, Paul needs a metaphor from the creation in which an object moves downwards, withers, and then moves upwards into a better form. The sowing metaphor thus perfectly provides Paul's following argument the fundamental image schema of reversal and the core idea of bodily transformation by God's power. That is, through a reversal pattern, God's creative power can transform a body that goes downwards and dies beneath earth to a new form of body that grows upwards in its new life. Nevertheless, the two schemas do not contradict each other. Rather, while the downward movement and the turning point are simply assumed in the traditional schema, they are addressed and highlighted in the reversal schema.

The second blend is also built upon the sowing metaphor and its reversal pattern. After the first blend between resurrection and the reversal pattern of seed sowing and growing, in 15:39–44a, Paul then develops this reversal image of resurrection by introducing another input, the cosmic polarity, and so enacts the second blend. I maintain that the cosmic polarity mentioned in 15:39–41 is not another illustrating metaphor or analogy of resurrection provided by Paul. Rather, it was taken by many people in antiquity as reality and as an important basis for their rejection of bodily resurrection.[74] As Asher observes, the theme of cosmic polarity actually creates a

---

[74] Relying on Rodolphe Morissette, Bonneau has noted the structural parallels between Paul's argument in 15:35–44a and the similar metaphorical or analogical teachings about the resurrection body found in rabbinic literature. Bonneau thus indicates that, in parallel with the rabbinic teachings on resurrection, Paul's argument in 15:35–44a is a didactic unit that consists of three parts: the objecting question from dissenters (15:35), the metaphor or analogy based on common experiences (15:36–41), and the application (15:42–44a). I agree with Bonneau's analysis of this passage as one unit with these three parts and his insightful emphasis on Paul's didactic use of common human embodiment (seed sowing in Paul's case) from which a recurrent pattern of reversal emerged. However, by treating 15:36–38 and 15:39–41 as two distinct analogies, Bonneau has missed both Paul's strategy of accommodation and the driving force of the sowing metaphor. See Bonneau, "Resurrection Body," 80–3. Cf. R. Morissette, "La condition de ressuscité, 1 Cor 15, 35–49: Structure littéraire de la péricope," *Biblica* 53 no. 2 (1972): 208–28.

problem (rather than an illustration) for bodily resurrection since the perishable things on earth cannot inherit the imperishable things in heaven (15:50).[75] It is thus more reasonable to argue that polarity is a problem of resurrection raised by the dissenters that Paul needs to resolve on the basis of the sowing metaphor. Indeed, with the repeated pair of verbs in 15:42–44a (it is sown … it is raised), Paul develops the ideas of transformation and the reversal pattern that have been introduced in the sowing metaphor in order to clarify how resurrection might be possible in the context of cosmic polarity.[76] Therefore, in 15:39–41 Paul does not provide another illustrating analogy, but further exposits the reversal schema of the sowing metaphor by 'blending' it with the concept of cosmological polarity.[77] In so doing, Paul intends to show that resurrection is not in conflict with cosmic polarity. In other words, Paul accommodates the dissenters' cosmology by a conceptual blend of that cosmology and his sowing metaphor for imagining resurrection. As Asher states, Paul's purpose is to demonstrate that "bodily resurrection of the dead is fully compatible with the very basis on which the dissenters had challenged it."[78]

Thus, as will be detailed in the blending analysis below, when Paul again uses the verb σπείρεται in 15:42–44a, a new meaning has been generated through conceptual blending. That is, driven by the sowing metaphor, at the application part of the metaphor (15:42–44a, see my outline of 15:35–58) Paul has reached the new idea that he intends to use to instruct the Corinthians: through the reversal pattern, bodily transformation would result in temporal polarity (rather than cosmic polarity) before and after resurrection. The generation of this important idea requires a detailed analysis applying conceptual blending theory.

The third blend is that between the whole argument of metaphor (15:36–44a) and the argument of scripture (15:44b–49). As Bonneau notes, Paul ends his metaphorical style at 15:44a and begins "argument based on Scripture" at 15:44b, and this scriptural argument in 15:44b–49 is aimed to defend and to develop the new idea of temporal polarity of the body, an idea that emerges from the first and second conceptual blends enacted in 15:36–44a.[79] According to Paul's scriptural interpretation, there is a temporal polarity between the first Adam and the ἔσχατος Adam. That is, Paul applies the temporal polarity, his new message, to a Christological and eschatological framework. Thus, in 15:50–54, Paul is finally ready to offer his solution to the question stated in 15:35 concerning the mortal body: in the eschatological redemption, we who belong to Christ will be transformed and the

---

[75] Asher, *Polarity and Change*, 82.
[76] Ibid., 82–3.
[77] See Bonneau, "Resurrection Body," 88. Bonneau has noted that Paul's message emerges from the "blending" of 15:36–38 and 15:39–41: the "before-after transformation" that results in the "below-above distinction." I call this emergent message "temporal polarity."
[78] Asher, *Polarity and Change*, 63.
[79] As Bonneau argues, the repetition of the phrases "psychical body" and "pneumatic body" from 15:44a, together with the εἰ … καὶ construction in 15:44b, indicates that 15:44b serves to reassert the message delivered in 15:42–44a and to anticipate the supporting argument in what follows. Moreover, introduced by the connective phrase οὕτως καὶ, it is also clear that the scriptural citation of Gen 2:7 in 1 Cor 15:45 functions to support and explain the immediately preceding contents. See Bonneau, "Resurrection Body," 82.

dead will be raised in an imperishable form. Nevertheless, as I will analyze below, by introducing the scriptural typology of Adam and Christ, Paul enacts the third blend, which adds a tone of war and victory into the idea of temporal polarity (15:54–57). For Paul, this warlike and dualistic sense of polarity seems to be helpful for marking community boundaries.

In sum, Paul's change from a traditional image schema of resurrection to an alternative schema of reversal corresponds to his rhetorical purpose and thus directly addresses the circumstantial issues. Starting from 15:35, the sowing metaphor and its reversal pattern is central to Paul's answer to the dissenters' challenge of resurrection at 15:35, a challenge that largely arose from the vivid experience of body-decomposition. Moreover, based on the reversal pattern, Paul enacts three conceptual blends to deal with issues related to body-decomposition. In the following, I will apply conceptual blending theory to analyze Paul's use and exposition of the sowing metaphor and its reversal pattern.

3.4 "What You Sow Is Not the Body That Is to Be": A Conceptual Blending Analysis

Four input mental spaces are constructed through the flow of Paul's argument in 15:35–50 and are all involved in a complex network of conceptual blending that achieves a human scale. These four spaces in sequence are resurrection of the dead (I_1, 15:35), seed sowing and growing (I_2, 15:36–38), cosmological polarity (I_3, 15:39–41), and the Adam-Christ typology (I_4, 15:45–48). As this passage unfolds, one blended space (B_1) first emerges from the blend between I_1 and I_2 and frames the imagination of resurrection within the reversal pattern. This blended space (B_1) then in turn functions as an input space (denoted as I_{B1}) to be blended with I_3. As Gilles Fauconnier and Mark Turner indicate, a blended structure in a previous blending network can become an input for another blending network.[80] The second blended space (B_2) thus emerges from the blend between I_{B1} and I_3 and conveys Paul's core message of temporal polarity through the new structure emergent from the second blending operation. This insightful blended space (B_2) also in turn functions as an input space (denoted as I_{B2}) to be blended with I_4. With the blended space (B_3) emerging from this third blending operation, Paul's innovative idea of temporal polarity is applied to Jewish eschatological scenario and conveys a warlike sense that is different from the hierarchal sense in Hellenistic comic polarity. The three parts of the whole network (the first blend of I_1 and I_2, the second blend of I_{B1} and I_3, and the third blend of I_{B2} and I_4) can function interactively as the whole discourse unfolds. In order to trace the function of these conceptual blends in Paul's rhetorical flow, it would be helpful to assess each of the blends in sequence.

---

[80] G. Fauconnier and M. Turner, *The Way We Think: Conceptual Blending and the Mind's Hidden Complexities* (New York: Basic Books, 2002), 139–59.

3.4.1 The First Blend: Resurrection and the Metaphor of Seed Sowing and Growing

The blend of resurrection and bodies (I_1) and the sowing metaphor (I_2) is a necessary preparation for Paul's innovative message because this blend provides the alternative structure of reversal for imagining resurrection. Thus, before employing this reversal structure of resurrection and blending it with the concept of cosmic polarity (the second blend), Paul needs first to build the sowing metaphor as a legitimate analogy for resurrection so that his argument will be persuasive. Paul accomplishes this first task through a "single-scope conceptual blend" in 15:35–38 (the first blend).[81] At 15:35, Paul introduces the theme of resurrection and the body with two questions: "How are the dead raised? With what kind of body do they come?" After stating these two questions, he immediately describes the sowing metaphor in 15:36–38. In so doing, Paul is arguing that the way that the dead are raised and the body that they come with (I_1, 15:35) is just like (cf. 15:42) the way that a seed was sown and will grow with a different form of body (I_2, 15:36–38). As Fauconnier and Turner indicate, the single-scope network of blend is the "prototype" of source-target metaphors and makes us feel that "one thing is giving us insight into another thing."[82] Here, the sowing metaphor functions as the "framing input" (or the source domain in terms of metaphorical projection) of a single-scope network that informs and structures the issue of resurrection and the body, the "focus input" (or the target domain).

The first input space (I_1), resurrection and bodies, is formed in 15:35. As shown in Figure 3.2, this input is the "focus input" to be framed through the blending network and consists of two kinds of bodies: the former body of the dead and the later resurrected body. In 15:35, Paul's second question amplifies the first general question about resurrection and addresses the problem that the Corinthian dissenters' have with resurrection—the body. The existence of a resurrected body appears impossible according to their common and ritual experience. However, while the dissenters are not convinced of the existence of the resurrected body, Paul skillfully realigns their focus onto the nature of the resurrected body with the second question: what sort of body is that? Paul thus reveals his intent of defending bodily resurrection by considering the nature of the resurrected body. In other words, this second question has assumed the existence of the resurrected body and implicitly suggested that its nature might be somehow different from the former body. Therefore, in Figure 3.2, I denote the resurrected body in I_1 with an ambiguous shape and a question mark. The nature of this body is still in question. Moreover, Paul also identifies the resurrected bodies with the same dead people: with what kind of bodies do "they" come after their former bodies are destroyed? Thus, in I_1, the dead body is the former body and the resurrected body is the later body of the same person. These two bodies share the same identity. However, the structure that frames the relationship between these two bodies is still ambiguous in this leading question. There is no clue offered in 15:35 of the way that the

---

[81] A single-scope network has two input spaces with distinct organizing structures, and only one of the structures is projected to organize the elements in the blended space (ibid., 127–9, 312).
[82] Ibid., 129.

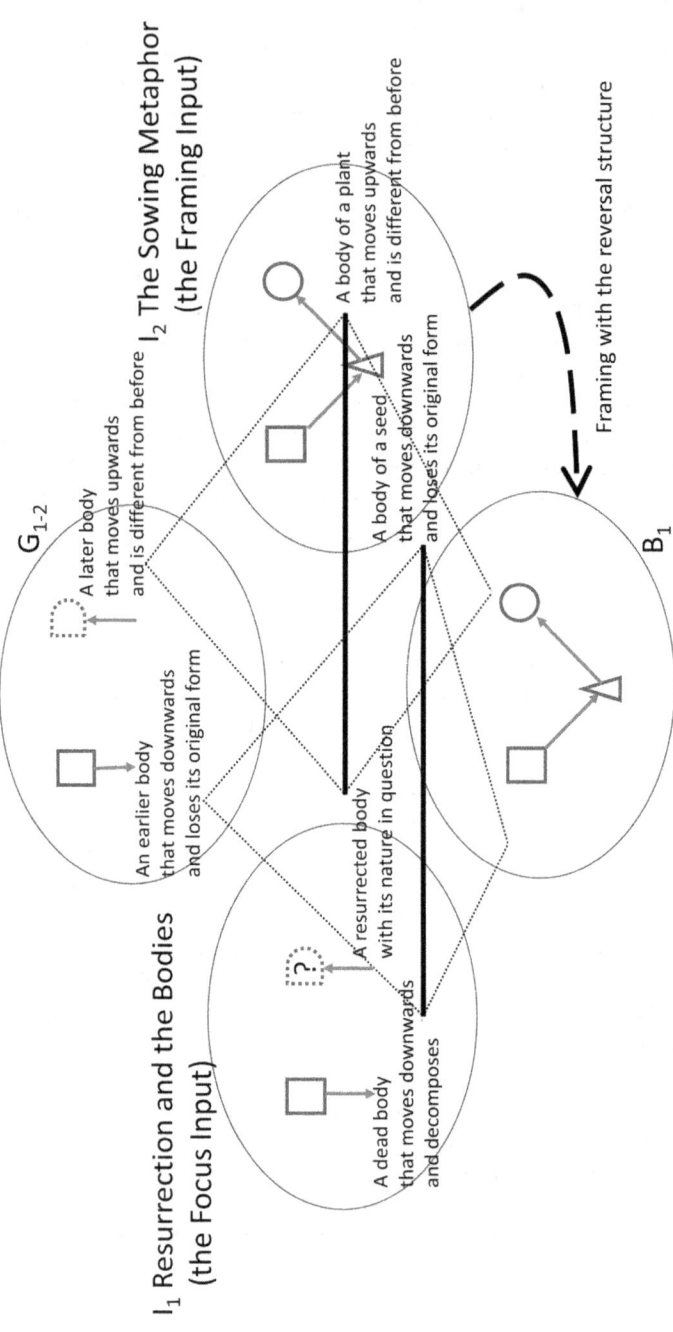

Figure 3.2 The Resurrected Body and the Sowing Metaphor.

resurrected body can come into existence while the dead body must move downwards, decomposes, and reduces into the earth. Paul has so far only raised the question of how these two bodies might relate to one another, while assuming they do, and has yet to answer the question. In other words, I_1 is a rather unstructured mental space and its elements remain diffuse. As Fauconnier and Turner indicate, in a single-scope blend, it is the framing input that offers the structure to organize the diffuse elements in the focus input.[83]

The second input (I_2), the sowing metaphor, functions as just such a frame. By employing this metaphor, Paul frames the mental space of resurrection and bodies (I_1) with the reversal schema. The skeletal structure of I_2 consists of a downward path, an upward path, and a turning point. The body of the seed moves through this reversal pattern and changes into the body of the plant. While these two bodies are indeed the same entity, they are visibly and qualitatively different from each other (15:37). Thus, I denote these two bodies in the sowing metaphor (I_2) with distinct shapes, a square and a circle, respectively. In fact, I_2 itself is a blended space, where the complexity of seed sowing and plant growing (different species, sizes, appearances, times, weather, locations, even the results of sowing, etc.) is compressed into the simple reversal schema. This compressed schema serves to frame the diffuse elements in the mental space of resurrection and the bodies (I_1) and organize them into the blended space (B_1). The generic space (G_{1-2}) portrays the elements or structures shared by both inputs, a sharing that facilitates the blend between the image of resurrection and the bodies (I_1) and the sowing metaphor (I_2): two distinct bodies; death as a downward movement; one body moves downwards to perish; another body moves upwards. There is no indication in G_{1-2} of the way that the new form of body comes into existence. Facilitated by the generic space, in the blended space (B_1), the body of the dead is identified with the body of the seed since they are both the former bodies, and the resurrected body with the body of the plant since they are both the later bodies. The relationship between the two different bodies in B_1 is organized through the reversal schema taken from the sowing metaphor (I_2). More importantly, the turning point of the schema accounts for the transformation of the same person from the former body to the later, visibly different body (15:37). Paul explicitly states that this transformation at the turning point is made by God (15:38). This temporal difference of the body of the same person is crucial for the further conceptual blend between I_{B1} and the concept of cosmic polarity (I_3).

At this point (15:38), by employing the sowing metaphor, Paul has shown that God is able to reverse the downward moment and the decomposition of the body and to transform the body into a better form. As implied in the reversal pattern, the idea of "bodily transformation occurring at resurrection" is already generated in this first blend before the concept of cosmic polarity is introduced. This is itself an important development in Paul's ideas. As seen in Paul's wording, by 15:42a (what is sown … what is raised [ἐγείρεται]), the sowing metaphor and its reversal structure has been blended with "the resurrection of the dead" before it is further blended with the idea of polarity projected from 15:39–41 (I_3). Starting from 15:39, Paul attempts to explain the

[83] Ibid., 130.

manner of the bodily transformation and why it can happen in a hierarchical cosmos by forming the second blend between I_{B1} and I_3.

3.4.2 The Second Blend: The Reversal Resurrection and Cosmic Polarity

I have argued that 15:39–41 is not another analogy of resurrection offered by Paul but reflects the worldview of cosmic polarity based on which the Corinthian dissenters had challenged the idea of bodily resurrection. Through this passage, Paul attempts to further exposit the sowing metaphor and its reversal pattern in order to correct the dissenters' evaluation of resurrection within the framework of that cosmology. Paul accomplishes this strategical exposition by constructing the mental space of cosmic polarity (I_3) in 15:39–41 to be blended with the reversal pattern of resurrection (I_{B1}, as emergent in B_1) and, at the same time, by continuing in these three verses the theme of God's creative power that was already introduced in the sowing metaphor. Thus, I suggest that 15:39–41 reflects Paul's own accommodating interpretation of cosmic polarity, in which his idea of God's creative power is implied and functions as an element in the generic space to link these three verses (I_3) with I_{B1}. In so doing, Paul lays the groundwork for the conceptual blend between what he has achieved in I_{B1} (God's creative power shown in the reversal pattern of resurrection and transformation) and the idea of cosmic polarity (15:39–41, I_3). In other words, Paul's main purpose in continuing the theme of "God's creative power" in 15:39–41 is to introduce this very theme into the Corinthians' understanding of cosmic polarity. Thus, Paul can overcome the challenge based on polarity by resorting to God's creative power.

It is usually suggested that Paul's purpose in 15:39–41 is to demonstrate the varieties of bodies within God's creation.[84] This suggestion accurately describes Paul's rhetorical purpose in part. As many have noted, Paul's enumeration of animals in 15:39 and the celestial bodies in 15:41 alludes to the Priestly account of creation in Gen 1.[85] For Paul, the various "bodies" in the hierarchically arranged cosmos are all created by God. As Archibald Robertson and Alfred Plummer state, "the God who made these myriads of differences in one and the same universe can be credited with inexhaustible power … God finds a suitable body for every type of earthly life and every type of heavenly life."[86] However, Paul's main purpose in 15:39–41 is not simply, as suggested by this line of interpretation, to demonstrate God's creative power and to infer that God is also capable of creating a resurrected body.[87] Such a suggestion has limited the rhetorical function of this passage and misses Paul's didactic technique of accommodation and correction. In fact, Paul has expressed the theme of God's creative power much more explicitly in the sowing metaphor (15:38), whereas in 15:39–41, Paul's concern is rather

---

[84] Fee, *Corinthians*, 865–7; A. Robertson and A. Plummer, *A Critical and Exegetical Commentary on the First Epistle of St Paul to the Corinthians* (2nd ed; Edinburgh: T&T Clark, 1971), 371; A. T. Lincoln, *Paradise Now and Not Yet: Studies in the Role of the Heavenly Dimension in Paul's Thought with Special Reference to His Eschatology* (Cambridge: Cambridge University Press, 1981), 338–39.

[85] C. Burchard, "1 Korinther 15, 39–41," *ZNW* 75 (1984): 237; K. Usami, "'How Are the Dead Raised?' (1 Cor 15,35-58)," *Bib* 57 no. 4 (1976): 468–93; Fee, *Corinthians*, 783.

[86] Robertson and Plummer, *First Epistle*, 371.

[87] See Asher, *Polarity and Change*, 102–3.

on the sharp, hierarchical distinction between the bodies in the celestial sphere and the bodies in the terrestrial sphere even when he delineates the varieties of bodies in a way similar to the Priestly account of creation.

We can observe that Paul's major concern in 15:39–41 is cosmic distinction by looking at these three verses and the later application of these three verses in 15:42–44a and 15:44b–49. First, the language and structure of 15:39–41 itself suggests that, with his purpose of accommodation, Paul intends to classify the varieties of bodies into two categories that were understood as belonging to two opposite ends of a hierarchical cosmos: the celestial and the terrestrial.[88] Asher has demonstrated that 15:39–41 follows an XYX' chiasmus pattern.[89] The peak of the chiasm (Y), 15:40, divides the cosmos into two opposite realms of habitation and offers a general term for all things in these two realms: body (σῶμα). There are terrestrial bodies and celestial bodies. Another two verses, 39 and 41, correspond to the two opposite realms divided in 15:40, respectively.[90] Bonneau also indicates that the contrast of 15:39 and 15:41 is accentuated by placing the terms σάρξ and δόξα on either side of 15:40. Second, Paul's latter application of 15:39–41 shows that his concern is the heaven-earth polarity rather than the varieties of bodies in each realm. In 15:42–44a, initiating with οὕτως that immediately follows the description in 15:39–41, Paul clearly distinguishes the forms of the body before and after resurrection into only two opposite categories. Similarly, in 15:44b–49 when he applies the whole argument of the sowing metaphor (15:36–44a) to an eschatological scenario, Paul also draws on only two types of bodies—the celestial and the terrestrial—and does not pick up the wide varieties of the bodies listed in vv. 39 and 41. In other words, judging from Paul's expressions and the whole argument, what Paul really attempts to deal with concerning the description in 15:39–41 is the sharp distinction between the celestial and the terrestrial.

Moreover, by using the general term "body" in 15:40, Paul also recalls the second question in 15:35 and the metaphor of sowing (15:36–38). Thus, through 15:39–41, Paul has constructed a mental space of cosmic polarity (I_3) to be blended with the "reversal imagination of resurrection and bodily transformation" (I_{B1}). As shown in Figure 3.3, various bodies listed in 15:41 are categorized as heavenly bodies and

---

[88] Ibid., 104.
[89] Ibid., 100, 103.
[90] In 15:39 (X), Paul lists four forms of flesh (σάρξ) corresponding to their habitation: human, animal (dry land), bird (the air), and fish (the sea). For Paul, stating the difference among the varieties of the terrestrial fleshes is important because he needs to justify his use of the sowing metaphor, in which God's creative power is shown in the transformation of one terrestrial form into another terrestrial form. Nevertheless, while there are differences among these fleshes on earth, Paul does not consider them as opposite in 15:39. Instead, the varieties of fleshes are all categorized as earthly bodies in 15:40 and as opposite to heavenly bodies. As Asher indicates, Paul's language in 15:39 shows that "he is clearly differentiating these varieties into a comprehensive scheme of fleshly bodies" (ibid., 103). Similarly, in 15:41 (X'), Paul lists three forms of heavenly bodies that are distinct in terms of glory (δόξα): sun, moon, and stars. Thus, in both verses Paul links the varieties of bodies by the location of their habitation (the earthly realm in 15:39 and the heavenly realm in 15:41) and by the corresponding composition or quality (flesh in 15:39 and glory in 15:41, albeit both with differences in Paul's view). As Duane F. Watson also notes, the function of 15:40 is twofold. It not only delivers the polarity between heaven and earth but also makes a transition between the earthly bodies in 15:39 and the heavenly bodies in 15:41. See D. F. Watson, "Paul's Rhetorical Strategy in 1 Corinthians 15," in *Rhetoric and the New Testament: Essays from the 1992 Heidelberg Conference* (ed. S. E. Porter and T. H. Olbricht; Sheffield: Sheffield Academic Press, 1993), 245.

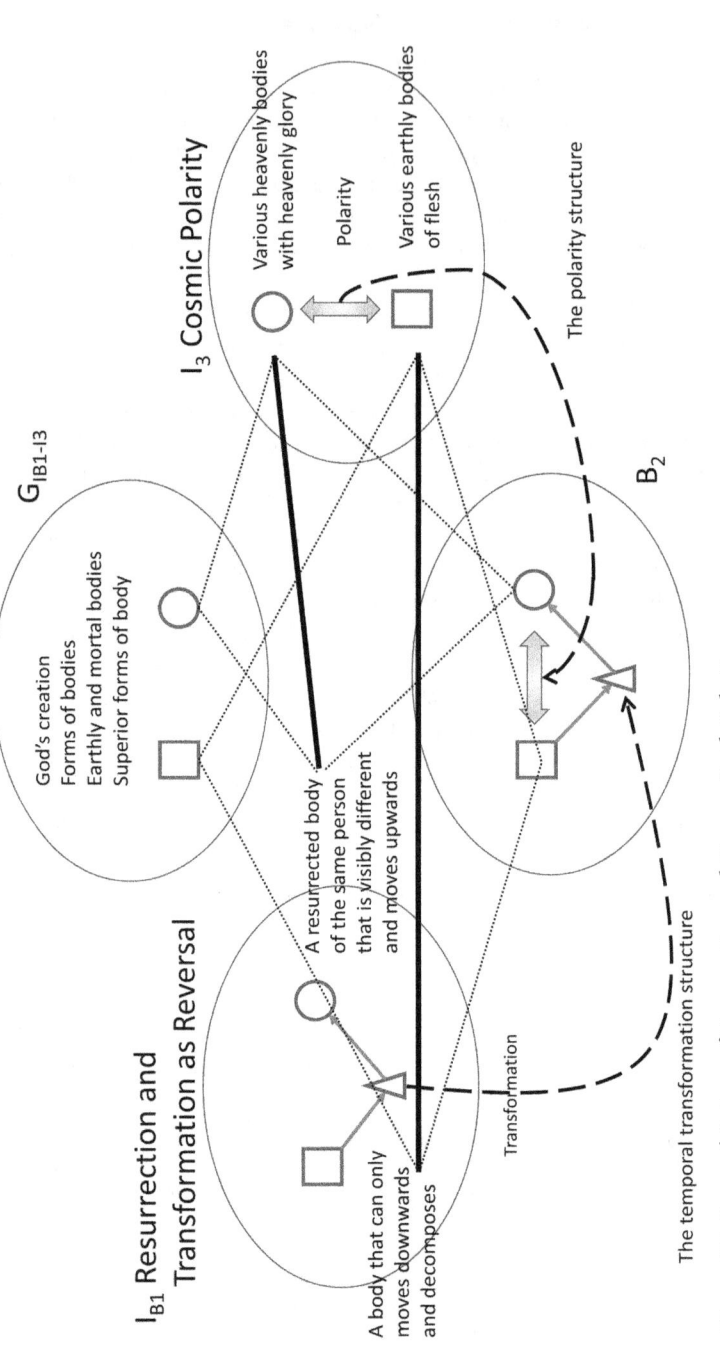

Figure 3.3 Reversal Pattern of Resurrection and Heaven-Earth Polarity.

bodies listed in 15:39 as earthly bodies. There is a sharp polar distinction between these two categories of bodies. They are discontinuous with each other. Nevertheless, I_{B1} shows the continuation between two bodies by linking them in a reversal schema. The two bodies with different qualities are identified with the same person, and a transformation enabled by God's creative power that happens at the turning point makes this continuation of two distinct forms possible. The relation between these two bodies in I_{B1} is temporally sequential rather than discontinuous, as in I_3. The former one is the present body of a deceased, a corpse, and the latter one is the body that is to be in the future. The generic space (G_{IB1-I3}), then, consists of two distinct bodies in God's creation with different qualities. One body appears to be superior to another.

In the blended space (B_2, as revealed in 15:42–44a), the repeated pair of two verbs of opposite movements (σπείρεται and ἐγείρεται) recalls the sowing metaphor and reflects the reversal structure in this space. This reversal structure is projected from I_{B1}. Each time, the pair of verbs is followed by an antithetical expression: ἐν φθορᾷ and ἐν ἀφθαρσίᾳ, ἐν ἀτιμίᾳ and ἐν δόξῃ, ἐν ἀσθενείᾳ and ἐν δυνάμει, and σῶμα ψυχικόν and σῶμα πνευματικόν. As Asher notes, these antithetical expressions clearly recall the polar structure of the cosmic locations of various bodies in 15:39–41. That is, the polar structure is projected from I_3. It is noteworthy that, in the blended space (B_2), the bodies with opposite qualities are no longer arranged according to cosmological locations or discontinuous with each other (as in I_3). Rather, they are linked with the two verbs, σπείρεται and ἐγείρεται, and show a consequential and temporally successive relation.[91] This successive relation is framed by the reversal structure rather than by cosmic polarity. More importantly, the reversal structure in the blended space is also different from the reversal in the input. While transformation does happen in the sowing metaphor and the blend of the metaphor with resurrection, what is sown and what is to be are still both earthly in the metaphor itself. There is no plant that is not earthly and there is no idea of cosmological polarity in I_{B1} and in the first blend (Figure 3.2). As Bonneau also observes, 15:42–44a combines the temporal aspects of 15:36–38 with the spatial ones of 15:39–41 in their application to the resurrection of the dead.[92] Thus, what Paul enacts through 15:39–44a is a "double-scope network" since the blended structure is not identical with that of either input space.[93]

In the blended space (B_2, 15:42–44a), contributed by both inputs, there is an emergent structure of temporal polarity that is resulting from a reversal transformation.

---

[91] Asher argues that 15:42–44 is still about locative polarity since the οὕτως καὶ in 15:42 suggests that the verse fills out what precedes in 15:39–41 and that temporal issue only starts after 15:45 with 15:44b as a transition (*Polarity and Change*, 113). However, the temporal relation is clearly revealed in Paul's use of verbs "is sown" and "is raised up." A thing must be sown first before it is raised up. Driven by the seed-sowing and growing metaphors, the temporal sense is always effective throughout the course of 15:36–44, and the locative sense in 15:39–41 is a problem of resurrection that Paul adds into this passage to be solved by the logic of the sowing metaphor. Moreover, 15:45 also begins with οὕτως καὶ. Thus, if 15:45 can introduce a new aspect of transformation to support previous contents, 15:42 can do it as well. See ibid., 98, 106–16.
[92] Bonneau, "Resurrection Body," 79–92.
[93] More complex blends like this are called *double-scope* or *multiple-scope networks*, in which more than one input contributes to the organizing structure in the blended space (Fauconnier and Turner, *The Way We Think*, 131).

The (moving down) body before resurrection is earthly, and the (moving up) body after resurrection is heavenly. There are both discontinuity in terms of the form of the body and continuity in terms of identity and temporal succession. With this emergent structure, Paul is now able to explain how resurrection is possible in a hierarchical cosmos with the heaven-earth polarity. Paul's answer is a reversal transformation that changes a person into an imperishable form (15:50–51).

As mentioned, the new structure of "temporal polarity resulting from a reversal transformation" that emerges from the second blend (Figure 3.3) is not in conflict with Paul's previous teachings and the traditional imaginations of resurrection. Rather, this new structure deals with the body issue by highlighting the downward movement of the body that is only assumed and implied in the traditional schema. Thus, the new structure helps Paul to develop the received traditions and to convince the Corinthians of the received traditions. First, the reversal pattern in this new structure, which is projected from I_{B1}, recalls Christ's own pattern of death-burial-resurrection described in 15:3–4. For Paul, the resurrection of Christ is the prototype of general resurrection (cf. 15:20). However, Paul cannot not rely on the model of Christ to make his argument in 15:35–58. It appears that body-decomposition was not a problem for the resurrection of Christ as it would be for general resurrection. As McCane indicates, body-decomposition was usually understood as starting on the fourth day after death (cf. John 11:39), and so it would not be considered hindering the resurrection of Christ.[94] Paul has to find another way to make sense of general resurrection. Indeed, it is clear in 1 Cor 15 that, instead of the Christ model, the sowing metaphor is the means by which Paul deals with the issue of the body for general resurrection. The idea of bodily transformation occurring at resurrection is generated through the use of this metaphor. Thus, building upon the sowing metaphor, Paul is able to recall the Christ pattern in 15:3–4 and to describe Christians' bodies in afterlife in the form of Christ: "as is the man of heaven, so are those who are of heaven. Just as we have borne the image of the man of dust, we will also bear the image of the man of heaven" (15:48–49).

Second, Paul uses the last antithetical pair of temporal polarities in 15:42–44a—σῶμα ψυχικόν and σῶμα πνευματικόν—as a transition from the second blend to the third blend. Through the third blend, Paul situates the temporal polarity within the framework of a Christological, eschatological scenario in 1 Cor 15:44b–49, a scenario that is compatible with his previous depiction in 1 Thess 4:13–18. Indeed, Paul's purpose in 1 Cor 15 is to defend the gospel tradition of resurrection. In the first half of ch. 15, Paul shows that the Corinthians' denial of resurrection is inconsistent with what they received. In the second half, up to 15:44a, he employs the sowing metaphor to offer a new idea—transformation—by which he is able to directly deal with the challenge against the resurrection tradition. Thus, at this point, Paul still attempts to show that his new idea is consistent with the received traditions. More analysis is needed below to explore Paul's peculiar language of this ψυχικός-πνευματικός opposition and the way that this opposition contributes to Paul's conceptual blend and argument.

---

[94] McCane, *Death and Burial*, 111.

3.4.3 The Ψυχικός-Πνευματικός Opposition and the Third Blend

In 15:44b–49, resorting to scriptural support from Gen 2:7, Paul applies the whole argument of metaphor about the body in 15:35–44a to the contrasting of two figures, Adam and Christ. He characterizes Adam as earthly (a living ψυχή according to Gen 2:7) and Christ as heavenly (the ἔσχατος Ἀδάμ), and restates the idea of temporal polarity (as delivered in 15:42–44a) as corresponding to these two opposite figures. In so doing, Paul forms the third conceptual blend in 1 Cor 15 between the structure that emerges in 15:42–44a and the contrast of Adam-Christ. It is the last pair of temporal polarities in 15:42–44a—σῶμα ψυχικόν and σῶμα πνευματικόν—that allows Paul to introduce the Adam-Christ typology and enacts the third blend.[95] Paul offers four pairs of opposites in 1 Cor 15:42–44a to describe the temporal polarity. With the repeated ἐν + dative construction, the first three pairs describe two contrasting states through the container schema. These states correspond to either the earthly or the heavenly realms (the containers). Nevertheless, the last opposition is phrased differently. It consists of a contrasting pair of adjectives (ψυχικός and πνευματικός) that qualify the noun σῶμα. Paul is now characterizing the body itself. The body that is in the earthly state and possesses earthly qualities is a "ψυχικός body," and the body that is in the heavenly state and possesses heavenly qualities is a "πνευματικός body" (cf. 15:47).[96] By directly characterizing the body, here in 15:44 Paul is preparing to offer his answer to his leading question in 15:35: with what kind of body will the resurrected come?

What is left before offering the answer (15:51) is to situate the innovative idea of reversal transformation that results in these two distinct bodies within a more traditional eschatological framework, in which the hope of resurrection is typically embedded. Thus, as shown in Figure 3.4, the third conceptual blend is a blend between the temporal polarity resulting from a reversal transformation (I_{B2}) and the scriptural typology of Adam-Christ (I_4). With this blend, Paul weds the structure of temporal polarity to a traditional end-time scenario and recalls his argument in the first half of this chapter that all people die in Adam and will be made alive in Christ, who is the first fruits of resurrection (15:20–22). Paul therefore strengthens his own innovation emergent from the sowing metaphor with support from scripture and gospel traditions.

The third blend is a double-scope network because both input spaces contribute significantly to the organizing structure of the blended space (B_3). The first input (I_{B2}) reuses the structure that emerges from the second blend (B_2). However, the structure projected from the second input (I_4), the Adam-Christ typology, differs from that of the first input (I_{B2}) regarding the continuation of identity. That is, while it is the same person in I_{B2} that undergoes transformation and comes to have a different form

---

[95] The origin of the ψυχικός-πνευματικός opposition is uncertain. It is difficult to determine whether the Corinthians already used these terms or the opposition itself. In either case, I agree with Asher that a clearer reason for Paul's use of this opposition is that the scripture cited in 1 Cor 15:45 uses the term ψυχή. The term πνευματικός, then, is added by following the principle of polarity in 14:42–44a. See Asher, *Polarity and Change*, 112. Thus, the ψυχικός-πνευματικός opposition allows Paul to transit from temporal polarity to scriptural argument and so to situate his new idea within a traditional framework.

[96] As Bonneau notes, these two adjectives "recapitulate the preceding states" and "apply them to the body itself as attributes." See his "Resurrection Body," 87.

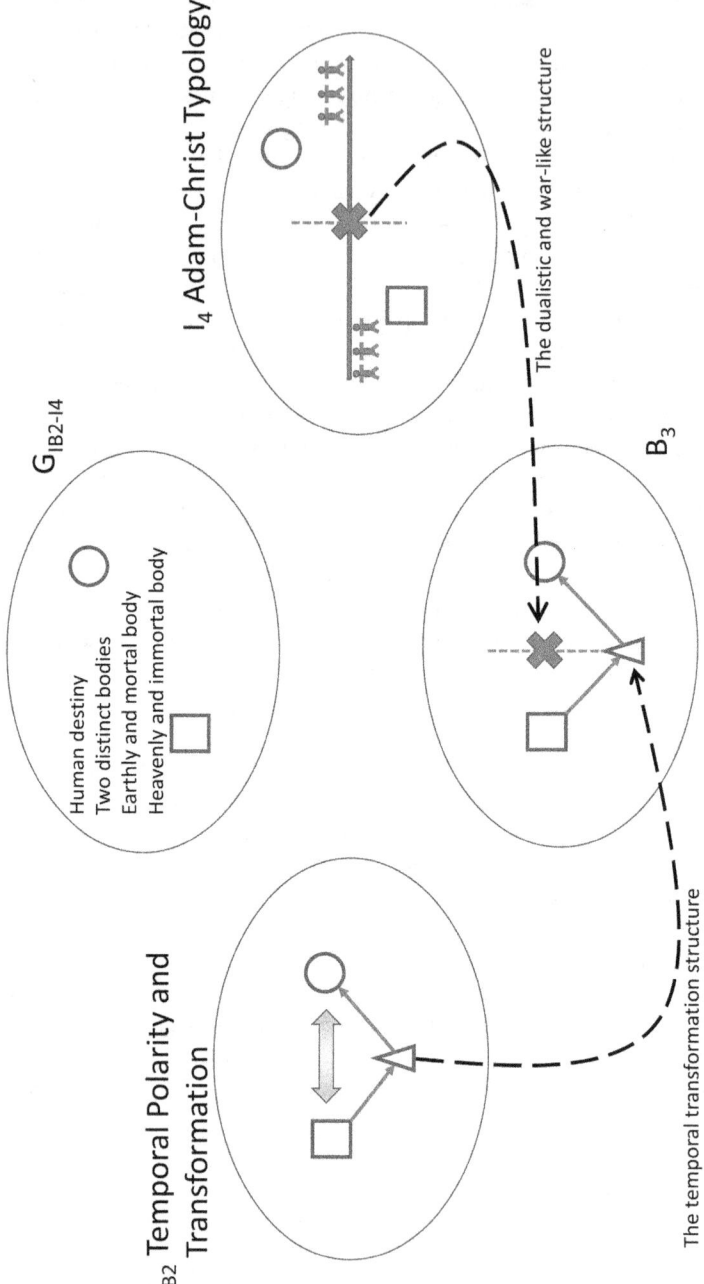

Figure 3.4 Temporal Polarity from Transformation and the Adam-Christ Typology.

of body, the two figures in I$_4$ that represent two distinct somatic forms are in fact distinct and so are discontinuous in terms of identity. Adam is not Christ and is never transformed to be Christ. Rather, the continuity in I$_4$ and in the blended space (B$_3$, as reflected in 15:49–54) is reflected on the people who belong to these two figures in sequence. According to the context in 15:20–27, the sovereignty of Christ defeats the sovereignty of death and other enemies and consequently takes over the kingdom. This war and replacement of sovereignty is the reason that the same people who used to die in Adam will be resurrected and transformed in Christ. Here (15:22), the immediate context suggests the understanding of the preposition ἐν in the sense of influence or sovereignty. Adam and Christ do not share the same identity but exert influence on the same people. The influence of Christ comes after the influence of Adam and stops it (15:21–22, 46–49), and therefore enables the same "we" to be transformed into the form of Christ (15:51). This logic of temporally sequential sovereignty is clearly reflected in the third blend and frames the continuity in the blended space (B$_3$). In other words, the continuity and temporal succession projected from the Adam-Christ typology (I$_4$) is not offered by identifying the two figures as the same but by a warlike scenario between the two figures in this context. Through a war, the same person can belong to new kingdom that is in conflict with their former kingdom and experience a different destiny (hence a different form of body).

Therefore, instead of the hierarchical sense of polarity projected from Hellenistic cosmology, a dualistic sense of polarity arises from the third blend as shown in Figure 3.4. In the blended space (B$_3$), unlike the logic of cosmic polarity, the resurrected have to be transformed not because they ascend to the heavenly realm but because they are brought into "God's kingdom," which will come later than the current powers (15:24–25, 50). This kingdom is not a higher stratum of the current world. Through this blend, Paul further develops the structure of temporal polarity into a more Jewish and dualistic view of eschatology (projected from I$_4$), in which two powers are at war. In this war, God gives victory to Christians through Christ, who has swallowed death (15:54–57). The images of victory and swallowing, which continue the metaphor in 15:25–26 of death as an enemy destroyed by Christ, convey a stark dualistic distinction between the current world and the world to come. For Paul, the relationship between the ψυχικός and the πνευματικός is not as hierarchical as it is dualistic.

3.5 Conclusion

With the aid of cognitive linguistic tools, we are able to ground human conceptualizations and articulations of death and afterlife on recurrent patterns of somatic experience. I have demonstrated that the common observation of body-decomposition was a central element in the experience and procedure of ancient death rites, and so the verticality schema was fundamental for understanding death and imagining afterlife. In this regard, the seed-sowing metaphor provides an alternative image schema of reversal to deal with the downward movement of the body. Applying conceptual blending theory, I have also explained the generation of two significant ideas through Paul's use of this metaphor: that transformation occurs at resurrection and that the polarity is to be understood in a temporal and dualistic sense. In short, the common experiences in death rites and in seed sowing had an unneglectable influence on the formation of Paul's resurrection thinking. Indeed, in Paul's argument of resurrection in 1 Cor 15:35–58, these experiences play a more fundamental role than the philosophical idea of hierarchical cosmology.

Thus, for two reasons, I identify the structure of temporal polarity resulting from a reversal transformation as indicating a crucial development in Paul's ideas. First, as seen in this chapter, this innovative structure emerged as directly responding to a specific contextual issue and related experiences. Thus, Paul had a contextual reason to develop and introduce this structure at this moment, a structure that as we have seen in this chapter is different from the traditional structures of resurrection. Second, as will be discussed in the following chapters, this structure—the reversal pattern and the idea of bodily transformation—became an important element in Paul's later thoughts and further generated more innovations responding to particular issues and experiences of his later letters.[97] Some further innovations could not have emerged within the traditional structures of resurrection. In other words, this new structure of reversal proved to be not just a contingent expression that only responded to the specific issues in 1 Corinthians but a milestone that had a continual effect in Paul's thoughts. Thus, on the basis of the emergent structure analyzed in this chapter, we will go on to examine Paul's diverse ideas about resurrection and transformation in 1 Corinthians, 2 Corinthians, and Romans.

---

[97] As Asher notes, Paul conceives resurrection as occurring together with transformation in Phil 3:20–21 and appears to have an idea of eschatological transformation in Rom 8:18–25. Also, in 2 Cor 3:18, he understands transformation as part of Christian religious experience. See Asher, *Polarity and Change*, 173. I will deal with these ideas in the following chapters.

4

"We All Are Being Transformed": Experienced Transformation

The differences between 1 and 2 Corinthians is an intriguing topic in studies of Paul's development. This stage in Paul's life is particularly relevant to my study since Paul reflects two different aspects of bodily transformation in these two letters, and the coexistence of these two aspects will further fuel the development of Paul's resurrection thought in a later stage. In Chapter 3, I have examined 1 Cor 15 and explored the emergence of Paul's idea of bodily transformation occurring at resurrection (rather than occurring during the heavenly ascent after resurrection). However, in 2 Cor 3:18, Paul appears to consider transformation as not only in the future but also experiential and ongoing: "We are being transformed into the same image [of the Lord] from one degree of glory to another." While Charles H. Dodd insightfully demonstrates Paul's radical mental shift (a "spiritual crisis") when he was writing 2 Corinthians, in this chapter I will instead focus on 1 Corinthians to explore another factor that more directly contributed to Paul's development between these two letters about transformation.[1] That is, I will argue that Paul already showed clues and a tendency toward such a development in 1 Corinthians even though he only came to explicitly speak of the experiential aspect of transformation in 2 Corinthians.

To begin this argument, I will demonstrate that the idea of bodily transformation occurring and experienced in the present was not unimaginable in ancient perspectives on the body. As Dale B. Martin presents, the body was considered in Greco-Roman culture as a "microcosm" that was "malleable" because it was subject to both influence from the cosmic environment and molding from social activities.[2] In other words, according to its cosmic and social correlation, the body was conceptualized and even experienced to some extent as moldable or transformable. Thus, Greco-Roman perspectives on the body provide cultural conditions for understanding the early Christian ideas and experiences of the body. As Frederick S. Tappenden accurately notes, while human experiences are always embodied and therefore "constituted by somatic and neurobiological functions," they are at the same time "culturally mediated."

---

[1] C. H. Dodd, "The Mind of St. Paul: Change and Development," *Bulletin* 18 no. 1 (1934): 101; "The Mind of St. Paul: A Psychological Approach," *Bulletin of the John Rylands Library* 17 no. 1 (1933): 97, 103.
[2] D. B. Martin, *The Corinthian Body* (New Haven, CT: Yale University Press, 1995), 16, 25.

We make sense of our embodied experiences partly on the basis of cultural mediation.[3] Thus, based on cultural understandings of the malleable body, I will further rely on Colleen Shantz's neuroscience work on Paul to indicate that certain neurobiological phenomena in the experience of religious ecstasy could have been interpreted as, among other interpretations, the transformation of the physical body.[4]

Next, on the basis of the cultural understandings of the body and interpretations of religious ecstasy, I will apply conceptual blending theory and argue that Paul conceived an important conceptual blend in 1 Cor 12:13, a blend that would eventually direct him and/or other early Christians to interpret their ecstatic experience as ongoing bodily transformation. With this conceptual blend, Paul's purpose was to construct his ideal image of the Christian social body—the body of Christ. As will be analyzed below, one of the input spaces of this conceptual blend is the common ancient metaphor of the physical body for a political or social organism (e.g., *corpus imperii* as a metaphor for the Roman Empire), and Paul employed this body metaphor in order to achieve social union in the Corinthian community.[5] The typical ancient concept of the correlation between the physical body and its social environment is prominent in this metaphorical image. Specifically, as I will demonstrate, the Corinthians believed that their reception and possession of the Spirit gave rise to their various phenomena of religious ecstasy, which played a founding role in the formation of their community. Nevertheless, the diversity of the phenomena had ironically led to divisions among them. Thus, it was for the sake of concord in Corinth that Paul blended the contemporary metaphor of the social body with the common experiences shared among the Corinthians—the reception of the Spirit and baptism (12:13). Thus, the experience in baptism will be treated in relation to the experience of the Spirit. Conceptual blending theory will help us demonstrate how this blended image of Christ's body contributed to Paul's rhetorical purpose of concord, and how this image would in time encourage the interpretation of ecstatic experiences as ongoing bodily transformation (cf. 2 Cor 3:18).

4.1 Intellectual Context: The Concept of the Body

Greco-Roman conceptions of the cosmos and the body reveal a similar hierarchical structure. Martin and Troels Engberg-Pedersen have argued against the understandings of ancient cosmologies through strict oppositions such as "matter versus nonmatter, physical versus spiritual, or corporeal versus psychological." Instead, they have delineated the Greco-Roman conceptions of the cosmos as "a hierarchy of [material]

---

[3] F. S. Tappenden, *Resurrection in Paul: Cognition, Metaphor, and Transformation* (Atlanta: Society of Biblical Literature, 2016), 212.
[4] C. Shantz, *Paul in Ecstasy: The Neurobiology of the Apostle's Life and Thought* (Cambridge: Cambridge University Press, 2009).
[5] M. M. Mitchell, *Paul and the Rhetoric of Reconciliation: An Exegetical Investigation of the Language and Composition of 1 Corinthians* (Tübingen: Mohr Siebeck, 1991), 157–60. M. Squire, "*Corpus Imperii*: Verbal and Visual Figurations of the Roman 'Body Politic,'" *Word & Image* 31 no. 3 (2015): 305–6.

essence" rather than "an ontological dualism."[6] Moreover, as Tappenden states, Martin has also traced out the "cosmo-somatic mappings" by which the hierarchy of the cosmos is projected onto the conceptions of the body and the related practices.[7] Examining both elite philosophical teachings and popular ideas accessed from magical papyri, Greek tragedy texts, and medical works, Martin indicates that human beings (body and soul) were considered as constituted by exactly the same material elements as the universe around them.[8] These elements of the human person imitatively corresponded to the hierarchical arrangement of the universe. Thus, the natural principles that one could observe functioning in the external cosmos "could be read onto and into human body."[9] For example, according to Galen's report, Diogenes the Babylonian believed that the soul functioned in an integrated way with the body and was fed by vapors evaporating from the blood in the same way that stars were fed by vapors evaporating from water on the earth. Working with this view, Galen and other physicians believed that it was necessary to control the "weather inside the body" in order to maintain the balance of the body like maintaining the ecological balance of the cosmos.[10] Such cosmos-soma correlation is also seen in popular texts such as magical papyri.[11] As Martin concludes, "the human body was not *like* a microcosm; it *was* a microcosm—a small version of the universe at large."[12] In light of this literal sense of cosmos-soma correlation, the common contrast between the body and the soul seen in Greco-Roman discourses is not to be understood as an ontological dichotomy between the two but as a hierarchy that corresponds to the cosmos. The body and the soul were both made of cosmic elements yet were identical to distinct strata of the cosmos.

Moreover, the body is also related to society in a similar way that it is related to the cosmos. That is, the vertical hierarchy of both the cosmos and the society was mapped onto the body. With the body, the hierarchy might still be expressed in a vertical schema in which, for example, the head represents a father in a family and the foot represents a slave. It might also be expressed in a horizontal schema in which, for example, the right hand represents men in a family and the left women. As Martin indicates, the hierarchical construction of the body in Greco-Roman society clearly illustrates a close body-society correlation.[13] This correlation is also evident in the common body metaphor in the Greco-Roman political texts, in which various body parts represent various hierarchical classes or social roles in a social unit. In this way, while those texts typically argue for the common good for the whole political organism as a body, different body parts are assigned with different statuses according to the

---

[6] Martin, *Corinthian Body*, 15. See also the summary in T. Engberg-Pedersen, *Cosmology & Self in the Apostle Paul: The Material Spirit* (Oxford: Oxford University Press, 2010), 19–22.
[7] Tappenden, *Resurrection in Paul*, 98–99, 112. See Martin, *Corinthian Body*, 3–38.
[8] Martin, *Corinthian Body*, 16. See also R. Padel, *In and Out of the Mind: Greek Images of the Tragic Self* (Princeton, NJ: Princeton University Press, 1992), 48.
[9] Martin, *Corinthian Body*, 16.
[10] Ibid., 17.
[11] For example, Martin indicates that some magical papyri refer to a popular belief that the human body consists of 365 members and that these members reflect the body's structure corresponding to the cosmic structure. See ibid.
[12] Ibid., 16 (original emphases).
[13] Ibid., 28–34.

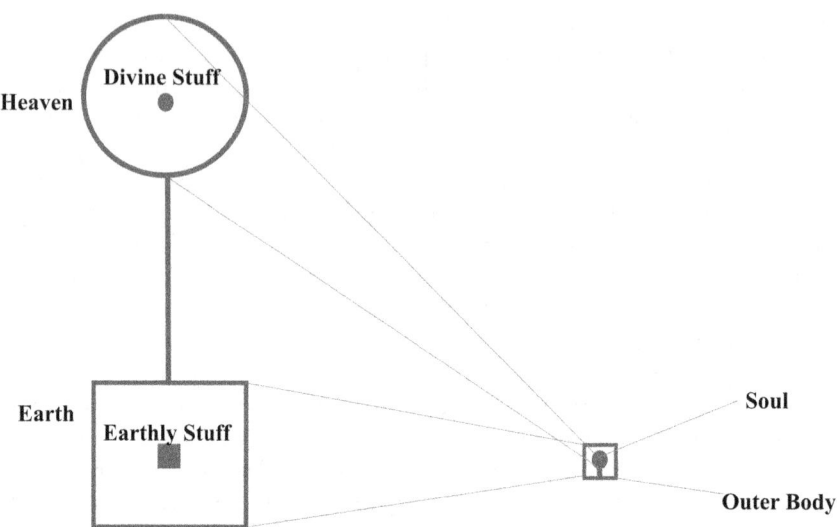

Figure 4.1 The Cosmo-Somatic Hierarchy.

hierarchy. To put it in Mary Douglas's words, "the social body constrains the way the physical body is perceived."[14]

Another common expression of the bodily hierarchy is more important for our study and is articulated through the in-out (container) schema. As illustrated in Figure 4.1, it refers to the inner mind or soul versus the outer body. The mind or soul was considered the highest-status component of a human being and functions as the command center (cf. Plato, Phaedo, 80A). Thus, as we have seen, Hellenistic philosophers such as Cicero considered the soul as composed of heavenly material and, consequently, located the afterlife abode of the blessed souls in the heavenly realms.[15] Also, there was a common deprecation of the body even though it was not ontologically opposite to the soul. The outer body would decompose into dust since it was made of earthly stuff and belonged to the lower strata of the hierarchy. The idea of different destinations in the afterlife for the body and the soul thus affirms the cosmos-soma correlation rather than a dichotomy of physical versus spiritual or matter versus nonmatter.[16]

---

[14] M. Douglas, *Rules and Meanings: The Anthropology of Everyday Knowledge, Selected Readings* (Harmondsworth: Penguin Education, 1973), 93. Martin notices that the Greco-Roman understanding of the body demonstrates Douglas's point (*Corinthian Body*, 30).

[15] G. Luck, "Studia Divina in Vita Humana: On Cicero's "Dream of Scipio" and Its Place in Greco-Roman Philosophy," *HTR* 49 no. 4 (1956): 214.

[16] Likewise, as Martin notes, the spells for heavenly ascent in magical papyri also reveal such cosmo-somatic correlations. The invocation typically starts by recalling the identity of the elements inside the magician's body with the elements of various cosmic strata. It is assumed in the spells that the magician has the right to traverse the cosmic hierarchy because of the identity of her inner body elements with the elements of the strata through which she intends to traverse. Martin, *Corinthian Body*, 17.

The ancient construction of the body as a real microcosm would integrate the presumed physical sense of the outer body and the mental sense of the inner soul or spirit. The mechanism and ideal balance of both the cosmos and the social body suggests the integrated way that the whole human being is supposed to work. Those of higher status (the constellations, the aristocracies, or the soul) do not function without those of lower status (earth, the labors, or the body or specific organs), and vice versa. Seneca tells Nero, for example, that he is ultimately hurting himself by harming his people because "you are the spirit of your republic, and republic is your body" (Clem. 1.5.1).[17] Seneca's body metaphor maps the social hierarchy upon a person through the schema of the outer (body) versus the inner (spirit) yet also assumes the union of the whole person. Similar body metaphors are common in Greco-Roman texts, a topic to which we will return.

Moreover, Martin indicates that the body is not only an isolated, imitated version of the cosmos or society. Rather, the functions of the whole microcosmic body are really embedded in the cosmos at large and constantly influenced by one's surroundings through the surface of the body.[18] The concept of *poroi* was an important way to conceptualize this intense cosmos-soma relation. As Martin summarizes, *poroi* are channels both on the body to allow external matters to enter and go around the whole body, and within the body to enable psychic and nutritive processes. Thus, the body is "of a piece with the elements surrounding it and pervading it" because "the surface of the body is not a sealed boundary" but is "porous."[19] Resorting to *poroi* that allow the soul to move through the body, the Hippocratics explain the various characteristics of human souls (such as "quarrelsome" or "benevolent") as affected by either the nature of the body or the nature of the environmental objects that the soul "meets and with which it mixes." This might happen through breathing and sweating.[20] With a similar logic, madness (mania) is considered a symptom of the soul that requires treatment on the body. Galen, following Aristotle, also considers the quality of blood as reflecting the state of the soul and as depending on the appearance and surface of the body.[21] In short, the "inner" of a person is constantly influenced by the "outer," including the outer surface of the body itself and its social or cosmic environment.

The constant influence of the outer on the inner would suggest that the body is "malleable." The body is not only constituted by the same elements as the cosmos but also able to be pervaded and continually shaped by environmental elements and forces. These concepts of intense cosmos-soma correlation and the malleability of the body were held by people from different social strata even though they showed different attitudes and practices concerning these concepts. Martin insightfully points out the correlation between people's attitudes toward environmental influences and their social positions. On the one hand, lower-class people, who were usually helpless

---

[17] See also M. V. Lee, *Paul, the Stoics, and the Body of Christ* (Cambridge: Cambridge University Press, 2006), 42.
[18] Padel, *Mind*, 42. See also Martin, *Corinthian Body*, 17.
[19] Martin, *Corinthian Body*, 16–18.
[20] Padel, *Mind*, 58, 86; cited in Martin, *Corinthian Body*, 18.
[21] E. C. Evans, *Physiognomics in the Ancient World* (Philadelphia: American Philosophical Society, 1967), 23.

in the face of the power exerted by the other classes, showed much fear of the invasive influence from the environment. The upper class, on the other hand, valued the stability of a society and the balance of various social forces. They tried to manipulate environmental influences and to achieve balance of the body.[22] For example, based on the malleable understanding of the body, the upper class seemed to pay much attention to the massaging procedures by which young male bodies may be shaped into beautiful, balanced, and "masculine" bodies that conform to their social class.[23] The perfectly balanced body that is nearest to divine beauty, then, was located at the highest end of the vertical social spectrum.[24]

In sum, while people of different social strata and different social experiences show different attitudes toward the cosmos-soma pervasion, the body is commonly considered as constantly pervaded by cosmic forces and continually molded by those forces. As will be shown below, this ancient construction of the body provides intellectual backgrounds for interpreting the neurobiological phenomena of early Christian experience of the Spirit. It also provides an important framework for understanding Paul's idea of spirit possession and the related experience of bodily transformation in the present. Paul, like others of his time, assumes the correlation between the individual body and its cosmic/social environment. For Paul, the experience of receiving the otherworldly Spirit of Christ (1 Cor 2:12; 6:17; 2 Cor 3:17-18) in the inner body is in parallel with being molded by a peculiar outer community, which he calls "the body of Christ" (1 Cor 12:13).

4.2 Experiential Context: The Perception of the Body in Pneumatic Experience

Susan Grove Eastman astutely observes that Martin's analysis of the ancient construction of the body shows "intriguing convergences" with modern theories on the topics of "personhood, human cognition, and relatedness."[25] As she indicates, in 1995, Martin asks his readers "to try to imagine how ancient Greeks and Romans could see as 'natural' what seems to us bizarre: the nonexistence of the 'individual,' the fluidity of the elements that make up the 'self,' and the essential continuity of the human body with its surroundings."[26] Nevertheless, such a correlation between the

---

[22] Martin, *Corinthian Body*, 159-60. Cf. M. M. Lock, *East Asian Medicine in Urban Japan* (Berkeley: University of California, 1980), 3-45. Martin's model of two kinds of attitudes relies on her work.

[23] The manipulation of bodily formation began before birth and continued through childhood, adolescence, and even to the later parts of life. Central to this manipulation was the idea of bodily balance. For example, since women, infants, and younger men were moister and softer than older men, the manipulation of the young male body was a process of properly "drying and hardening" so that the body could gradually arrive at and maintain the correct balance of moist/dry and soft/hard that corresponded to the age and demonstrated the aristocratic beauty. See Martin, *Corinthian Body*, 25, 27-9.

[24] Ibid., 34-5.

[25] S. G. Eastman, *Paul and the Person: Reframing Paul's Anthropology* (Grand Rapids, MI: W. B. Eerdmans, 2017), 2, 95.

[26] Martin, *Corinthian Body*, 21.

inner self and its outer environment through the body is no longer bizarre in today's scientific analysis of the self and the human body.[27] It has become increasingly clear from scientific data that our consciousness is always interacting with the environment through the functioning of our body, and neuroscience is one of the modern tools that can help to account for the mechanism of such experiential interaction.[28]

The intriguing intersection between neuroscience and ancient ideas is particularly relevant to our concern with the idea of bodily transformation occurring in socialization or religious activities. While this idea is not inconceivable according to the Greco-Roman construction of the body, modern neuroscience stresses the "universality of the human brain"[29] and indicates that the disturbance of body perception and self-boundaries is in fact a cross-cultural phenomenon and is usually experienced in religious ecstasy. Shantz has pioneered the application of neuroscience to analyze religious ecstasy as reflected in early Christian texts and to argue for the constitutive role of such ecstatic experience in Paul's ideas of bodily transformation. Following her work, I will first consider how Paul and his congregations might share similar pneumatic-ecstatic experiences caused by the Spirit and then explore how those common experiences might influence his rhetorical strategies and contribute to his ideas.

4.2.1 The Ecstatic Experience of the Spirit Shared by Paul and His Congregations

First of all, Shantz emphasizes the experiential aspect of Paul's religious life. As she enumerates, Paul frequently talks about various experiences of the Spirit: inexpressible prayer aided by the Spirit (Rom 8:26; cf. 1 Cor 14–15), praying or singing with the Spirit rather than the mind (1 Cor 14:14–15), signs and wonders performed by the power of the Spirit (Rom 15:18–19), and spiritual gifts such as revelation (ἀποκάλυψις), prophecy, and glossolalia in assemblies (1 Cor 14:6, 26). Paul also talks about the way that he received revelations (ἀποκαλύψεις) and visions through his "ecstatic journey" to heaven (2 Cor 12:1–4; cf. Gal 1:12 "a revelation of Jesus Christ").[30] Applying models from neuroscience, Shantz has demonstrated that these passages about experience of the Spirit reflect various ecstatic forms, including "worship, visions, spirit possession, glossolalia," and different types of altered states of consciousness (ASC).[31] She points out

---

[27] Eastman, *Paul and the Person*, 12, 86.
[28] An example is neurologist Antonio R. Damasio's description of the way in which our brain perceives and recalls something other than the self: "We store in memory not just aspects of an object's physical structure … but also aspects of our organism's motor involvement in the process of apprehending such relevant aspects: our emotional reaction to an object; our broader physical and mental state at the time of apprehending the object." See A. R. Damasio, *The Feeling of What Happens: Body and Emotion in the Making of Consciousness* (New York: Harcourt, 1999), 183. As Eastman points out, "many of the insights from neuroscience and experimental psychology sound eerily similar to views of the body in the Hellenistic world." See Eastman, *Paul and the Person*, 86, 104–5.
[29] Shantz, *Paul in Ecstasy*, 71.
[30] Ibid., 2.
[31] Ibid., 2, 87–93, 145–97.

that these passages of pneumatic experience "suggest that ecstatic religious experience was a frequent and significant aspect of Paul's life and his apprehension of the divine."[32]

Thus, it would not be surprising that pneumatic-ecstatic experience had been a crucial element not only in Paul's own religious view but also in Paul's evangelizing work and community-building. As Shantz notes, Paul repeatedly mentions his undeniable experience of the Spirit when he speaks of himself founding the Christ-believing communities (1 Thess 1:4–5; 1 Cor 2:4–5; Gal 3:1–5).[33] Philip Esler also notes that Paul pictures himself as "powerfully manifesting the Spirit in preaching, miracle-working, and glossolalia."[34] Moreover, focusing on Galatians, Engberg-Pedersen observes a pattern of transmitting pneumatic-ecstatic experience from Paul to other believers in Paul's mission:

> In fact, just as Paul had had Christ revealed "in him" (1:16), when God called him through his grace (1:15), so the Galatians have had the crucified Christ drawn to their very eyes (3:1) when Paul proclaimed the gospel to them (4:13–14).[35]

It appears that the Christ event was transmitted to the Galatians in a very vivid and experiential way so that, as Engberg-Pedersen claims, the image of the crucified Christ was revealed "in a sort of *direct vision*." To an extent they had received Paul as "messenger of God, as Christ Jesus" (Gal 4:14).[36] Note that such experiential transmission is frequently described through the container schema. Because of such a strong experience and relationship, in the beginning of the letter, Paul is astonished that the Galatians have departed from the one who called them in grace (ἐν χάριτι) into (εἰς) another gospel (1:6). Now Paul is again in labor like a woman and eagerly expects that Christ would be formed like a fetus in them (ἐν ὑμῖν; 4:19).

Assuming the correlation between the inside of an individual and the outer environment or community, Paul considers his evangelizing work as transmitting what was revealed or given in him into individuals and as building up a corresponding group filled with what he transmits.[37] As Paul reminds the Galatians, God "was pleased to reveal his son in me (ἐν ἐμοί), so that I could preach him in the nations (ἐν τοῖς ἔθνεσιν)" (1:16). The Galatians thus received the Spirit into them when they believed his preaching (3:2; εἰς in 4:6) and had miracles in their group (ἐν ὑμῖν; 3:5). Such remarks on experiential transmission seem to indicate that Paul considers his evangelizing mission as a process of transmitting God's Spirit and the experiences of the Spirit as the features that demonstrate the presence of God's Spirit in a certain 'container,' either an individual or a group. Thus, Shantz's suggestion appears convincing: the demonstration of Paul's "apostolic power" that he usually resorts to (σημεῖα τοῦ ἀποστόλου; 2 Cor 12:12) is most likely his "ability to kindle ecstatic experiences in the communities he

---

[32] Ibid., 2.
[33] Ibid., 181.
[34] P. F. Esler, *The First Christians in Their Social Worlds: Social Scientific Approaches to New Testament Interpretation* (New York: Routledge, 1994), 48.
[35] T. Engberg-Pedersen, *Paul and the Stoics* (Louisville, KY: Westminster/John Knox, 2000), 144.
[36] Ibid., 144 (original emphasis).
[37] See also ibid., 332.

visited" and so to bring about the reception of the Spirit into each individual (see also 1 Cor 2:4–5; Rom 15:15–19).[38]

Therefore, it seems justified to suggest that Paul and his communities shared common ecstatic experience of the Spirit or at least similar perceptions and articulations of what they experienced. In addition to the Galatians, this commonality in experience is found in the Corinthian community. One significant experience shared by Paul and the Corinthians is glossolalia, a phenomenon that both Paul and the Corinthians understood to be a result of possessing the indwelling Spirit.[39] The accounts from Acts also suggest that glossolalia was a widely recognized sign of receiving the Spirit in the early stage of the spread of Christianity (Acts 10:44–48; 19:1–6). Although Paul has to argue in 1 Corinthians that glossolalia is not the only, nor even the most important, manifestation of the Spirit (1 Cor 14:5–6; 28–30; c.f. 12:1–11), he affirms that it comes from the Spirit.

In light of modern studies, the Corinthian phenomenon of glossolalia appears to be a form of possession trance—the trance state caused by spirit possession. As Paul says, a glossolalist utters mysteries by the Spirit when "the mind is fruitless" (νοῦς μου ἄκαρπός ἐστιν; 14:2, 14). This description coheres with the idea of the spirit taking over or possessing the person's mind.[40] In the absence of interpretation, such speech is unintelligible to others present (14:9) and might be considered madness by outsiders (14:23). It only edifies the speakers (14:4) since they speak only to God "in the spirit" or "by the indwelling Spirit" (πνεύματι; 14:2). Paul's description is highly coherent with the "dissociative" state of the glossolalists described in Felicitas Goodman's cross-cultural study of glossolalia. Goodman finds that modern glossolalists enter an "altered state of consciousness" to dissociate themselves from the realities surrounding them, withdraw into inner functioning, and break out into the practice of glossolalia.[41] In light of similar modern phenomena, it seems appropriate to place the practice of glossolalia in Corinth within Goodman's cross-cultural findings and understand it as occurring in trance.[42] Shantz also affirms the dissociative nature of glossolalia utterances and argues that glossolalia appears to be a "predominant form of spirit possession" in the Corinthian community.[43]

Goodman's work further indicates that dissociative states are transmittable. For example, modern Pentecostal evangelists who are able to powerfully manifest glossolalia can in turn kindle a similar phenomenon among new groups in which such a phenomenon has not previously existed or been popular.[44] This kind of

---

[38] Shantz, *Paul in Ecstasy*, 180.
[39] D. B. Martin, "Tongues of Angels and Other Status Indicators," *JAAR* 59 no. 3 (1991): 551–6.
[40] As Esler indicates, "This unusual expression may refer to the disengagement of the consciousness from everyday reality." See Esler, *Social Worlds*, 45–6.
[41] F. Goodman, *Speaking in Tongues: A Cross-Cultural Study of Glossolalia* (Chicago, IL: University of Chicago Press, 1972), 59–60, 126–34.
[42] Esler suggests that underlying Paul's argument in 14:22–25 seems to be a claim by the Corinthians that God is among them in glossolalia. Esler then argues that, if his suggestion is correct, the Corinthians likely understood glossolalia as occurring during states of dissociation since the idea that religious trances and ecstasy were the manifestation of possession by a god was popular in Greek and Near Eastern religions. See Esler, *Social Worlds*, 46.
[43] Shantz, *Paul in Ecstasy*, 157–9.
[44] Goodman, *Speaking in Tongues*, 87–92.

transmission is also in parallel with the picture provided in Acts and the way in which Paul established his communities. Thus, based on Goodman's description and Max Weber's model of charismatic leadership, Esler suggests that Paul ignited the practice of glossolalia when he converted the Corinthians and established their community, and that the Corinthians' glossolalia "closely mirrored Paul's own."[45] Esler's suggestion seems reasonable because it may explain why Paul still highly values the practice of glossolalia (14:18) and only instructs conditional restrictions on glossolalia (4:28) even though it appears to be a cause of current divisions (1 Cor 14:5-6, 28-30; c.f. 12:1-11).[46] At the current stage in Corinth, Paul promotes prophecy as the preferable practice and divine manifestation in public worship for the sake of community-building, yet still emphasizes that he gives thanks to God for speaking in tongues more than all the Corinthians (14:18-19). It would not be wise to totally dismiss Paul's claim of common glossolalia experience as ironic or simply a polemical defense of Paul's spirituality.[47] As Gordon D. Fee states, "The fact that [Paul] can say it at all, and say it as a matter for which he can thank God, and do so without fear of contradiction to some believers who are quite taken by this Spirit gifting, must be taken seriously."[48]

Moreover, Shantz suggests a better understanding of Paul's conditional restrictions on glossolalia, an understanding that recognizes Paul's concern for social formation. She observes that Paul describes the neurological phenomenon of prophecy as under the control of the prophets (the spirits of prophets are subject to the prophets; 1 Cor 14:32), and that at the same time he promotes a type of prayer or worship practice in which both the mind and the spirit can function (14:15). Thus, as Shantz indicates, Paul appears to be contrasting "two kinds of ecstatic functioning": the first is "straightforward spirit possession accompanied by the displacement of personality or partial amnesia," and the second is "comparable to mediumship marked by modest control of the trance experience."[49] Relying on Michael Winkelman's analysis of ASC societies, Shantz indicates that "a movement away from spirit possession toward mediumship is coupled with an experience of a relatively complex sociopolitical

---

[45] Esler, *Social Worlds*, 47-8.

[46] See G. D. Fee, *The First Epistle to the Corinthians* (rev. ed.; Grand Rapids, MI: W. B. Eerdmans, 2014), 748. As he states, "[Paul's] concern throughout has been with *uninterpreted* tongues in the assembly, because what is said cannot edify the church" (original emphasis).

[47] Shantz has indicated the invalid circularity of arguments that dismiss the "face value" of Paul's statements in favor of ecstatic experience based on the assumption that Paul opposes such experiences. See Shantz, *Paul in Ecstasy*, 43-4. We should also note that there is no evidence in either 1 Corinthians or Galatians suggesting that Paul had been accused of not having pneumatic experiences, as reflected in 2 Cor 10-13. On the contrary, in Galatians, Paul argues against his opponents' position about circumcision on the very basis of his ability to bring about pneumatic experiences. In 1 Corinthians, Paul's style is not polemic but rather didactic, and his teachings and instructions usually presume the common ground of experience of the Spirit (e.g., 1 Cor 2:10-12; 6:11; 9:11). See also H. Conzelmann, *1 Corinthians: A Commentary on the First Epistle to the Corinthians* (trans. J. W. Leitch; ed. G. W. MacRae; Philadelphia: Fortress Press, 1975), 239. Moreover, even if Paul has to defend his authority in offering instructions by appealing to his ability to speak in tongues, his argument is effective only if his description reflects a common understanding of the experience of glossolalia (whether he has that experience or not).

[48] Fee, *1 Corinthians*, 748.

[49] Shantz, *Paul in Ecstasy*, 191-4.

arrangement" in which the structure of governance is still being formed.[50] In other words, when a religious community becomes more developed and stratified, the second type of practice that can be used to endorse leadership structures and authoritative discourses is preferable.[51]

I believe that Shantz's suggestion is coherent with the picture revealed in 1 Corinthians. Appealing to reconciliation and social union among the Corinthians, Paul needs and attempts to promote a form of social organization that can resolve divisions (c.f. 6:1–5; 11:18–34). Note that Paul arranges various spiritual gifts in a hierarchical order in which the apostle is on top and the positions for authoritative teachings are highlighted (12:28). It appears that Paul attempts to manage the religious practices (including those of ASC) according to the current stage of societal growth in which the group has become more stratified. Besides, since Paul has to lead the Corinthians from a distance, he would also prefer a social organization that emphasizes the authority that has been set (likely by him). Similarly, as I will show in the next section, Paul's conceptual blend between the reception of the Spirit and baptism (12:13) reveals his ultimate concern for social formation in dealing with pneumatic experience. Thus, in line with Shantz, I would suggest that what is reflected in Paul's claim of having much glossolalia experience is not hyperbole or polemic but a more rudimentary stage of social formation and the corresponding practice of ASC, a stage in which Paul most likely participated as a leader and from which he is ready to move on. At the stage at which Paul wrote 1 Corinthians, he would rather evaluate pneumatic experience on the basis of its contribution to the community.

Another important parallel pneumatic-ecstatic experience between Paul and the Corinthians is that of revelation and special knowledge. As John M. G. Barclay observes, the Corinthians value their experiences of the Spirit, especially their accessibility to spiritual wisdom and esoteric speech (cf. 1 Cor 2:10–14; 14:37–39).[52] It is the Spirit indwelling in the Corinthians that reveals special knowledge to them (2:10–11; 12:6). They thus consider themselves πνευματικοί and τέλειοι and thus different from the ordinary people outside of their community.[53] Like in Galatians, the container schema is frequently used here to conceptualize possessing the Spirit and belonging to a certain group (or a spiritual level in this case). The Corinthians' emphasis on esoteric knowledge is in fact in parallel with the way that Paul endorses his apostleship and teaching by resorting to his revelatory visions and heavenly journey. As Shantz notes, Paul's ecstatic experiences of revelation appear to give him "some of the content (particularly his certainty that Christ was raised) and much of the conviction of the gospel" (see 1 Cor 9:1; 15:8; 2 Cor 12; cf. Gal 1:12).[54] In the next section, I will discuss

---

[50] Ibid., 202–3, also 165–76; cf. M. Winkelman, *Shamans, Priests, and Witches: A Cross-Cultural Study of Magico-Religious Practitioners* (Anthropological Research Papers 44; Tempe: Arizona State University, 1992).

[51] In addition to the hierarchy in the Corinthian community, as Shantz indicates, each member of the community is a part of the stratified society of Corinth that is imbedded in the hierarchical structure of the empire. Shantz, *Paul in Ecstasy*, 195–6.

[52] J. M. G. Barclay, "Thessalonica and Corinth: Social Contrasts in Pauline Christianity," in *Pauline Churches and Diaspora Jews* (ed. J. M. G. Barclay; Tübingen: Mohr Siebeck, 2011), 192.

[53] Ibid.

[54] Shantz, *Paul in Ecstasy*, 183.

the association between experiences of attaining to the divine sphere and the idea of bodily transformation.

4.2.2 The Disturbance of Body Perception and Its Cultural Interpretations

Second Corinthians 12:1–4 is the fullest account of Paul's heavenly journey and revelation. Shantz places this account among the cross-cultural descriptions of ecstatic experiences and indicates that it shares two significant features with those from various times and places: the inability to put one's experience into expression (unutterable words; 12:4) and the confusion of the status of one's own body (in or out of the body; 12:2–3).[55] In this case, Paul's defense of his apostolic status might make one question whether this account only reflects the polemic against his opponents.[56] However, even if the context were polemical to some extent, Paul's argument must be conceivable and reasonable. Thus, that the two ideas of the inability to express himself and the confusion about his body even come to Paul is itself intriguing. This demands both experiential and cultural considerations because the two ideas would not be intelligible to the Corinthians if no one in their time has experienced or expressed similar feelings. Indeed, Paul expresses his uncertainty in a rather certain way. He explicitly states that he does not know whether he was in the body or out of the body as if his uncertainty supports his argument. As Shantz states, "there is something in the character of the experience itself that must precede the repeated uncertainty."[57] In the following, I will argue that Paul's report reflects not only certain characteristics that are common to the neurobiological effects of human ASC but also the common cultural understandings in Paul's time about such effects. Otherwise, Paul's claim would not be valid to the Corinthians. Moreover, as will be discussed below, some clues in the account suggest that Paul most likely has reported what he really went through, even if he shaped it for the immediate purposes of the letter.

Shantz applies Eugene d'Aquili and Andrew Newberg's neurobiological model to account for Paul's report of somatic bewilderment.[58] She indicates that one's normal consciousness can be altered by the combination of the intensification of particular aspects of neural functioning and the muting of some other aspects. She also indicates that examining the experience of both healthy and brain-damaged people helps us to figure out how our biological systems may be implicated in religious ecstasy. That is, through religious activities, some aspects of the sense and sensations of the body are intensified while others are restrained (similar to the cases of brain-damaged). The

---

[55] As Shantz summarizes from cross-cultural descriptions of ecstatic experiences, the disturbance of body perception is often experienced and perceived as bodily changing, disembodiment, ineffability, unlimitedness, and blurred self-boundaries, or, in other words, "a sense of participation in a greater category of being." Ibid., 71, 90–6.

[56] See A. T. Lincoln, *Paradise Now and Not Yet: Studies in the Role of the Heavenly Dimension in Paul's Thought with Special Reference to His Eschatology* (Cambridge: Cambridge University Press, 1981), 81. R. Jewett, *Paul's Anthropological Terms: A Study of Their Use in Conflict Settings* (Leiden: Brill, 1971).

[57] Shantz, *Paul in Ecstasy*, 91.

[58] See E. G. d'Aquili and A. B. Newberg, *The Mystical Mind: Probing the Biology of Religious Experience Theology and the Sciences* (Minneapolis, MN: Fortress Press, 1999).

sensation of this kind of neural phenomena is often described by ecstatics as "floating or flying without physical boundaries."[59] Shantz suggests that this sensation might be experienced when some sensory input from the body—such as weight, touch, boundaries, and pain—is largely blocked, yet the "orientation association area" is more activated than when functioning normally, an area in the brain that is responsible for providing body perception by synthesizing and processing somaesthetic (the sense of touch and position), visual, and auditory information channeled to it from other brain areas.[60] Such neural combinations might explain the confusing ecstatic conditions in which the presence of the body or the self in a space is strongly felt, yet the bodily sensations are atypical or even absent.[61] It is not surprising that heavenly ascent is one of the most common interpretations of ecstatic experiences in Paul's time since heaven is identified as lightness and earth as heaviness according to the idea of cosmic polarity and hierarchy.[62] It is also not surprising that two notions concerning body status are associated with the experience understood as heavenly ascent: the transformation of the body (thus conceptualized as ascent with the body) and the escape from the body (non-bodily ascent). As Shantz states, both notions can make sense of the neural phenomena in religious ecstasy.[63]

In Paul's report of ascent, the uncertainty of being whether in or out of the body reveals the very nature of ecstatic experience.[64] First, comparing to non-bodily ascent, the notion of bodily ascent is more familiar to Jewish thought. As we have seen in the ancient construction of the body, the fleshly and earthly body is of the lower status of the cosmo-somatic hierarchy and so not compatible with the heavenly, divine strata (see Figure 4.1; cf. Figure 2.5). Within a similar logic of the heaven-earth polarity, the body is at times presented in Jewish literature as either transformed (1 En. 71:11; 4Q491; see also Dan 1–3 in afterlife) or clothed with glorious garments (2 En. 22:8) in one's experience of heavenly ascent. Whatever change to the body, the experience is usually accompanied with the sense of infinity.[65] Second, the notion of non-bodily ascent is another way to conceive of an ascent journey within the framework of cosmo-somatic hierarchy and is found in Greek works. For example, in a story of Plato (Republic X 614B-621B), Er's corpse was not damaged after his death, and he revived

---

[59] Shantz, *Paul in Ecstasy*, 98.
[60] D'Aquili and Newberg, *Mystical Mind*, 33–4; P. W. Brazis et al., *Localization in Clinical Neurology* (3rd ed.; Boston: Little, Brown, 1996), 497.
[61] Shantz, *Paul in Ecstasy*, 98.
[62] Jeffrey R. Asher, *Polarity and Change in 1 Corinthians 15: A Study of Metaphysics, Rhetoric, and Resurrection* (Tübingen: Mohr Siebeck, 2000), 177–8.
[63] Shantz, *Paul in Ecstasy*, 96.
[64] Regarding two interpretations of body bewilderment in ascent experiences, Alan Segal indicates that Paul's comment about his uncertainty about his body status provides a valuable insight into the evolution of the mystical ideas in Paul's cultural context. Segal argues that Paul's uncertainty "demonstrates either a disagreement in the community or more likely a first-century mystic's inability" to distinguish between bodily and non-bodily journeys. See A. Segal, *Paul the Convert: The Apostolate and Apostasy of Saul the Pharisee* (New Haven, CT: Yale University Press, 1990), 38–39.
[65] Infinite time is a common expression regarding ascent in Jewish thought (e.g., Dan 12:2–3). As for infinite space, see 1QH^a xi 21–25, where the hymnist says that he is only "a vessel of clay" and is limited in a "wicked boundary" (בגבול רשע). But God has lifted him up to an "eternal height" (לרום עולם) and so he "walks about on a limitless plain."

on the day of his own funeral. He then described the journey of his soul (without his complete body) to the entrance of heaven and the underworld. Although Er's journey occurs after his death and does not include heaven itself, Margaret E. Thrall rightly notes that this example still attests to "the notion of extrabodily translation to some sphere beyond that of ordinary earthly life, followed by return to the body."[66] In his *Concerning the Face which Appears in the Orb of the Moon*, Plutarch also writes that a man's head was struck and so "the sutures parted and released his soul." The soul then "mingled joyfully with air that was translucent and pure" and went on for a heavenly journey.[67] Again, the sense of lacking the boundary of the body or even the self is clear. Given the Corinthians' consistent deprecation of the body and the carelessness of bodily activities (cf. 1 Cor 6:11–20; 8:1–8), it is very likely that they would lean toward the non-bodily view of heavenly ascent. For them, Robert Jewett suggests that spiritual ecstasy meant release from the prison of the inferior body.[68]

It is intriguing that Paul, who is familiar with Jewish concepts of ascent (e.g., 1 Thess 4:13–18) and earnestly advocates for bodily resurrection in 1 Cor 15, would even allow the possibility of non-bodily ascent.[69] Regarding this kind of seeming contradiction, some have argued that Paul's idea about the body in 2 Corinthians is different from that in 1 Corinthians because he has developed his idea between the time of these two letters. As mentioned in Chapter 1, the Pleiderer-Teichmann line of interpretation argues that Paul's development is a process of getting rid of the somatic aspects of his Jewish heritage, and that the difference between the two Corinthian letters witnesses to a crucial stage of this developmental process. However, I have indicated that this line of interpretation falsely assumes a sharp Jewish-Hellenistic dichotomy and so downplays the somatic aspects of Paul's thought.

Without assuming this false dichotomy, Dodd focuses on Paul's experiences and the way they may have contributed to the change in Paul's thinking. Dodd argues that humiliation (2 Cor 10–13) and illness (1:8–10) have made Paul more aware of his mortality and limitedness, so that he shows a "quiet self-abandonment" in 2 Cor 4–5.[70] Although Dodd indeed observes a sort of mental development revealed in 2 Cor 4–5, this does not adequately account for Paul's expression in 2 Cor 12. On the one hand, a "self-abandonment" does not necessarily lead to non-bodily ideas. Admittedly, Paul talks about escape from the body in 5:8: "being away from the body and at home with the Lord." Nevertheless, as Enberg-Pedersen and Richard N. Longenecker note, Paul still insists on the bodily existence in front of God (5:10), especially when he states that he is not willing to be "found naked" or "unclothed" and expects that we will be "further clothed" (ἐπενδύσασθαι; 5:4).[71] On the other hand, as I will demonstrate in

---

[66] M. E. Thrall, "Paul's Journey to Paradise: Some Exegetical Issues in 2 Cor 12,2-4," in *The Corinthian Correspondence* (ed. R. Bieringer; Leuven: Leuven University Press, 1996), 354.
[67] Martin, *Corinthian Body*, 14.
[68] Jewett, *Paul's Anthropological Terms*, 278.
[69] As Thrall also notes in "Paul's Journey," 354.
[70] Dodd, "Change and Development," 92–3.
[71] R. N. Longenecker, "Is There Development in Paul's Resurrection Thought?" in *Life in the Face of Death: The Resurrection Message of the New Testament* (ed. R. N. Longenecker; Grand Rapids, MI: W. B. Eerdmans, 1998), 195.

the next chapter, Paul has a clear idea and coherent logic about the body in 2 Cor 5 (his ideas in 2 Cor 3–5 require further analysis), and this is not what he expresses in 2 Cor 12—he does not know.[72] What Paul repeatedly emphasizes in 2 Cor 12:1–4 is his lack of comprehension of the event.

I maintain that the uncertainty that he describes (or claims) in 12:1–4 is a common sensation itself. Paul does not choose one position as if he is defending that position. Actually, what Paul is defending is his revelatory knowledge and apostleship (11:5–6), and he argues from the description of his experience and uncertainty.[73] Nor does he express his uncertainty in a way of concession as if he is in the process of changing his mind or intends to leave the question unanswered to be accepted by people of both positions. Rather, he repeats his uncertainty in a very certain way and claims that only God knows the mechanism—"I do not know, God knows."[74] Paul's uncertainty directly serves his polemic goal, which is to convince the Corinthians of the divine origin of the revelation to him. It was God who lifted him and gave a special revelation to him despite his weakness (cf. 12:10). Paul achieves this polemical goal by describing the genuine sensations in his pneumatic-ecstatic experience and by interpreting the sensations as transcendent. His description may function in this way precisely because these sensations are how ecstatics commonly feel—floating without boundaries and being ignorant of one's own body status. Paul then interprets these well-known sensations and ignorance of body status as demonstrating God's power and the authenticity of the revelation that he receives. Paul is not in charge; God is. Thus, based on these sensations, Paul goes on to argue that his suffering and weakness, as well as his ignorance of body status, show God's transcending power (12:5–9).

In sum, the experience of the Spirit is an important common ground between Paul and his congregations. Their common experiences include miracles and ecstatic states such as glossolalia, inexpressible prayers, singing with the Spirit, and body bewilderment in ascent. Through the container schema, these overwhelming experiences are conceptualized as the works of the indwelling Spirit, or, in modern terms, as the phenomena of spirit possession. Moreover, Paul shows his concerns for community growth in promoting a movement away from practices of straightforward possession trance toward practices with proper control of the trance state. While Paul emphasizes a genuine sensation of body bewilderment in 2 Cor 12:1–4, such sensations could be interpreted as either the escape of the body or the transformation of the body. Both interpretations are neurologically probable and culturally intelligible. As will be demonstrated below, being concerned with social formation, Paul enacts a conceptual blend between the reception of the Spirit, baptism, and the common body metaphor of his time. This blend would encourage the interpretation of pneumatic-ecstatic experience as bodily transformation.

---

[72] Besides, what Paul recalls in 2 Cor 12:1–4 is his experience fourteen years ago. It is less likely that his development occurring during his interaction with the Corinthians would have been the reason for his report of confusion about an event a long time ago.
[73] Shantz has made this point in *Paul in Ecstasy*, 90–109.
[74] Thrall, "Paul's Journey," 356. Shantz, *Paul in Ecstasy*, 91.

4.3 "The Body of Christ": Re-Picturing Pneumatic Experience with Ritual Experience

Paul's goal in enacting the conceptual blend in 1 Cor 12:13 is to construct his ideal image of "the body of Christ" and to lead the Corinthians to re-picture the reception of the Spirit according to this image. The famous "body of Christ" metaphor is important for the teachings about Christian community life in the Pauline groups (see also Col 1:24; Eph 4:12) and is largely built on the conviction of the presence and work of the Spirit in their groups. This metaphor in 1 Corinthians provides a vivid image for understanding Paul's construction of the Christian social body and its correlation with individual bodies. For Paul, it is within this distinct social body that the individual bodies of the members are supposed to be embedded and by which they are to be molded. This image of Christ's body is first introduced in 1 Cor 6:15 (see also 1:13) and is fully elaborated in ch. 12. Throughout 1 Corinthians, Paul expounds his ideal picture of community life largely on the basis of this image (cf. 6:12–20; 10:14–22; 11:29).[75] Specifically, it is noteworthy that the reception and the experience of the Spirit is the particular aspect of community life that Paul emphasizes in both 6:15 and the full exposition of the body metaphor in chapter 12. Regarding the body of Christ, in 1 Cor 6:15–19, Paul stresses the connection between the individual body and the social body on the very basis of the possession of Christ's spirit (6:17): you have (ἔχετε) the Holy Spirit from God (6:19). Based on the physical connection resulting from having the Spirit, he explains the incompatibility between individual fornication and the social body as Christ's body (6:15): a man's fornication would cause the sexual union between Christ and the prostitute who had been sexually united with the man.[76] In ch. 12, after his full exposition of the image of Christ's body (12:14–27), Paul immediately applies this image to the use of spiritual gifts such as prophecy and glossolalia (12:28–14:40)—apparently the two dominant types of spiritual experience in the Corinthian community. Thus, the experience of the Spirit characterizes the Corinthians' community life and Paul's construction of the body of Christ.

However, while the usually overwhelming experience of the Spirit has a founding role in the establishment and growth of Pauline groups, it ironically becomes an important source of divisions among the Corinthians (1 Cor 12:1–3, 25; 14:36–38). Thus, I will apply conceptual blending theory to demonstrate that, appealing to social unity, Paul exploits both a contemporary metaphor of 'the body for a society' and the immersion image taken from baptismal practices to blend with the image of receiving the Spirit into one's own body (12:13). In so doing, he innovatively argues that receiving the Spirit is not only receiving it into one's physical body (the image of drinking in 1 Cor 12:13) but also an immersion into a special social body, the body of Christ (12:27).

---

[75] As Mitchell observes, "the body of Christ image runs throughout 1 Corinthians, and is, alongside the metaphor of the building, the predominant image in Paul's extended argument for church unity." See Mitchell, *Rhetoric of Reconciliation*, 161–2.

[76] As Martin observes, "Paul's rhetoric implied that sexual intercourse between the Christian man and the prostitute enacted sexual intercourse between Christ and the prostitute" (Martin, *Corinthian Body*, 178).

In other words, by blending the social body metaphor with two experiential images—the reception of the Spirit and baptism—Paul constructs his ideal image of the body of Christ. Both Spirit-reception and water-immersion are common physical experiences shared by the Corinthians. The former is the issue that Paul attempts to deal with, and the latter provides him with the pivotal image by which he can associate the former with the social body metaphor.

Before turning to the overall blending network formed in 12:13 and its conceptual effects, we need to look at all three inputs of this blend. For the sake of analysis, I will discuss the concepts in these three inputs in turn in the order below. The first input is a contemporary metaphor of the body for a social or political organism, a metaphor that is in many ways parallel to Paul's image of the body of Christ. The second input is a metaphorical image of "being baptized in the Spirit." I will indicate that it is a pre-blended image based on the concrete bodily experience of the boundary-crossing rite of water baptism. The third input, receiving the Spirit metaphorically conceptualized as drinking water, is of course also a pre-blended image. Moreover, based on the neurological phenomena of spirit possession and the ancient concept of cosmos-soma correlation analyzed above, I will argue that the new idea of drinking the Spirit into the body and simultaneously being immersed into "the body of Christ" would suggest a sort of bodily transformation of each individual.

4.3.1 The First Input: The Body Metaphor

I will first look at the metaphorical expression of "one body" (ἓν σῶμα) in 1 Cor 12:13 because this expression reveals Paul's rhetorical purpose in constructing the overall conceptual blend in this verse. In her classic work *Paul and the Rhetoric of Reconciliation*, Margaret M. Mitchell has indicated that the metaphor of the body for a social unity is very common in the ancient political rhetoric of homonoia and that its function is to achieve social union and oppose factionalism.[77] In texts of both Greco-Roman political literature and Hellenistic Jewish appropriation of this metaphor, it is always connected with disputes and factions. This metaphor is typically used to argue that, just like the human body, a society is also hierarchically constituted of different members (representing social classes) assigned naturally to different positions in the body and is supposed to function with harmonious integrity. Thus, the body metaphor is usually used to support social hierarchy and to argue that inequality is natural and necessary for the common good of the whole. Therefore, division or any disruption of the balanced order is like a disease that can weaken the whole body and make all members suffer. For example, the famous fable of Menenius Agrippa (Livy 2.32.12-33.1) tells of a revolt of body members such as the limbs, mouth, and teeth (representing the plebs who did all the work) against the belly (representing patres, the governing class), which eventually results in the distress of the whole body. With this fable, Menenius attempts to persuade the plebs who are striking to return to their social position and their labor. In some other cases, the ruling class represents the soul or mind that rules

---

[77] Mitchell, *Rhetoric of Reconciliation*, 157–60.

over the body yet is also integrated with the body and will suffer together with the body (cf. Seneca's words to Nero in Clem. 1.5.1).

Referring to Menenius's body metaphor, Arnaldo Momigliano notices that "1 Corinthians 12:12–27 is the striking translation into Christian terms."[78] Following Momigliano, Mitchell also argues that Paul applies the common body metaphor to the situation in Corinth. As Mitchell shows, Paul's use of the body metaphor conforms with ancient political writers in multiple aspects: the use of the same body parts, the personification of the body parts, the description of the weak body parts as necessary (ἀναγκαῖά), the idea of sharing one spirit or soul (cf. Dio Chrys. Or. 39.5), the theme of co-suffering and co-rejoicing, and the rhetorical purpose.[79] Paul explicitly states his purpose of combating factionalism in 12:25: in order that there may be no division in the body (ἵνα μὴ ᾖ σχίσμα ἐν τῷ σώματι). In fact, this purpose of homonoia recalls 1:10 (the πρόθεσις of the whole letter according to Mitchell) and the multiple references to division all through the letter (cf. 1:18–19; 8:1–3, 10–13; 11:18–22).[80]

Moreover, the way that Paul applies the body metaphor to the Christian community also finds parallels in his time. As Mitchell indicates, Paul "christianizes" the body metaphor by "transference" to the body of Christ.[81] This transference seems to be similar to the way that the image of the body of the emperor is used to conceptualize the Roman Empire as an integrated unity. Michael Squire draws out the development of the body metaphor from early Greek authors to those of the early Roman Empire and indicates that, by the time Augustus came to power, "the emperor emerged as an emblematic symbol of the imperium that he embodied."[82] That is, as we have seen in Seneca's words to Nero, the empire is the emperor's body and is thought to embody the *corpus imperii*.[83]

In addition to tracing the formation of this idea of embodiment, Squire further explores the public visual experience of such embodiment in the empire. He indicates that the statues of Augustus represent the emperor's body to the public as not only the actual body of Augustus but also the metaphorical *corpus imperii*. For example, analyzing the statue of Augustus from Prima Porta, Squire observes that while Augustus's body is represented as an actual body with "nipples, belly-button, iliac crest, and pectoral muscles" under the cuirassed chest, the cuirass also "aligns that body with a series of additional figures portrayed on the Augustan chest," such as the mythmaking of important political events and "personifications of the celestial Sun, Sky, and Moon."[84] In this way, Squire argues that Augustus's "ribcage marks the limits of the terrestrial world and his chest marks the respective limits of the cosmos."[85] Through visual experience, the statue strengthens the political ideology about the

---

[78] A. Momigliano, "Camillus and Concord," *The Classic Quarterly* 36 no. 3 (1942): 117.
[79] Mitchell, *Rhetoric of Reconciliation*, 159–60.
[80] Ibid., 198.
[81] Ibid., 160.
[82] Squire, "Body Politic," 305–10 (esp. 306).
[83] See also Suetonius's report about the cosmic markings on Augustus's physical chest (*Aug.* 80) and about Caligula's body that symbolizes weakness and corruption (*Calig.* 50); Squire, "Body Politic," 310.
[84] Squire, "Body Politic," 318, 320.
[85] Ibid., 320.

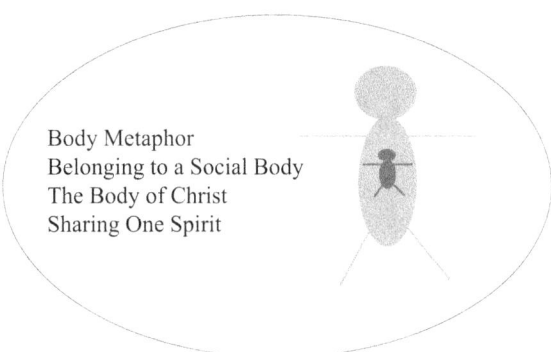

Figure 4.2 The First Input of the Overall Blend in 1 Cor 12:13.

imperial body by inviting viewers to see the body of Augustus as a manifestation of the *corpus imperii* and the "Augustan political and cosmic order."[86]

In 1 Cor 12:12–13, Paul also conceives the Christian community as the body of its leading figure (Christ). In so doing, as shown in Figure 4.2, Paul conveys an image in which each individual member in the Corinthian community belongs to a collective body, the body of Christ, and is part of this body. This is the first input of the overall blend in 12:13, an input that provides the fundamental idea of belonging to the body of Christ for the blend. Nevertheless, it is through the verb "baptize" that Paul introduces the political body metaphor. With the verb "baptize" and the preposition "into," Paul maps a clear in-out orientation onto the metaphorical body and conceptualizes it as a body-container. Members enter this body. As I will argue below, the bodily and visual experience of baptism (of both the baptizand and the audience) provides another input space that concretizes and visualizes the entrance of each individual into the body of Christ.

4.3.2 The Second Input (1): Applying Conceptual Blending Theory to Baptism

The second input of the overall blend in 1 Cor 12:13 describes the entrance into Christ's body by referring to both the Spirit and baptism: "In one Spirit we were all baptized/immersed" (ἐν ἑνὶ πνεύματι ἡμεῖς πάντες ... ἐβαπτίσθημεν) into the body of Christ. Thus, in the following two sections, I will apply conceptual blending theory to consider baptism and its connection with the experience of the Spirit. I will first discuss the cognitive way ritual performance (such as baptism in the Corinthian community) enacts conceptual blends, and, based on this discussion of ritual, I will consider the role of baptism in Paul's argument about the Spirit by focusing on the physical experience of baptism itself and the cultural understanding of the physical experience.

---

[86] Ibid.

In his influential work *Ritual Criticism*, ritual theorist Ronald L. Grimes states the way ritual analysis should proceed: "Ritual studies ... begins with the act of describing the performance events themselves ..." and "[extends] to the cultural occasion and social circumstances in which [the performances] are embedded."[87] Following Grimes, Richard E. DeMaris has emphasized the performance of the ritual itself and the ritual's cultural context in his treatment of early Christian baptism.[88] On this point, conceptual blending theory provides a cognitive basis for considering both the physical and the cultural aspects of a specific ritual performance. Cognitive linguist Eve Sweetser has discussed the significant relationship between conceptual blending and ritual practice. She indicates that one purpose of ritual activities is to represent a particular scenario and to affect that represented scenario by acting in it, and that rituals achieve this purpose through conceptual blending.[89] For example, according to George Lakoff and Sweetser, it used to be a custom in some Italian villages to carry a newborn infant upstairs right after birth, so that the child might rise socially in real life.[90] Thus, through a conceptual blending of physical elevation by ascending stairs and socially rising in complex human society, a new scenario of the child's later social life is created and imagined as being affected by the activity of climbing the stairs. As Gilles Fauconnier and Mark Turner state, "the blend of cause [here walking upstairs] and effect [rising in society] is often the central motivation of ritual."[91] Another example is a Catholic Holy Communion. The consumption of bread and wine, being blended with the body and the blood of Christ, is designed to causally achieve a spiritual union with Christ. That is, through conceptual blending, the ritual of consuming bread and wine is conceptualized as a cause that affects the participants by creating the union between participants and Christ. Thus, as Vyvyan Evans and Melanie Green indicate, rituals often provide "material anchors" and conceptual structures for the blending.[92] In the case of Holy Communion, the bread and wine are material anchors, and the act and bodily experience of consuming something into one's body (an act that always affects the body) provides the conceptual structure. In short, ritual provides embodied grounds and patterns for blending, and, through blending, creates a scenario and physically makes a change in the scenario.[93] In order to explore the blending enabled by ritual, we will need to look directly at the material and physical aspect of a ritual.

---

[87] R. L. Grimes, *Ritual Criticism: Case Studies in Its Practice, Essays on Its Theory* (Columbia: University of South Carolina Press, 1990), 219 and 90. Cf. R. L. Grimes, "Research in Ritual Studies: A Programmatic Essay," in *Research in Ritual Studies: A Programmatic Essay and Bibliography* (ed. R. L. Grimes; American Theological Library Association Bibliography Series 14; Metuchen, NJ: American Theological Library Association & Scarecrow Press, 1985), 1–33.

[88] R. E. DeMaris, "Funerals and Baptisms, Ordinary and Otherwise: Ritual Criticism and Corinthian Rites," *BTB* 29 no. 1 (1999): 25.

[89] E. Sweetser, "Blended Spaces and Performativity," *Cognitive Linguistics* 11 no. 3 (2001): 305–33.

[90] Ibid., 312.

[91] G. Fauconnier and M. Turner, *The Way We Think: Conceptual Blending and the Mind's Hidden Complexities* (New York: Basic Books, 2002), 80.

[92] V. Evans and M. Green, *Cognitive Linguistics: An Introduction* (Edinburgh: Edinburgh University, 2006), 418.

[93] This is also how Paul understands the physical actions of eating and drinking in the Lord's Supper (1 Cor 11:27).

However, cultural context is another aspect to be considered in addition to physical experience. The created scenario and the constructed meaning of a ritual through conceptual blending are also largely determined by the ritual's social and cultural contexts. Fauconnier and Turner have pointed out that conceptual blending is a kind of meaning construction that happens locally and dynamically "as thought and discourse unfold."[94] Thus, on the one hand, how a certain ritual practice is physically performed is usually scripted and how it is perceived is limited according to social purposes. On the other hand, new meanings can also emerge unintentionally or even unconsciously through local blending operations based on the social and cultural context of the practice.[95] As Fauconnier and Turner describe, a ritual "takes place embedded in the full richness of human life, and the principle of emergent meaning [through conceptual blending] can always recruit from that richness."[96]

Fauconnier and Turner's claim that the conceptual blend formed in a ritual practice is embedded in its sociocultural context is evident in the passages about baptism in the New Testament. Although both John the Baptist (Mk 1:8) and Paul (1 Cor 12:13) had baptismal practice in mind when they tried to deliver metaphorical messages of "being baptized in the Spirit," the ways that their baptismal rites were perceived and the meanings of their metaphorical messages were different from each other due to different contexts. At a time and location where the expectation of the coming Messiah was in the air, John's baptism focused on the experience of purification by water and so enacted the remission of sins and escape from the coming judgment (Mark 1:4; Matt 3:7–8).[97]

The situation for Paul is very different. At Paul's time and in a city like Corinth, the pervasive issue was the formation of a community that was recruiting people from various social strata. Most scholars agree that it is clear in 1 Cor 1:11–17 that baptism had become a well-known initiatory rite for Christian communities.[98] Thus, being concerned with the unity and growth of the community (1 Cor 12:25), Paul focused

---

[94] Fauconnier and Turner, *The Way We Think*, 102.
[95] Ibid., 86; R. Uro, *Ritual and Christian Beginnings: A Socio-Cognitive Analysis* (Oxford: Oxford University Press, 2016), 156.
[96] Fauconnier and Turner, *The Way We Think*, 86. As social anthropologist Stanley Tambiah also emphasizes, "A rite is never conducted in vacuum, but in the context of other activities" (S. J. Tambiah, *Culture, Thought, and Social Action: An Anthropological Perspective* [Cambridge: Harvard University Press, 1985], 48).
[97] See M. Smith, *Clement of Alexandria and a Secret Gospel of Mark* (Cambridge, MA: Harvard University Press, 1973), 208. However, Joan E. Taylor argues that John's baptism is a purification of the body that does not itself mediate the forgiveness of the sins of the baptizand. Rather, forgiveness comes from repentance. This argument is in agreement with the common bathing rites in Jewish society and Josephus' account of John's baptism (*Ant.* 18.117); see her *The Immerser: John the Baptist within Second Temple Judaism* (Grand Rapids, MI: W. B. Eerdmans, 1997), 88. Regarding Taylor's argument, Risto Uro points out that Taylor's reading of Mark 1:4 is problematic, where the phrase εἰς ἄφεσιν ἁμαρτιῶν (for the remission of sins) is better understood as referring to βάπτισμα μετανοίας (baptism of repentance) than to repentance alone; see his *Ritual*, 83.
[98] E.g., E. Ferguson, *Baptism in the Early Church: History, Theology, and Liturgy in the First Five Centuries* (Grand Rapids, MI: W. B. Eerdmans, 2009), 149; G. R. Beasley-Murray, *Baptism in the New Testament* (London: Macmillan, 1963), 93–9; A. J. M. Wedderburn, *Baptism and Resurrection: Studies in Pauline Theology against Its Greco-Roman Background* (Wissenschaftliche Untersuchungen zum Neuen Testament 44; Tübingen: Mohr, 1987), 59, 357.

on the experience of being immersed into a larger entity when he mentioned baptism. This baptism then enacted the entrance into a social body and the initiation of a new belonging. Thus, the same physical experience of going into water created different ritual scenarios by John and Paul through conceptual blending, and they accordingly affected their scenarios in different ways. While John washed the baptizands through immersion, Paul considered the baptizands as immersed into a social body with new social connections. With different understandings of the ritual practice itself, their metaphorical messages would also be different.

4.3.3 The Second Input (2): Baptized in the Spirit

Now, by focusing on the physical experience of being immersed in baptism and the cultural understanding of this immersion as belonging to a new social body, I will apply conceptual blending analysis to baptism as it is used metaphorically in 1 Cor 12:13. In doing so, I will demonstrate the connection between water-baptism and the experience of the Spirit as reflected in Paul's argument, and will argue that the ritual experience of baptism is crucial to Paul's rhetorical purpose in enacting the overall blend in this verse.

First, let us consider the most fundamental element of baptismal experience: the physical experience of immersion. The word ἐβαπτίσθημεν in this verse delivers the sense of being immersed and overwhelmed. Everett Ferguson offers a thorough survey of the words from the βαπτ- root in both Classical and Hellenistic Greek.[99] As he demonstrates, the basic meaning of the verb βαπτίζω is "to dip," usually through submerging in liquid. In addition to the action itself, this word can also refer to a state or condition of being surrounded by something (usually liquid, such as water, wine, or blood).[100] In metaphorical usages, this word usually describes a state of being overwhelmed by more abstract things, such as affairs in life (Plutarch, Sign of Socrates 24), drunkenness and debauchery (Plutarch, Cleverness of Animals 23; Philo, Contemplative Life 5.46), or passion (Chariton of Aphrodisias, Chaereas and Callirrhoë 2.4.4).[101] Ferguson further indicates that Christian sources maintain the basic meaning of the word βαπτίζω.[102] With its basic meaning, in the New Testament, βαπτίζω mostly refers to the baptismal rite, either in a literal sense (e.g., Matt 3:7; 1 Cor 1:13-17; Acts 10:47) or as the reference of a metaphor (e.g. Mark 10:39). As Ferguson shows, a full immersion is involved in "all the possible Jewish antecedents" to the baptismal practices of both John the Baptist (whose practice is consistently considered in Christian texts as the antecedent to their own baptismal rite) and the early Christians.[103] Descriptions of baptism in the New Testament (e.g., Matt 3:7; Acts 8:39; Rom 6:3-4) also affirm an immersion image in which the baptizand goes down into water and comes up from it.

---

[99] Ferguson, *Baptism*, 38–59.
[100] Ibid., 47–8.
[101] Ibid., 52–5.
[102] Ibid., 59. He also indicates that actions of pouring or sprinkling are not represented by the word βαπτίζω but by different verbs, and Christian sources follow these usages as well.
[103] Ibid., 95. See also Taylor's thorough analysis of John's immersion rite in *The Immerser*, esp. 50.

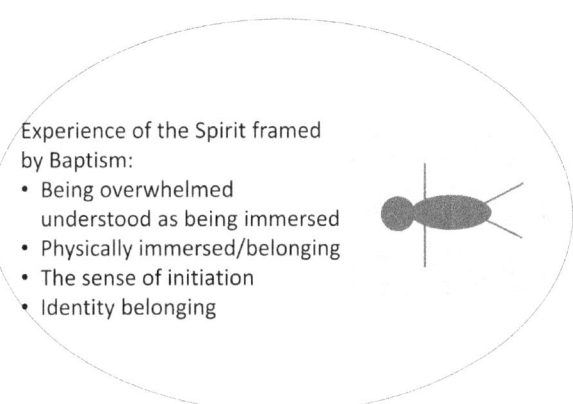

Figure 4.3 The Second Input of the Overall Blend in 1 Cor 12:13.

Here in 1 Cor 12:13, Fee has argued for the locative sense of the preposition ἐν. As Fee indicates, when Paul elsewhere uses ἐν with the verb βαπτίζω, he refers to the element "in which" one is immersed/baptized (see "all were baptized in the cloud and in the sea" in 10:2; see also Matt 3:11).[104] According to the context of this verse, I argue that the second input as shown in Figure 4.3, being immersed in the Spirit, is a pre-blended image that conceptually frames the experience of being overwhelmed by the Spirit (the target domain or the focus input) with the physical experience of being immersed in water (the source domain or the framing input). This pre-blend is a single-scope network in which one input provides the conceptual structure to reorganize another. Later in this verse, Paul specifies the general overwhelming experience of the Spirit as the reception experience (12:13c), which is the concept that he attempts to reconfigure with the overall blend. Thus, in addition to being immersed/overwhelmed, the element of "the Spirit" in the second input is also crucial for the overall blend. This element links the second input with the first input (the body metaphor) through the idea of sharing one spirit. It also links and expects the third input—the reception of the Spirit, which is the rhetorical target of the overall blend.

However, the question of what Paul means when he states that people were immersed in the Spirit as in water has been controversial. Some scholars suggest that Paul refers to a particular rite or experience as being overwhelmed by the Spirit for the first time, the so-called Spirit-baptism.[105] In other words, it is simply another way to talk about the same thing that is mentioned at the end of this verse, the reception of the Spirit, without referring to water-baptism. However, as Geoffrey W. H. Lampe rightly indicates, there is no evidence for special ritual activity of "Spirit-baptism" in

---

[104] Fee, *1 Corinthians*, 671 (original emphasis).
[105] J. D. G. Dunn, *Baptism in the Holy Spirit: A Re-Examination of the New Testament Teaching on the Gift of the Spirit in Relation to Pentacostalism Today* (London: S. C. M. Press, 1970); H. D. Hunter, *Spirit-Baptism: A Pentecostal Alternative* (Lanham, MD: University Press of America, 1983), 39–42.

the New Testament.[106] Indeed, Paul never, as James D. G. Dunn suggests, refers to a specific practice of "Spirit-baptism" that is widely recognized and distinct from water-baptism.[107] On the contrary, it is clear that Paul has in mind the image of water-baptism when he mentions the bodily experiences of reclothing (Gal 3:27) and being buried/immersed (Rom 6:4).[108] In fact, Paul's wording and logic in 1 Cor 12:13 is in close agreement with Gal 3:27–28, which undoubtedly refers to water-baptism according to the vast majority of commentators.[109] Since there is no special ritual practice as "Spirit-baptism," such an idea or event, even if it is intended, would be metaphorical and most likely articulated on the basis of the water-baptism image.

Despite downplaying water-baptism, Dunn is insightful in exploring the metaphorical force of the baptismal image in the New Testament. Indeed, as he shows, baptism is frequently used as the source domain for metaphors (cf. Mark 10:38–39; 1 Cor 10:2).[110] We have seen that in John the Baptist's expression "He will baptize you

---

[106] G. W. H. Lampe, *The Seal of the Spirit: A Study in the Doctrine of Baptism and Confirmation in the New Testament and the Fathers* (London: Longmans, Green, 1951), 307.

[107] So ibid., 306.

[108] Lars Hartman complains that "Dunn is virtually alone in regarding 'baptize' as a metaphor here [Gal 3:27]." I would say that the problem is not the recognition of metaphorical force but rather the overlook of the ritual act in this verse. As Dunn rightly notes, to "put on" Christ is a metaphor for sure. However, he is incorrect in saying that this expression in Gal 3:27 does not describe a ritual act at all (*Baptism*, 110). In fact, metaphorical force is exactly how ritual activities are performed and received. Through metaphorical imagination, people create a scenario and deem their ritual activities in the scenario to be effective. This is also how Paul understands eating and drinking in the Eucharist (1 Cor 11:27). See L. Hartman, *'Into the Name of the Lord Jesus': Baptism in the Early Church* (Edinburgh: T&T Clark, 1997), 55 note 7; cf. Dunn, *Baptism*, 109–10. For others on water rite in Gal 3:27–28, see R. N. Longenecker, *Galatians* (Nashville: Thomas Nelson, 1990), 154–8; D. A. deSilva, *The Letter to the Galatians* (Grand Rapids, MI: W. B. Eerdmans, 2018), 336–7; F. F. Bruce, *The Epistle of Paul to the Galatians: A Commentary on the Greek Text* (Exeter: Paternoster Press, 1982), 185; H. D. Betz, *Galatians: A Commentary on Paul's Letter to the Churches in Galatia* (Hermeneia; Minneapolis, MN: Fortress Press, 1979), 186–93; M. C. de Boer, *Galatians: A Commentary* (Louisville, KY: Westminster John Knox Press, 2011), 242–7; J. L. Martyn, *Galatians: A New Translation with Introduction and Commentary* (New York: Doubleday, 1997), 374–83; L. A. Jervis, *Galatians* (Grand Rapids, MI: Baker, 2011), 105–7.

[109] As Wayne A. Meeks argues, some evidence may suggest that Paul is quoting a traditional formula of baptism in Gal 3:28:

1. The motif of opposite groups of people being baptized into Christ and the language of reunification occur three times in Pauline texts (Gal 3:38; 1 Cor 12:13; Col 3:11).
2. The declaration is related with baptism even though baptism itself is not under discussion in the contexts.
3. The opposite pairs in the declaration are also out of the context. For example, the issue in Galatians is the relationship between Jews and Gentiles. The pairs of social-political status (slave and free) and gender (male and female) play no role in the context.

Thus, in light of the clear parallelism with Gal 3:27–28, it is reasonable to suppose that 1 Cor 12:13 would have called to the Corinthians' minds the well-recognized tradition of the initiatory water rite and their somatic experience in the water rite. See W. A. Meeks, "Image of the Androgyne: Some Uses of a Symbol in Earliest Christianity," *History of Religions* 13 no. 3 (1974): 180–1. Cf. H. D. Betz, "Spirit, Freedom, Law: Paul's Message to the Galatian Churches," *Svensk Exegetisk Årsbok* 39 (1974): 145–60; and his *Galatians*, 181–201; E. Schüssler Fiorenza, *In Memory of Her: A Feminist Theological Reconstruction of Christian Origins* (New York: Crossroad, 1983), 208–9.

[110] J. D. G. Dunn, "'Baptized' as Metaphor," in *Baptism, the New Testament and the Church: Historical and Contemporary Studies in Honour of R. E. O. White* (ed. S. E. Porter and A. R. Cross; Sheffield: Sheffield Academic Press, 1999), 294–6.

with [ἐν] the Holy Spirit" (Mark 1:8), John metaphorically exploits the image of water-baptism provided by his own action and clearly uses this image as the basis to deliver his message about "the coming one" who will baptize with the Spirit.[111] According to the Gospels, serving as a metaphorical figure to deliver an additional message is exactly the function of John's mission of water-baptism. Just as John the Baptist uses his own water-baptism as the reference of his metaphorical message, Paul also uses the image of Christian water-baptism as the reference for his metaphorical expression in 1 Cor 12:13. Nevertheless, as we have seen, the water-baptism of Paul's context is not exactly the same as John's baptism in the Jordan River. Therefore, instead of directly resorting to the meaning in John's expression of "βαπτίσει ὑμᾶς ἐν πνεύματι" and so regarding it as not being about water at all (as Dunn does, see below), a proper interpretation of Paul's similar metaphorical expression of "ἐν ἑνὶ πνεύματι ἡμεῖς ... ἐβαπτίσθημεν" requires the consideration of the water-baptism itself in Paul's time and communities.

Unfortunately, in terms of both the physical/material and the cultural aspects of ritual, Dunn's metaphorical analysis of baptism has downplayed the role of the source domain (in this case, water-baptism itself) and sharply divided the source and the target. Based on this sharp division, Dunn insists on interpreting some Pauline texts about baptism as a distinct event of "Spirit-baptism" that has nothing to do with water or water-baptism. He claims that "for Paul βαπτίζειν has only two meanings, one literal and the other metaphorical: it describes either the water-rite pure and simple (1 Cor 1:13–17) or the spiritual transformation which puts the believers 'in Christ,' and which is the effect of receiving the gift of the Spirit (hence 'baptism in the Spirit')." However, even if Paul at times speaks of certain spiritual events as Dunn suggests, we still have to acknowledge that Paul chooses to express such events metaphorically as baptism/immersion. Dunn's sharp division between a metaphorical expression and its reference is most evident when he states that Paul is thinking only about the Spirit in 1 Cor 12:13 and "is not speaking about water at all."[112] This statement is inconsistent with his (correct) observation elsewhere that this very verse echoes traditional metaphors in which the Spirit is spoken of in water imagery (Isa 44:3; Ezek 39:29; Joel 2:28).[113] As Anthony R. Cross indicates, "there has to be an underlying reality" to make the metaphor of baptism or immersion intelligible.[114] Following Dunn in his metaphorical interpretation, Fee still has to concede that "the point of reference for the metaphor would be their own baptism [immersion] in water" in 1 Cor 12:13.[115] Indeed, cognitive linguistic theories have taught us that bodily experiences provide a basis for complex and metaphorical thinking. Based on this cognitive insight, I have also suggested that ritual activities provide embodied grounds and patterns for complex conceptual

---

[111] Dunn notes that John's baptism in the Jordan River serves as the reference point for the metaphorical imagination of being immersed into a river of the Spirit (*ruah*), which recalls the image of God's anger in Jewish traditions (c.f. Isa 30:27–28). See ibid., 304–5.

[112] Dunn, *Baptism*, 129–30.

[113] Dunn, "'Baptized' as Metaphor," 308. See also Cross's critique in A. R. Cross, "Spirit- and Water-Baptism in 1 Corinthians 12.13," in *Dimensions of Baptism: Biblical and Theological Studies* (ed. S. E. Porter and A. R. Cross; London: Sheffield Academic Press, 2002), 129.

[114] Cross, "Spirit- and Water-Baptism," 129.

[115] Fee, *1 Corinthians*, 670.

blending operations. Thus, the role of water-baptism is foundational for the meaning and rhetorical effect of Paul's metaphorical expression.

In addition to the physical experience, the cultural understanding of this common ritual immersion as a new belonging is also crucial to Paul's strategical metaphor that seeks social union. Dunn is misleading when he insists on a particular "Spirit-baptism" in contrast to the water rite and asks, "Were this [1 Cor 12:13] the only Pauline text using the verb 'baptized,' would anyone have doubted that it was directly indebted to the imagery created by the Baptist—'he will baptize in Holy Spirit' (Mk 1:8 pars.)?"[116] However, it is precisely because of those other Pauline texts about baptism that we come to know that the understanding of (water-)baptism itself had changed since the time of John the Baptist. Again, according to the Gospels, the function of John's water-baptism is the remission of the baptizands' sins in order to allow them to flee from the coming wrath (Mark 1:4; Matt 3:7–8). Coherent with this understanding of the ritual itself, as Dunn rightly notes, John's metaphorical expression of "baptize you in Spirit and fire" (Matt 3:11) is most likely a metaphor of "judgment and tribulation" that he expects "the one who is coming" to bring about. Immediately in the next verse, John expresses this expectation with the imagery of trees without good fruit being cut down and burnt, and wheat winnowed together and the chaff burnt. Through judgment, the coming one will clean out his threshing floor (3:12). Having John's own service of water-baptism in the Jordan River as the source domain, the metaphorical image of being immersed into a river of the Spirit (ruah) and fire recalls a familiar expression of God's terrifying anger and judgment in Jewish traditions in which God's "breath (ruah) is like an overflowing stream that reaches to the neck" (Isa 30:27–28).[117]

However, judging from Paul's letters and Acts, baptism had become an established boundary-crossing rite for entering Christian communities and the common initiation of a new belonging in Paul's time. As Agnes Choi notes, the sense of boundary-crossing and belonging is evident since baptizands are commonly considered as baptized "in(to) the name of Jesus" (Acts 2:38; 8:12, 16; 10:47–48; 19:5; 1 Cor 1:13, 15; 6:11; Gal 3:27; see also Rom 6:3–4; Matt 28:19).[118] In addition to purification in water, the bodily experience of being immersed into a larger entity has become more prominent in the meaning of the ritual practice itself. Furthermore, Choi relies on Richard E. DeMaris's work on the use of water in the early Roman period to emphasize the sense of belonging in baptism. She argues that baptism not only positively conveys the idea of a new belonging but also negatively distinguishes the Christian communities from other groups through their different use of water.[119] As DeMaris demonstrates,

---

[116] Dunn, "'Baptized' as Metaphor," 309.

[117] Ibid., 304–5.

[118] She emphasizes that baptism signifies "the unity of the Christian community." See A. Choi, "Boundary-Crossing in Christian Baptism," in *Early Christian Ritual Life* (ed. R. E. DeMaris, J. T. Lamoreaux, and S. C. Muir; New York: Routledge, 2018), 84. However, this strong sense of belonging does not necessarily lead to social union. As DeMaris notes, Paul shows "ambivalence about baptism" in 1 Corinthians and "implies that the conflicting loyalties that threaten group unity stem at least in part from *who* baptized whom" in 1:11–17. See R. E. DeMaris, "Backing Away from Baptism: Early Christian Ambivalence about Its Ritual," *Journal of Ritual Studies* 27 no. 1 (2013): 12 (emphasis added).

[119] Choi, "Boundary-Crossing in Christian Baptism," 82.

water was frequently used by various groups for cultic purposes in Hellenistic Corinth. However, the cultic use of water declined significantly and abruptly when the Romans destroyed Corinth. Instead, when Corinth was rebuilt as a Roman colony, various water projects were carried out to control the use of water and signal the sovereignty of the Romans.[120] The Corinthian Christians' ritual use of water in baptism, then, conveyed a subtle resistance and the idea of a new belonging in a negative way. This is particularly the case in 1 Cor 12:13 when the verb "baptize" is used with the political body metaphor: by being immersed into the water that was ritually used in their own way, the baptizands belonged to the body of Christ rather than the *corpus imperii*. This idea of new belonging is also clear in the parallel passage in Gal 3:27–28, where Paul similarly (see 1 Cor 12:13a) announces that people from different social statuses—"Jews or Greeks, slaves or free, male or female"—were all "baptized into Christ" and so became "one in Christ."

Moreover, the role of the ritual itself in the baptismal metaphors highlights another methodological weakness of Dunn's analysis: meaning does not move unidirectionally in conceptual blending. Metaphor theory explains how the target domain (the experience of the Spirit) is conceptualized through the source domain (baptism in water). Nevertheless, the inputs are still conceptually linked (online) with the blended space and so can generate a significant cognitive phenomenon called backward projection. Thus, we can explain how the meaning of the source domain might also be modified in a metaphorical expression since the expression forms a conceptual blend. Through backward projections, the input spaces of a blend (here particularly the input of baptismal practice, which is the source domain according to metaphor theory) can be influenced by the blended image and so produce new effects. The effect of backward projection is particularly prominent when one of the inputs in a blend is a ritual practice because ritual provides a repeated embodied basis that conveys meaning, and in this way the meaning of the ritual can be developed. Here in the second input in 1 Cor 12:13 (Figure 4.3), Paul conceptualizes the overwhelming experience of the Spirit according to the immersion experience of water-baptism. Thus, through backward projection, the understanding of the baptismal rite itself is also enriched by being linked with the Spirit. This connection might have encouraged an understanding of baptism as the ritual bestowal of the Spirit or a ritual control of receiving the Spirit.[121]

---

[120] R. E. DeMaris, *The New Testament in Its Ritual World* (London: Routledge, 2008), 46–49. These projects included, as DeMaris lists, the renovation and expansion of the harbor at Lechaion, the building of nymphaea, public fountains, and public baths. The Peirene Fountain, the most famous public source of water in Corinth, was remodeled as a grotto according to Roman tastes. Moreover, these water projects, together with other Roman constructions, largely reduced "the availability of water in and around sanctuaries and other cultic sites in the Corinthia." Thus, for example, the water basin in front of Corinth's Temple of Asklepios that used to supply water for cultic purification was covered by new constructions. Cf. C. Roebuck, *Corinth vol. 14: The Asklepieion and Lerna* (Princeton, NJ: American School of Classical Studies at Athens, 1951), 27, 46–51, 79–82; B. A. Robinson, "Fountains and the Formation of Culture of Water at Roman Corinth," in *Urban Religion in Roman Corinth: Interdisciplinary Approaches* (ed. D. N. Schowalter and S. J. Friesen; HTS 53; Cambridge, MA: Harvard University Press, 2005), 116–25.

[121] For example, Richard E. DeMaris notices that, in the narrative of Mark's gospel, Jesus's baptism that he receives from John (Mark 1:9) functions to present Jesus's Spirit possession (1:10–11) as ritually controlled and hence a positive possession. See his "The Baptism of Jesus: A Ritual Critical Approach," in *The Social Setting of Jesus and the Gospels* (ed. W. Stegemann, B. J. Malina,

Moreover, through backward projection in the overall blend, we will see that baptism will be further linked with the ideas of bodily transformation and being united with Christ. These conceptual links appear to prepare Paul's later development in Rom 6, where one is baptized into Christ's death.

In sum, I maintain that the common ritual experience of water-baptism is always in effect and has a continuing influence on Paul's metaphorical expression in 1 Cor 12:13.[122] Considering the practice itself and Paul's context, water-baptism provides two crucial elements to Paul's metaphorical expression "you were baptized in one Spirit": the physical experience of being immersed or overwhelmed and the contextual understanding of this ritual immersion as a new belonging. With these two crucial elements, Paul forms the second input in 1 Cor 12:13 as the pivotal mental space of the overall blend. First, the element of new belonging links the second input with the first input, the metaphor of one body. Indeed, Paul is not as concerned with eschatological judgment as the Baptist is. Rather, like in Gal 3:27–28, Paul's point in 1 Cor 12:13 is clearly about boundary-crossing and common belonging. The Corinthians were baptized into one body. Second, based on this common belonging, Paul then tries to argue that the various spiritual gifts were distributed by the same Spirit. The physical experience of being immersed and overwhelmed in water-baptism then provides a strategic way to describe the experience of the Spirit. For those who boast about glossolalia or other special experience, this physical immersion might vividly represent their intense experience of being taken over by the Spirit. Water imagery also links the second input with the third input (the reception of the Spirit). As we will see, by the end of this verse, the experience of being overwhelmed is considered the effect of the Spirit that a person intakes into the body.

4.3.4 The Third Input: Receiving the Spirit Conceptualized as Drinking Water

The third input space of the overall blend is cued at the end of 1 Cor 12:13: "We were made to drink (ἐποτίσθημεν) of one Spirit." Here, Paul finally addresses his rhetorical target. With the elements and images provided by two previous inputs, Paul's purpose for the overall blend is to re-picture the reception of the Spirit and so to argue that every member has received the same Spirit. As shown below, the way that Paul conveys

---

and G. Theissen; Minneapolis, MN: Fortress Press, 2002), 137–52. It is indicated that, in cultures with spirit possession as the dominant type of altered state of consciousness, this phenomenon is usually associated with ritual activity. As Goodman observes, "All religious communities where the religious trance is institutionalized have rituals to induce it, and those participating learn to react to them." See F. Goodman, *Ecstasy, Ritual, and Alternate Reality: Religion in a Pluralistic World* (Bloomington: Indiana University Press, 1988), 34–8. E. Bourguignon, *Psychological Anthropology: An Introduction to Human Nature and Cultural Differences* (New York: Holt, Rinehart & Winston, 1979), 243–5.

[122] "Physical" is a wording based on Dunn's distinction of Paul's uses of the verb "baptized": one is in a literal sense denoting the physical ritual activity that uses water, and another is in a metaphorical sense denoting the spiritual reality. See Dunn, *Baptism*, 129–30. Although I do not agree with the physical versus spiritual division, here I use the wording "physical" in order to emphasize the role of the ritual activity itself.

the concept of receiving in the third input is also helpful for forming the overall blend. That is, he metaphorically describes the experience of receiving as a common act of drinking. In so doing, he conceives of the body of a member as a container.

However, a number of interpreters suggest that the verb ἐποτίσθημεν here reflects the image of "watering" or "saturating" (cf. 3:6–7) instead of "drinking" (cf. 3:2), thus referring to the traditional motif of the "pouring out" of the eschatological Spirit on the land, as in Isa 29:10.[123] Countering this interpretation, E. R. Rogers has indicated that the verb ποτίζω has its primary meaning of "to give or to cause to drink." This basic meaning remains effective in its metaphorical expressions of "watering or saturating." For example, in 1 Cor 3:6–7, a plant is personified as needing to drink to subsist and grow.[124] More decisively, while the Septuagint Isa 29:10 has the Spirit in dative, the verb ποτίζω in 1 Cor 12:13 takes two accusatives and so clearly delivers the connotation "to cause someone to drink something" (cf. Paul's own use of the accusative "milk" in 3:2).[125] John 7:37 is an example from the New Testament that likens the Spirit to water and its reception to drinking (cf. Eph 5:18).[126] Thus, I maintain that Paul delineates the reception of the Spirit as the physical act of drinking water by saying "drink of one Spirit" and so delivers a conceptual blend of these two experiences.[127] This is a pre-blend that provides the third input for the overall blend in 1 Cor 12:13, as shown in Figure 4.4.

This pre-blend is a single-scope network in which one of the two inputs, the physical act of drinking water, provides the conceptual structure to reorganize and reimagine another input, the reception of the Spirit. Thus, in the blended space, the Spirit enters one's body in the way that one drinks water into the body. As linguist John Newman indicates, drinking is an ordinary human act and experience and is widely used as a source for metaphorical expressions in English and various languages.[128] Drawing upon his analysis of the way that drinking experience is used in metaphors, here I list four basic components that constitute common drinking experience. People come to drink when they, first, have a degree of thirst or desire for liquid. They then, second, take the drink into the mouth and swallow it through the throat into the body, and so, third, they experience an enjoyable or disgusting taste. Fourth, a certain effect

---

[123] E.g., Dunn, *Baptism*, 130–1; R. Schnackenburg, *Baptism in the Thought of St. Paul: A Study in Pauline Theology* (trans. G. R. Beasley-Murray; New York: Herder and Herder, 1964), 84–6; G. J. Cuming, "Ἐποτίσθημεν (I Corinthians 12.13)," *NTS* 27 (1981): 283–5.
[124] E. R. Rogers, "Ἐποτίσθημεν Again," *NTS* 29 (1983): 139–42.
[125] See also Fee's comment on the accusative usage in his *1 Corinthians*, 670.
[126] In fact, the idea of drinking the Spirit is compatible with Jewish traditions. For example, Sir 15:3 mentions "drinking the water of wisdom," which, as Rogers states, "is not far from 'drinking the Spirit.'" See his "Ἐποτίσθημεν Again," 142.
[127] This blend emphasizes the in-out schema, which is important for the overall blend. The in-out schema is also used to describe the reception of the Spirit in Gal 4:6 and Rom 8:11. Nevertheless, Paul's focus on the body of Christ is the reason that I treat this blend as a "pre-blend" rather than one of the inputs that directly interacts in the overall blend. As I mentioned, the purpose of Paul's overall blend in 1 Cor 12:13 is to construct "the body of Christ" *by* blending two crucial aspects of the initiation of a member's participation in Christ's body. Drinking water is not one aspect of Christian initiation.
[128] J. Newman, "Eating and Drinking as Sources of Metaphor in English," *Cuadernos Filología Inglesa* 6 no. 2 (1997): 213–14.

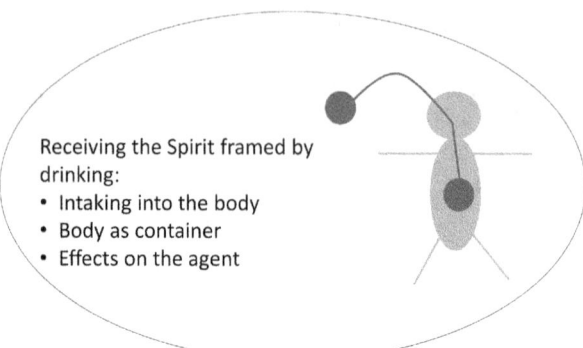

Figure 4.4 The Third Input of the Overall Blend in 1 Cor 12:13.

of the drink on the body is usually expected, such as nourishment, refreshment, or being poisoned or drunk.[129] All four components might be applied to metaphorical understandings of the experience of receiving the Spirit. For example, the thirst or desire might represent the need of a Christian to receive the Spirit, the intaking process the reception experience itself, and the taste the emotion or even ecstasy at or after the receiving moment. Furthermore, particularly relevant to my topic is the effect of the drink on the body. As Åshild Næss observes from different languages, although the verb "drink" is often taken as transitive, it is characterized by having an "affected agent": drinking is an act "performed by an agent in order to achieve an effect on [the agent]."[130] In fact, the effect on the agent caused by drinking can be intended or unintended. In this sense of affected agent, when the reception of the Spirit is taken as analogical to drinking liquid into the body, the ecstatic experience of body confusion would more likely be perceived as certain effects of the Spirit on the body rather than the escape of the person from the body.

Thus, this pre-blend contributes to Paul's overall rhetorical purpose in three ways. First, the blended image links the Spirit with the water imagery in the unfolding of the discourse and so helps Paul to link the reception of the Spirit (as drinking water) with the baptismal image in order to bring about the overall blending network (as discussed below). Second, the blended image emphasizes the in-out schema in which the body is conceptualized as a container to receive the Spirit/water. The body-as-container schema provides an important conceptual structure in the overall blend that makes sense of Paul's proposed mechanism of being immersed into the body of Christ. Third, based upon the body-as-container schema, I will argue that the blend of the acts of drinking the Spirit and being immersed into the Spirit would generate the idea of bodily transformation according to the Spirit. This idea is already implied in the experience of drinking in the third input and will be reinforced in the overall blend.

---

[129] Newman lists seven components. Here I only list four according to my own purpose. See ibid., 215–18.

[130] Å. Næss, "How Transitive Are Eat and Drink Verbs?" in *The Linguistics of Eating and Drinking* (ed. J. Newman; Amsterdam: John Benjamins, 2009), 27–43.

4.3.5 The Overall Conceptual Blend and Its Effects

While the body metaphor is commonly used for the argument of concord, blending this metaphor with the images of both baptism and the reception of the Spirit is necessary for Paul's situation. Particularly, baptism plays a pivotal role in this blend. It is not only because the baptismal rite is associated with the theme of social union but also because Paul attempts to reconceptualize the reception of the Spirit with the image of immersion.[131] As already stated in 1 Cor 12:1–11, Paul's rhetorical purpose in 12:13 is to make the Corinthians know that all members have received/drunk "the same Spirit" into their bodies even though they display various outer phenomena. Dunn and Fee are right in indicating that it is in "one Spirit" (a phrase that is repeated) not in one baptism that all become one body.[132] However, as many have argued, the differentiation of spiritual experiences and gifts has resulted in disputes and even divisions in the Corinthian community (c.f. 12:1–4, 25, 29–30; 14:5–6, 27–40). In other words, "one Spirit" is what Paul intends to argue for when various outer phenomena are exactly the reason for the divisions that Paul is addressing (12:1–4, 25–30). Paul needs another basis to argue from and to support his claim of sharing one Spirit and being united in one body. The text shows that Paul's strategy is to depict the reception of the Spirit as not only inwardly about the individual body but also outwardly about the one social body—the body of Christ. It is through the immersion image that Paul applies the body metaphor to this situation in Corinth and achieves his strategic depiction: regardless of whatever outer phenomena we display, we were all baptized/immersed in one Spirit and, in this sense, into one body.

It is now clear that Paul's statement in 12:13 is a conceptual blend consisting of three input spaces. Paul cues all three inputs in this verse. As shown in Figure 4.5, the common elements between I_1 and I_2 include the idea of belonging to the body of Christ and the idea of one spirit (hence G_{1-2}). In I_1, one belongs to a social body that embodies Christ; in I_2, a baptizand comes to belong to Christ through a rite. Additionally, as mentioned, such an idea of belonging might be conceived in the contemporary body metaphor (I_1) through various hierarchical schemas, including vertical (e.g., head-feet), horizontal (e.g., right hand-left hand), and in-out schemas (e.g., spirit/mind-body). In I_2, the verb ἐβαπτίσθημεν, the prepositions ἐν and εἰς and the bodily experience of being immersed in water would all suggest the in-out schema. Thus, we might also count the in-out schema as in G_{1-2}. The elements in G_{1-3}, then, include the body, the idea of becoming part of the body, and the body-as-container schema if the in-out schema is also reflected in I_1. As for G_{2-3}, both I_2 and I_3 are important aspects of early Christian initiation and are common bodily experiences in early Christian groups. They both involve water imagery and the in-out schema.

Each input space contributes a significant conceptual structure to organize the blended space. The fundamental idea of belonging to the body of Christ is projected from I_1 to the blended space. The idea of belonging and the experience of being

---

[131] Paul also relies on baptismal imagery to argue for equality and social union in the parallel text Gal 3:27–28.
[132] Fee, *1 Corinthians*, 670.

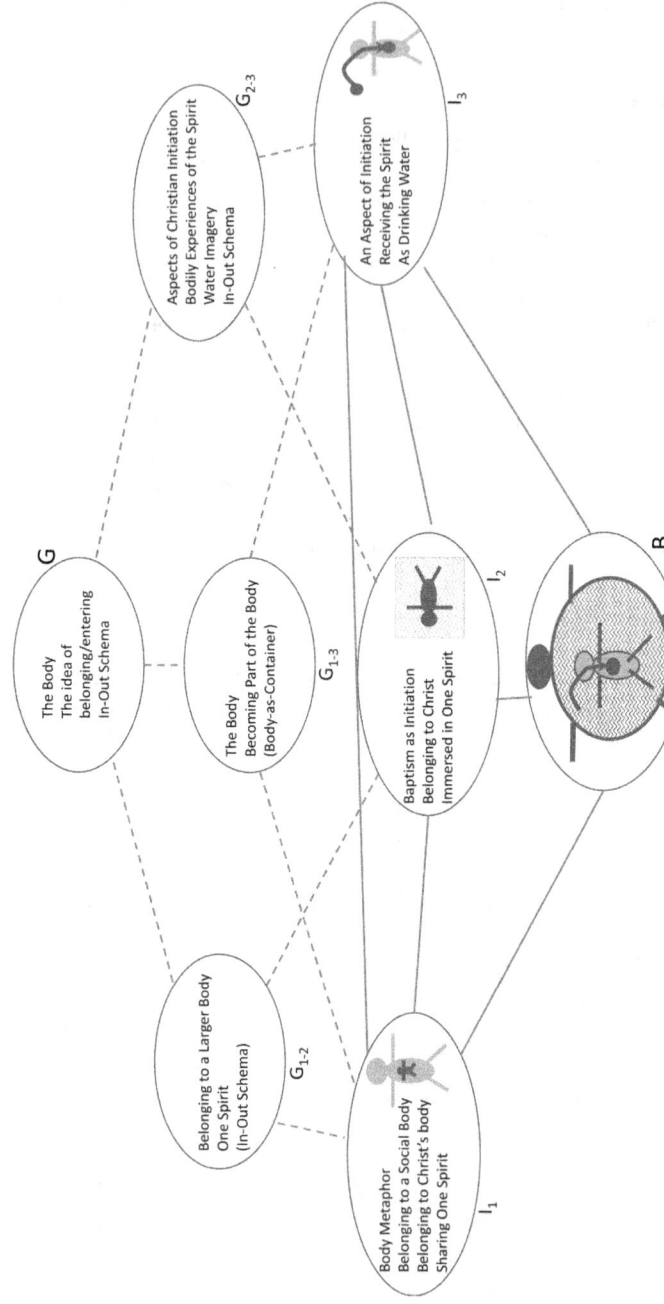

Figure 4.5 The Conceptual Blend between the Reception of the Spirit and Baptism in 1 Cor 12:13.

immersed into a larger entity are projected from I_2. The body-as-container-for-Spirit image is projected from I_3. Thus, in the blended space (B), when an individual receives the Spirit into the body as stated in 12:13c, the person (or the person's body) is simultaneously baptized "in the Spirit" and so "into one body," which is the body of Christ (12:12–13, 27). Thus, this blended image depicts the "one body" as filled with the Spirit of Christ (cf. 2 Cor 3:17 where the Lord is the Spirit). In other words, while one's own body is still a container into which the Spirit enters to dwell, one is immersed into another larger body-container (Christ's body) in which the Spirit also dwells (cf. 2:16; 6:17–19; 15:45). Paul thus achieves his purpose of redefining the reception of the Spirit with the image in B: being immersed in one Spirit was what happened when one drank it into the body—which means the Spirit that various members received and revealed was indeed one.

By forming this conceptual blend, Paul successfully applies the body metaphor common in his time to his own situation and purpose. As Mitchell and Martin indicate, the body metaphor is usually used to support social hierarchy and to argue that inequality is natural and necessary for the common good of the whole.[133] Although Paul's concern at this point is not social position, his logic in using the body metaphor is similar to his contemporaries. That is, through the body image, Paul is able to say that the various phenomena of the Spirit correspond to the various "members" of the one body. Thus, similarly resorting to the common good of the one body, Paul appeals to the union and mutual care among the various "members" who have been given different spiritual gifts (15:25–26) instead of divisions. Nevertheless, it is based on the conceptual blend analyzed above that Paul can link the issue about spiritual gifts with the common political metaphor of the body and even equate the reception of the Spirit with the entrance into the body (as an immersion) on a cognitive level.

Furthermore, this conceptual blend has a couple of significant effects on Paul's ideas in addition to the contribution to his rhetorical purpose. First, according to the ancient construction of the body and the idea of soma-cosmos correlation, the blended image emergent from 12:13 would encourage the notion of a sort of bodily transformation, a notion that sometimes is already inherent in the ecstatic experience of the Spirit. As mentioned, the body in Greco-Roman understandings is porous and malleable, and is shaped by its environment. The body is "of a piece with the elements surrounding it and pervading it," and may be transformed according to its interaction with the environment, including specific social or cultural practices.[134] Here, in the blended space in Figure 4.5, the individual body has the indwelling Spirit inside of it and is simultaneously immersed in the Spirit in a special society, the body of Christ. Thus, this blended image would suggest that the body might be continually transformed according to what is in it and what is surrounding it—the Spirit. Moreover, in the blended image, the emergent notion of bodily transformation is associated with the experience of receiving the Spirit (I_3). As we have seen, the reception experience appears to be one's first ecstatic experience of the Spirit of Christ (1 Thess 1:6; Gal

---

[133] Mitchell, *Rhetoric of Reconciliation*, 159–60.
[134] Martin, *Corinthian Body*, 16–18.

3:5; 4:6). To conceptualize the reception experience as drinking water into one's body further suggests an effect on the body. Thus, the whole operation of conceptual blending would encourage the Corinthians and/or Paul himself to interpret their ecstatic experience of body bewilderment and self-boundaries blurring as bodily transformation instead of an escape from the body.[135] Such transformation into the form of the Spirit is inaugurated by the reception experience and can be repeated in multiple experiences of the Spirit.

While the idea of ongoing transformation or the interpretation of ecstatic experience as such is only encouraged in 1 Cor 12:13, Paul later explicitly speaks of this idea in 2 Cor 3:18: we all "are being transformed into the same image from glory to glory, as from the Lord, the Spirit."[136] This verse seems to indicate a development in Paul's thought at least partly triggered by the blend analyzed here. Similar to the logic suggested in the blend in 1 Cor 12:13, when Paul talks about the ongoing transformation in 2 Cor 3:18 and again in Rom 12:2, he also emphasizes the social aspect of the Spirit's transforming work in addition to the inward effects. In Romans, while saying that the transformation is induced by the renewal of the inner, he locates this idea in the same context about various members becoming one body in Christ. In 2 Corinthians, immediately after mentioning the ongoing transformation, in 4:12 Paul refers to a kind of effect that enacts the death of Jesus in some members and so enacts the life of Jesus in some others. This "life of Jesus" is a kind of ongoing transformation of an individual caused by the Spirit. And it is not only about the Spirit indwelling in that individual but also about the work of the Spirit collectively in all members in the body of Christ.[137]

The emergent idea of ongoing transformation in the body of Christ appears coherent with Paul's emphases on the boundaries of the social body and regulations on individual bodies. In 1 Corinthians, Paul consistently considers the Spirit as otherworldly (2:12) and is very concerned with cosmic invasions into the social body. For example, he clearly expresses his view of the dichotomy between the world and the Spirit (and so the body of Christ) in 1 Cor 5. He states that it is not possible in this world to avoid people who are sexually immoral and ethically corrupt (5:10). Nevertheless, he does not allow the existence of these immoral characters in the Christian social body (5:11) because "a little yeast leavens all the dough" (5:6). Thus, Paul instructs the Corinthians to deliver the incestuous person to Satan for the destruction of the flesh

---

[135] As Shantz describes, ecstatic experience can produce "a sense of participation in a greater category of being." See Shantz, *Paul in Ecstasy*, 71 and also 96. Here Paul defines the greater category not as the higher/heavenly realm in a hierarchical cosmos but rather as the body of Christ filled with the Spirit.

[136] This does not mean that Paul has to abandon or forbid the interpretation of ecstatic experience as the escape of the body since the transformation and the escape of the body are not necessarily exclusive of each other. In fact, he remains uncertain in his report in 2 Cor 12:1–4. As I will indicate in the next chapter, Paul describes the ongoing transformation of the body as only an inward transformation in 2 Corinthians when he faces the problem of physical mortality in the present life. Thus, it could be at least reasonable to conceive of the ecstatic escape of the body as the ongoing renewal of the inner person (4:16) and as enhancing the inward transformation.

[137] In the next chapter I will analyze Paul's full exposition of transformation in 2 Cor 4–5 and will argue that Paul seems to have the image of the "body of Christ" in mind.

"in order to save τὸ πνεῦμα in the day of the Lord" (5:5). This instruction shows Paul's understanding of the Christian social body as a container filled with the Spirit. As DeMaris notes, "Paul understands the Corinthian church's disorder as a symptom of pollution or defilement compromising community purity"—what Martin calls "the invasion etiology."[138] Given Paul's sympathy with socially lower-class members (1:26–28), it is not surprising that his idea of social body also evinces a fear of invasion and "a social position of helplessness in the face of outside power."[139] With this logic, while Paul has not talked about the ongoing transformation of the body in 1 Corinthians yet, he expects the community members to treat their bodies and to consider their bodily actions in a new way corresponding to the presence of the indwelling Spirit (6:10–17).

This leads to the second significant effect of the blend in 12:13. The idea of bodily transformation emergent from the blend is not associated with resurrection as it is in ch. 15. Rather, through backward projection, bodily transformation in 12:13 is associated with Christian initiation since two of the input spaces are about initiation experiences—baptism and the reception of the Spirit. In this regard, the conceptualization of bodily transformation emergent in 12:13 is different from what Paul explicitly states in ch. 15. The former is experienced while the latter is anticipated. In ch. 15, Paul has to describe the transformation through other experiences, such as the observation of seed sowing and plant-growing. In 12:13, on the contrary, religious experiences here and now are the most vivid references for constructing an imaginative social body. Nevertheless, in spite of the difference, these two ideas about transformation share the same schema of temporal polarity. I have demonstrated that, in ch. 15, Paul enacts a conceptual blend that creates the schema of temporal-polarity-resulting-from-a-reversal-transformation (15:42–44a). I have also indicated that Paul emphasizes a sharp distinction between the bodily statuses before and after eschatological transformation by his use of the ψυχικός-πνευματικός opposition (15:44b–49) and the war metaphors (15:24–26). Similarly, in the emergent image in 12:13, the transformation is conceptualized in a temporal sense (it is after initiation) and the transformed body is supposed to be in a form corresponding to the Spirit—very similar to the idea of σῶμα πνευματικόν (15:44). Besides, Paul also emphasizes the sharp distinction before and after both initiation experiences, receiving the Spirit and baptism (6:11). Thus, the two different aspects of bodily transformation still share several important elements. Since the experience of the Spirit and the practice of baptism are routinely repeated in Christian communities, they provide a constant material basis for the idea of experienced transformation to be further blended with the idea of anticipated transformation. Therefore, although Paul does not explicitly talk about bodily transformation in 12:13 when his focus is on social union, his conceptual blend in this verse would in time bring about developments of his ideas stated in ch. 15.

---

[138] DeMaris, *Ritual World*, 88; Martin, *Corinthian Body*, 159–60.
[139] Martin, *Corinthian Body*, 159–60.

4.4 Conclusion

In this chapter, we have seen how religious ecstasy could be experienced by a person in Greco-Roman culture and how Paul's conceptual blend might encourage one specific perception—the ongoing bodily transformation. However, while the idea of bodily transformation in ancient texts (both Jewish and Hellenistic) is usually associated with the ideas of a hierarchical cosmos and heavenly ascent, we have also seen that Paul's idea of transformation has gradually modified the idea of cosmic polarity and become less related to ascent. Instead, it has become more temporal and even ritualized. In Chapter 3, I have demonstrated that Paul exploits the seed-sowing metaphor to respond to the problem of body-decomposition. In so doing, Paul frames his idea of anticipated transformation within a schema of temporal polarity. The cosmic polarity between heaven and earth is projected to be a temporal one between two sequential kingdoms in an eschatological drama. In this chapter, I have indicated that Paul deals with the religious experiences related to Christian initiation and emphasizes the distinction between the world and the body of Christ. Consequently, Paul in fact imagines a special realm on earth and in the present, a realm that is marked by religious experience, a boundary-crossing rite, and ethical instructions for members. Thus, the earth-heaven distinction is projected to be the clear distinction (in Paul's mind or expression) between the world and the special realm of the body of Christ. Paul seems to express the ecstatic sensation of unlimitedness and boundary-blurring of the body as freedom in Christ/the Spirit instead of floating in heaven (2 Cor 3:17–18; cf. Rom 8:21). Again, the emergent idea of experienced transformation also becomes less related to heavenly ascent but rather associated with one's participation and experience in the Christian community. This experiential aspect of transformation also reflects a temporal sense since it is ongoing and inaugurated at the moment of entering the body of Christ. In the next chapter, I will delineate how Paul distinguishes anticipated transformation from experienced transformation in his full exposition in 2 Cor 3–5 and how the two aspects of transformation might converge in the boundary-crossing rite of baptism (Rom 6:3–4).

5

"Baptized into His Death": The Convergence of Two Aspects of Transformation

5.1 Paul's Two Aspects of Bodily Transformation

In previous chapters, I explored the role of ritual activities in the emergence of Paul's two different aspects of bodily transformation. Both aspects significantly contribute to the development of Paul's thought. As I argued, in 1 Cor 15, Paul innovatively delineates his idea of eschatological transformation as occurring at resurrection when he deals with the issue of body decomposition, an issue that was an integral part of ancient death rites. This idea is a crucial development because, through the reversal schema in the seed-sowing metaphor, transformation is linked with resurrection itself instead of its traditional connection with exaltation or heavenly ascent.[1] Also, the emphasized connection with resurrection is an important element for later thought-development that will be discussed in this chapter. The second aspect is seen in 2 Cor 3:18, where Paul mentions the ongoing and experiential aspect of transformation. As we have seen, Paul struggles greatly with the mortal body largely because his expectation in Christ is very much somatically oriented. In addition to his lengthy defense for the final resurrection of the body in 1 Cor 15, in 2 Cor 3:14–18 Paul explicitly speaks of the ongoing transformation of the body, a transformation that starts when one "turns to the Lord" (3:16) and participates "in Christ" (3:14). This idea of transformation experienced to an extent in the present was not incomprehensible in Paul's time. In light of the ancient concepts of the "porous body," I have argued that Paul's conceptual blend between baptism and the reception of the Spirit in 1 Cor 12:13 could direct the Corinthians and himself to interpret their ecstatic experience as the ongoing transformation of the body. Thus, for Paul, the body is not to be escaped or abandoned but to be transformed both in experiences and in the afterlife.

However, Paul still had to deal with the relationship between his two aspects of transformation—the experiential and the anticipated transformation of the body. In fact, as we will see, the interaction between these two aspects of transformation

---

[1] Cf. R. N. Longenecker, "Is There Development in Paul's Resurrection Thought?" in *Life in the Face of Death: The Resurrection Message of the New Testament* (ed. R. N. Longenecker; Grand Rapids, MI: W.B. Eerdmans, 1998), 190–1.

would in time generate more radical innovations as reflected in the New Testament (Romans and Colossians). In this chapter, I will demonstrate that two physical experiences common to Paul and his communities were particularly relevant to this generative interaction: the ongoing decay of the mortal body and the ritual experience in baptismal performance.

First, as demonstrated below, Paul faces the problem of the weakness and ongoing decay of the body in 2 Cor 4. This is a reasonable challenge to the idea of ongoing transformation especially when it is followed by a future transformation in the afterlife. If the body is already being transformed and will continue to be in existence in the afterlife in a glorious form, why is it obviously weak and wearing away in our present life? In fact, the issue of frailty is also a personal remark upon Paul. In chs. 10–13, Paul is evidently defending his apostleship against his opponents who question him partly on the basis of his suffering and physical weakness (see especially 12:7–12).[2] We will see that this context and experiential issue are shared by chs. 4–5 (esp. 4:12; 5:12). Here, Paul also has to respond to the challenge of frailty and to explain how his own weakness and suffering might be compatible with his alleged glorious ministry and the idea of glorious transformation depicted in his gospel (3:7–18).[3] Being concerned with such issues, Paul delivers his fullest exposition of transformation in these two chapters.

My first goal in this chapter, then, is to explore Paul's understanding of the two aspects of transformation in 2 Cor 4–5 and to properly locate this passage in his thought-development. Some scholars argue that this passage indicates a radical development in Paul. For example, Charles H. Dodd notices the role of personal experience in the change of Paul's attitude toward death and afterlife. He indicates that the experience of humiliation (cf. 10:10; 11:16–21; 12:10) and a grave illness that almost caused Paul's death, as mentioned in 1:8–10 (cf. 12:7–9), seemed to force Paul to reconsider his present existence and to figure out in a more nuanced way what would happen after his death.[4] In fact, Dodd suggests that Paul's attitude in 2 Cor 4–5 concerning his present condition is a kind of "quiet self-abandonment," which is different from what he shows in earlier letters.[5] Richard N. Longenecker also observes that, instead of looking forward to the Parousia in his lifetime as in 1 Thess 4:15–17, Paul considers himself in 2 Cor 4–5 as one who will go through death before the coming of Christ.[6]

---

[2] R. P. Martin, *2 Corinthians* (2nd ed.; Grand Rapids, MI: Zondervan, 2014), 144–5.
[3] Regarding 2 Cor 4:7–15, V. P. Furnish also argues that

> what is at issue in these verses is how Paul and his associates, exhibiting all the frailties of mortal existence and, more than that, suffering various indignities and afflictions which attend their apostolic work, can yet claim to be agents for the gospel of the glory of God. It is likely that the Pauline apostolate has been challenged in this regard, and it is possible that Paul's rivals for leadership in Corinth had based their own apostolic claims on attestations of their special power.

See his *II Corinthians* (2nd ed.; Garden City: Doubleday, 1984), 279.
[4] C. H. Dodd, "The Mind of St. Paul: Change and Development," *Bulletin of the John Rylands Library* 18 no. 1 (1934): 92–4.
[5] C. H. Dodd, "The Mind of St. Paul: A Psychological Approach," *Bulletin of the John Rylands Library* 17 no. 1 (1933): 104.
[6] Longenecker, "Development in Paul," 196.

However, while I agree with Dodd's and Longenecker's observations of the changes in Paul's mood and expectation regarding his own death and resurrection, I maintain that, specifically regarding the eschatological scenario of transformation and resurrection, Paul shows no essential thought-development in 2 Corinthians. On the contrary, in 2 Cor 4–5, Paul carefully retains his previous idea about eschatological transformation as depicted in 1 Cor 15 and distinguishes it from the ongoing transformation in the present. With such a distinction, he explains how the idea of glorious transformation of the body might be reconciled with the present mortality, especially his own weakness in sufferings.

As I will analyze below, Paul's argument in 2 Cor 4–5 relies on the conceptual blends arising from metaphors. He utilizes two sets of metaphors to delineate his answer to the problem of mortality in the present life, the metaphor of a treasure in clay jars (4:7) and the metaphors of dwelling and clothing (5:1–4). Both sets of metaphors largely rely on the container (in-out) schema that carries the concept of the inner and the outer. Paul's answer is that the two aspects of transformation are different, and each corresponds to a distinct set of metaphors. The ongoing transformation is the renewal of the inner person (4:16) and is paradoxically manifested through the weakness and decay of the outer mortality (4:11), while a decisive renewal of the outer still lies in the eschatological future (5:1–4). Thus, in 2 Corinthians, the conceptual blends arising from these metaphors contribute to and then confirm the understanding of the present transformation as only inwards. An essential thought-development would occur only later when two distinct aspects of transformation converge in another experience shared by Paul and his communities—the experience in baptismal practice.

Thus, regarding the generative interaction between the two aspects of bodily transformation, in this chapter I will demonstrate that rituals contribute not only to the emergence of these two aspects separately but also to the blend of them. Although Paul insisted in 2 Corinthians that the complete transformation still lies in the eschatological future (5:1–7) and that only the transformation of the "inner" is now experienced (4:16), the convergence of the two aspects of transformation later occurred in the conceptual blend formed in Rom 6:3–4 between baptismal rite and the narrative of Christ's death and resurrection. Also, the idea of co-burial and co-resurrection with Christ occurring at baptism (cf. Col 2:12–13) arose in this blend in Romans. In short, I will analyze Paul's ideas in both 2 Cor 4–5 and Rom 6:3–4 and explore how his ideas about transformation and resurrection have developed through these two letters.

5.1.1 Intellectual Context: A Blend of Traditions and Paul's Suffering

Addressing an experiential issue (the ongoing decay of the body, as we will see), Paul enacts a conceptual blend with the metaphor of "treasure in clay jars" (2 Cor 4:7) and integrates a few important traditions in Paul's intellectual background. The metaphor of "treasure in clay jars" provides a container (in-out) schema with a sharp contrast between the inner and the outer. This in-out contrast is a foundational image schema for the conceptual blend and its implications in the whole argument addressing mortality in 4:7–18. Margaret E. Thrall indicates the intellectual context of this metaphor: the contrast imagery of valuable or appealing commodities carried in valueless or unprepossessing containers was a common metaphor in both Jewish and Hellenistic traditions.[7] As clearly stated in a rabbinic saying (Gen. Rab. 14:7), pottery vessels cannot be repaired once they are broken.[8] Thus, unlike more valuable vessels that are made of glass or metal, pottery vessels are fragile and cheap. They are temporary and have no enduring value.[9] In the Old Testament and the Dead Sea Scrolls, pottery vessels are metaphorically used as symbols of lack of value (Lam 4:2) and mortality or disposability (Isa 30:14; Jer 19:11; 1QS xi 22; 1QH iii 20–21). They are also associated with human frailty and sinful nature in contrast to the heavenly beings (1QH^a xxvi 35). As Victor P. Furnish indicates, the description in Gen 2:7 that God "formed" Adam from "dust" seems to lead to the metaphorical picture of God as a potter and human beings as pottery vessels in Jewish traditions (Isa 64:8).[10] Nevertheless, valuable and enduring commodities, such as coinage, might be carried in earthenware containers.[11] This contrast between the inner and the outer is emphasized in the story in Sipre Deut. 48, where the Roman emperor's daughter mocks a wise but physically unappealing rabbi by saying "glorious wisdom in a repulsive earthen vessel."[12] In the text, a rabbinic saying then explains the story: "As it is not possible for wine to be stored in golden or silver vessels, but only in one that is least among the vessels, an earthenware one, so also the words of Torah can be kept only with one who is humble in his own eyes."[13] In this instance, the rabbinic message is delivered through a conceptual blend in which the contrast of value between wine and its vessel is projected to organize the relationship between the glorious words of Torah and the ugly rabbi. By conceptual blending, the worthlessness of the rabbi/container is defended against the mockery not only as compatible with the valuable treasure/Torah but also as a necessary character for carrying it.

Similarly, by employing this traditional imagery, Paul also enacts a conceptual blend in 2 Cor 4:7–11 to argue that his weakness and suffering are in fact necessary for carrying God's glorious strength. As shown in Figure 5.1, three input spaces are involved in the blending network, and the generic space (G) consists of the conceptual structure of contrast that is revealed in all three inputs. Paul delineates all three inputs in this passage, and they all interact with each other and blend simultaneously.[14] Gilles

---

[7] M. E. Thrall, *A Critical and Exegetical Commentary on the Second Epistle to the Corinthians* (Edinburgh: T&T Clark, 1994), 1:322.

[8] Quoted by W. D. Davies, *Paul and Rabbinic Judaism: Some Rabbinic Elements in Pauline Theology* (4th ed.; Philadelphia: Fortress Press, 1980), 313.

[9] Furnish, *II Corinthians*, 278.

[10] Ibid., 253.

[11] For example, Plutarch speaks of a vast amount of silver coins contained in jars (ἐν ἀγγείοις) in the triumphant parade celebrated by Aemilius Paulus (Plut., *Aemil.* 32). As Thrall deduces from the following passage that explicitly specifies the material when it is special (some in the procession carried "silver bowels"), most of these jars should be ordinary ones. See her *Second Corinthians*, 1:322.

[12] Ibid., 1:322.

[13] Quoted in Martin, *2 Corinthians*, 230.

[14] It might be helpful at this point to offer a methodological clarification: it is for analytical purpose and convenience that I treat this blending network as constituted of three inputs instead of regarding two of the inputs as "pre-blended" into one (as I did in Chapter 4). As we have seen, a blended image can be involved in a new blending network with new inputs. Thus, in some cases, we can treat the previous blending networks as "pre-blends." Of course, a pre-blend also contributes elements and structures from its inputs to the new blending network. Thus, it is not fundamentally different to

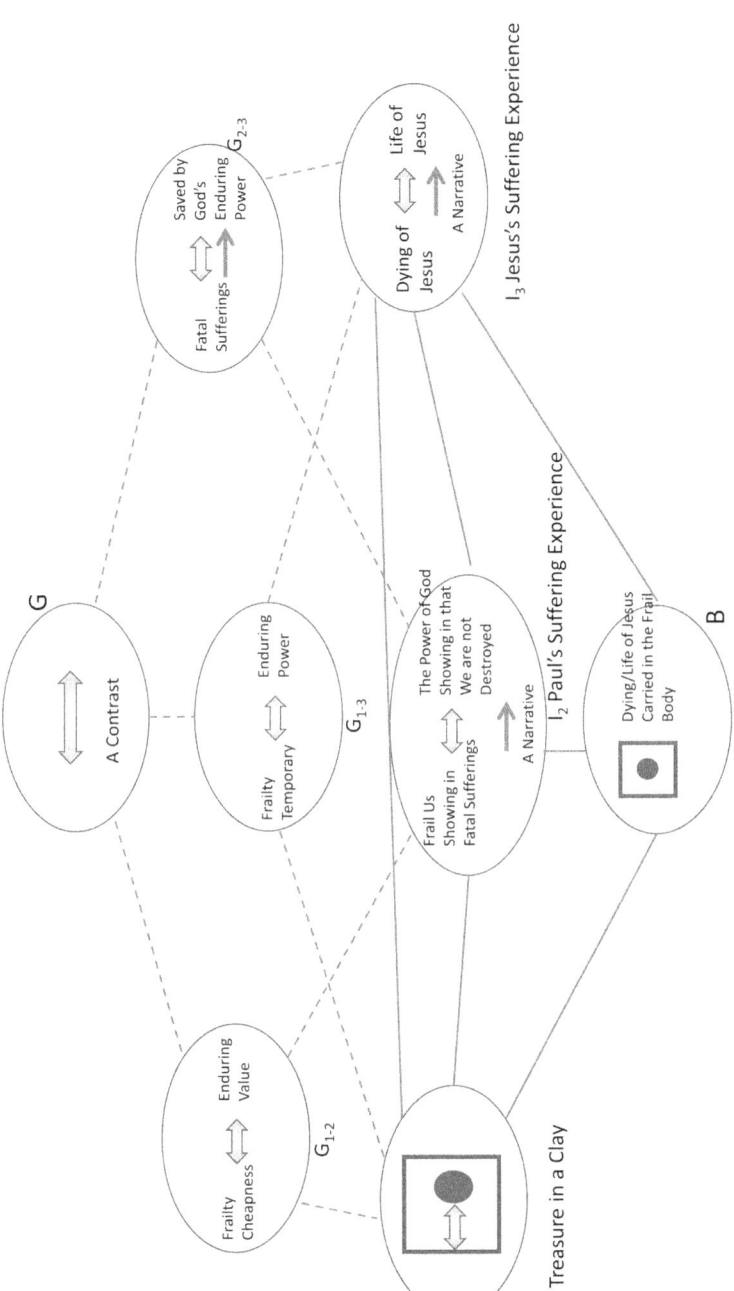

Figure 5.1 The Conceptual Blend Triggered by the Metaphor of Treasure.

Fauconnier and Mark Turner name this simultaneous phenomenon "cross-space mappings," one of the defining features of a blend with multiple inputs.¹⁵ The first input space (I_1) is the imagery of "this treasure in clay jars" (4:7a), which provides the container schema with a clear contrast between the inner and the outer. As we have seen, the outer is considered fragile and cheap, while the inner is superior and has enduring value.

The second input space (I_2) is a contrast revealed in Paul's suffering experiences (4:7b–9). This input is also constructed through a contrast schema, a contrast between the frail "us" who suffer to a fatal extent and "the power of God" that sustains our lives (4:7b). This input shows that Paul's use of the contrast between the treasure and clay jars in I_1 is in line with the traditions. As Paul states in 4:7b immediately after introducing the contrast imagery in 4:7a: "to show that the preeminent power as God's does not come from us" (ἵνα ἡ ὑπερβολὴ τῆς δυνάμεως ᾖ τοῦ θεοῦ καὶ μὴ ἐξ ἡμῶν).¹⁶ Thus, with Paul's own experiences in I_2, Paul associates "us" with the cheap "clay jars" and "God's power" with the superior "treasure." According to the previous verse, God's power is the divine glory that has been shone into our heart (4:6).¹⁷ Like the rabbinic saying in

---

treat some inputs as pre-blended into one than treating them as directly interacting in the ongoing blending network. However, an input of a pre-blend might not be a direct or immediate focal point of an unfolding discourse. Sometimes it is not even explicitly mentioned in the discourse but only functions as an assumed image in a certain community or tradition. Thus, it is more efficient to treat these kinds of images as pre-blended. For example, concerning 1 Cor 12:13 (see the I_1 in Figure 4.4), I have argued that the action of receiving the Spirit is pre-blended with the action of drinking water—hence Paul says, "We were all made to drink of one Spirit." I have indicated that Paul might draw this image from the Jewish traditions (e.g., Sir 15:3) in which the Spirit is usually spoken of in water imagery (see Isa 32:15; 44:3; Ezek 39:29; Joel 2:28). Without explicitly mentioning "drinking water," Paul's focal point is on the blend of two important aspects of early Christian initiation, the reception of the Spirit and baptism. He places the two images of initiation on the same level and blends them, so that he can re-picture Spirit-reception according to the baptismal image. Furthermore, for the sake of analysis, my treatment here is also different from what I have done in Chapter 3 concerning 1 Cor 15 (see Figures 3.2, 3.3, and 3.4). There, although I identify three inputs, I treat them as blending *in turn*: I_1 blends with I_2 first, and then the blended image blends with I_3. This is because Paul shows a clear sequence of rhetorical process in 1 Cor 15: he first deals with the issue of downward movement by employing the sowing metaphor, and then he turns to the issue of cosmic polarity. In order to recognize the rhetorical flow, it is more beneficial to analyze the multiple levels of the blend in 1 Cor 15 separately. In 2 Cor 4 (and 5, see below), however, Paul's rhetorical strategy is to convey his imagination by integrating multiple images. Thus, an important analytical purpose here is to explore the simultaneous interactions of the multiple inputs.

¹⁵ G. Fauconnier and M. Turner, *The Way We Think: Conceptual Blending and the Mind's Hidden Complexities* (New York: Basic Books, 2002), 279. For example, it would not be helpful to regard "Paul's sufferings and survivals by God's power" (I_2) and "Jesus's dying and life" (I_3) as pre-blended because all three inputs are on the same level and cross-map with each other. Paul describes his experiences with four pairs of antitheses (4:8–9) before he even mentions Jesus. When he refers to the dying and life of Jesus (I_3), he makes this image of Jesus interact with both the metaphor (I_1; hence the dying and life is carried) and his experiences (I_2; hence he suffers for Jesus and his survival is due to God's power) at the same time.

¹⁶ Martin's translation in his *2 Corinthians*, 231.

¹⁷ The precise reference for "this treasure" (τὸν θησαυρὸν τοῦτον) in the previous context is debated; see Thrall, *Second Corinthians*, 1:321–22. As Frederick S. Tappenden summarizes, it might be identified as the gospel (4:4), the ministry of the gospel (4:1), or the light of the knowledge of divine glory that shines into one's heart (4:6). I agree with Tappenden that the third option seems the most suitable for the in-out schema of the metaphor. See F. S. Tappenden, *Resurrection in Paul: Cognition, Metaphor, and Transformation* (Atlanta: Society of Biblical Literature, 2016), 199–200. Nevertheless,

Sipre Deut. 48, Paul uses traditional imagery to describe his frailty and worthlessness as necessary for the purpose of (ἵνα) manifesting the true value of God's power in him. Moreover, Paul claims this paradoxical manifestation on the basis of the fact that he survives. As seen in 4:8–9, Paul explains how "God's power" is shown in the weakness of "us" by describing the events in which Paul and his coworkers suffered ingloriously but were never totally destroyed. Paul depicts these experiences with antithetical pairs of participles: afflicted but not crushed, perplexed but not driven to despair, persecuted but not abandoned, and struck down but not destroyed/killed (ἀπολλύμενοι). In other words, Paul's life is sustained in all sufferings that could have killed him. It seems that Paul's purpose of introducing I_2 is to defend his inglorious experiences against his more powerful opponents and interpret the experiences as the manifestation of God's glorious power.[18] This logic in I_2 is very similar to what he says in 12:9–10: "for [God's] power is made perfect in weakness." Here in ch. 4, although he appears weak and frail in his suffering, God's power is manifested exactly through his weakness because his fragile life is kept (4:8–9) and so his glorious mission continues to give life (4:12–15). The generic space between the treasure metaphor (I_1) and Paul's experiences (I_2), then, consists of the common structure of the two inputs—the contrast of frailty and cheapness versus enduring value (G_{1-2}).

The third input space (I_3) is a simple, model contrast between "the dying of Jesus" (τὴν νέκρωσιν τοῦ Ἰησοῦ)[19] and "the life of Jesus" (4:10). In the blend space (B), this contrast is blended with the image of "person/body (projected from Paul's experiences in I_2) as the container (from the treasure metaphor in I_1)," and so these two elements are carried and manifested "in the body" (ἐν τῷ σώματι). Nevertheless, before blending, this contrast comes from the assumed, underlying intellectual background of Paul and his communities—the narrative of Christ's sufferings, death, and resurrection. Although Paul does not repeat the underlying narrative completely (see below about 4:14 though), the narrative is necessary for blending since it provides the link between Jesus's model contrast (I_3) and the other two inputs. In fact, the narrative is cued by Paul's wording and the context. The term νέκρωσιν, which is only found twice in Paul's letters, is not Paul's usual wording for Jesus's "death" on the cross (θάνατος; forty-six times). This term is used in texts of physicians to describe the "withering or mortification of the body or of a sick member."[20] Martin indicates that this term refers to "a process or a state of dying" rather than the act itself when death happens (cf. Rom 4:19).[21] On Paul's use of this term in 2 Cor 4:10, the majority of commentators regard Paul as portraying an extended process, "the course of events leading up to Jesus's death."[22] As for "the life of Jesus," as Furnish notes, the

---

as Furnish indicates, these three references are all interrelated since Paul apparently considers his ministry of gospel as delivering the gospel and as effecting "we all" to receive the glory of the Lord (see 3:18–4:1); see Furnish, *II Corinthians*, 279.

[18] Similarly, see Martin, *2 Corinthians*, 232.
[19] Martin's translation in ibid.
[20] R. Bultmann, "νεκρός, νεκρόω, νέκρωσις," *TDNT* (ed. Gerhard Kittel; trans. and ed. Geoffrey W. Bromiley; Grand Rapids, MI: W. B. Eerdmans, 1967), 4:895, citing Galenus 18.1; M. J. Harris, *The Second Epistle to the Corinthians: A Commentary on the Greek Text* (Grand Rapids, MI: W.B. Eerdmans, 2005), 345.
[21] Martin, *2 Corinthians*, 232.
[22] Harris, *Second Corinthians*, 346. See the summary of commentaries in Furnish, *II Corinthians*, 255.

context (specifically 4:14) shows that in 4:10 Paul is not referring to Jesus's earthly life but the resurrection life of Jesus.[23] Thus, the narrative of Jesus's dying and resurrection is cued and compressed into the two contrasting phrases that constitute I_3, "the dying of Jesus" and "the life of Jesus."

This underlying narrative provides the link for Jesus's model (I_3) with two other inputs. According to the narrative, Jesus appeared weak and frail in his dying process, but God's power raised him up into eternal life (4:14; cf. Rom 1:4). Thus, the structure of this narrative is very similar to that in Paul's experiences (I_2) despite that Jesus's life was not sustained but resurrected.[24] For Paul, in addition to resorting to God's sustaining power, another way to defend his inglorious sufferings (I_2) is to associate them with Jesus by introducing Jesus's model (I_3). As he explains in 4:11, it is "because of Jesus" that he is "constantly handed over to death" (ἀεὶ … εἰς θάνατον παραδιδόμεθα διὰ Ἰησοῦν). Furnish notices that Paul makes the same point in 12:10, that his sufferings are on behalf of Christ (ὑπὲρ Χριστοῦ).[25] Moreover, the γάρ in the beginning of 4:11 links it with 4:10 and further indicates that Paul considers his own sufferings (in I_2) as analogical to "the dying of Jesus" (in I_3). Similarly, "the life of Jesus" in I_3 also reveals God's power of raising Jesus up and is in parallel to the sustaining power in Paul's experiences (I_2). It is the same incomparable power of God that raised Jesus from the dead into resurrection life (4:14) and in turn sustained Paul's life (4:7b-9).[26] Thus, the generic space between Paul's experiences (I_2) and Jesus's model (I_3) consists of a contrast between fatal sufferings and God's power of life (G_{2-3}). The generic space of the treasure metaphor (I_1) and Jesus's model (I_3), then, is the contrast between frailty and enduring, superior value (G_{1-3}).

Now we are ready to focus on the outcome of the blend. As shown in Figure 5.1, all three inputs provide organizing structures for the blend space (B). As discussed, despite the difference between repeated survivals and a one-time resurrection, Paul's experiences (I_2) and Jesus's model (I_3) provide a similar narrative structure in which frail people suffer and are restored by God's power of life. Thus, in B, when Paul suffers and survives, it is the one-time event—the dying and the life of Jesus—that repeatedly manifests in his experiences. More importantly, while most of the elements in B come from the descriptions about Paul and Jesus (I_2 and I_3), the treasure metaphor (I_1) provides the most crucial container schema for Paul's expression. It is through the container schema that Paul proclaims, "We are carrying the dying of Jesus in our body, so that the life of Jesus may also be manifested in our body." This expression recalls 4:7b, where Paul associates "us" with the container, the clay jars. Here in 4:10-11, Paul emphasizes the bodily aspect of "us" since the issue of bodily transformation is still in Paul's mind and is already referred to in the previous context (3:18; see also 5:1-5 and following discussion). Not only "us" but also "our body" is described as "our mortal

---

[23] Furnish, *II Corinthians*, 283.
[24] Another difference is that Paul's experiences are not a one-time event but constantly repeated (2 Cor 4:11).
[25] Furnish, *II Corinthians*, 284.
[26] So Harris, *Second Corinthians*, 347.

flesh" (τῇ θνητῇ σαρκὶ ἡμῶν; 4:11) and conceptualized as an earthenware, fragile container. The life of Jesus, then, is of course the treasure because it shows God's power.

Note that this blending network is not a unidirectional metaphorical projection from the metaphor of clay jars. Rather, it is a more complex conceptual blend generating new structures that are not identical to all inputs. Two new structures in the blend are noteworthy. First, the static imagery of in-out contrast in the treasure metaphor (I_1) reorganizes both the repeated sufferings-survivals in Paul's experiences (I_2) and the one-time temporal sequence of dying-life in Jesus's model (I_3). Consequently, it is a persistent image in B instead of an event: the dying of Jesus is always (πάντοτε) carried in the body, and the life of Jesus is manifested simultaneously. This leads to the second new structure. In B, "the dying of Jesus" becomes a paradoxical element and does not have a clear position in the contrasting relation. It not only reveals the weakness of the body-container but also becomes an object to be carried in this body-container. After all, although Paul's body is frail in itself, his sufferings that show his frailty are "for the sake of Jesus." Thus, Paul maintains that his sufferings do not come from his own weakness but represent what happened to Jesus. They are not inglorious but something that Paul is willing and even honored to carry around in his body-container. In fact, these sufferings can reveal God's power in Paul (4:10) and so Jesus's life might be manifested (4:11). The logic seems to be that the fatal sufferings are not the clay, Paul is. These sufferings just confirm the fact that Paul is a clay vessel. This fact is paradoxically necessary for the manifestation of the treasure: life. In other words, while Paul's body is analogical to the clay jar because it appears cheap and frail in all his sufferings, these sufferings are surprisingly associated with treasure when they represent the dying of Jesus. They could be good things. In the emergent structure in B, the dying and the life of Jesus are tightly linked and are always carried simultaneously in the mortal body-container. Dying and life becomes two sides of the same coin. Thus, Paul argues that he is not ashamed of his sufferings. The treasure that Paul really expects to manifest in the body, however, is the life of Jesus.

5.1.2 Experiential Context: Mortality and Paul's Clarification of Experienced Transformation

Up to 2 Cor 4:11, through conceptual blending, Paul has argued that he carries the life of Jesus in his mortal body. However, he still has to explain the essence of this "life" in addition to the rather passive manifestation of surviving the sufferings. This is more the case in light of the experiential context: the ongoing decay of the body provokes a reasonable challenge to the combination of Paul's two aspects of bodily transformation. If Jesus's life is now carried in the body and if the body is already being transformed and will become a glorious existence in the afterlife, why is it so weak and obviously decaying? Paul addresses this experiential challenge in the rest of ch. 4. Based on the blended image emergent from 4:7–11, Paul offers two explanations regarding the essence of Jesus's life in the decaying body—an outward explanation and an inward one.

The first explanation is the outer, visible manifestation of the life of Jesus, that is, Paul's evangelizing ministry. Paul is constantly given up to death for this ministry (4:11), but this ministry gives life to the Corinthians (4:12). The tight connection and simultaneity between the dying and the life of Jesus as we have seen in the blend is also evident here. With this connection, the first explanation also serves as another defense of Paul's inglorious sufferings. Paul argues that it is for the lives of the Corinthians and thus for the glory of God (4:15) that he and his coworkers have suffered. In other words, Paul claims with the visible products of his ministry that, while he carries both in his body, "death is at work in us, but life is at work in you" (4:12). The evangelization of the Corinthians is how the life of Jesus might be manifested in Paul's dying—an undeniable fact for the Corinthians. Again, Paul's sufferings, like Jesus's dying, could be a good thing. They not only manifest life by providing contrast but actually produce life in the community. It is also noteworthy that here Paul's claim is coherent with his idea of "the body of Christ" that we have seen in 1 Cor 12:13. In one social body, as Frederick S. Tappenden notes, what happens to each individual body also influences other "members."[27] Given the body-as-container schema in 2 Cor 4:7–11, it is possible that Paul applies the blended image of carrying Jesus's dying and life in the body to the idea of one social body, and so the tight connection between dying and life might be understood as simultaneously effecting different members in the one social body, the body of Christ. In this sense, the outward manifestation of Jesus's life carried in Paul is at the same time carried inwardly in the social body. Ultimately, however, Paul is not content with "death at work in us." He expects his own resurrection life, like Jesus's, on the basis of possessing "the Spirit of faith" in himself (4:13–14).[28]

This expectation based on the indwelling Spirit leads Paul to the second explanation of his argument—the daily renewal of the inner (4:16–18). Here, Paul continues the container schema and distinguishes the outer and the inner person: even if (εἰ καὶ) our outer person (ὁ ἔξω ἡμῶν ἄνθρωπος) is wearing away, our inner (ὁ ἔσω ἡμῶν) is renewed day by day (4:16). As Martin notes, ἀλλ' εἰ καὶ (but even if) is a "disclaimer" granting the frailty of the body.[29] In this way, Paul directly addresses the visible issue of outer decay and inevitably resorts to the faith of the invisible renewal of the inner (cf. 5:7). As Furnish indicates, some argue that Paul's inner-outer contrast is "formally comparable" to the widespread distinction concerning afterlife, a distinction between the mortal physical body and the immortal mind or soul inhabiting the body.[30] However, in 4:16, Paul is talking about renewal in daily life rather than the afterlife. As we have seen, regarding the body in daily life in Paul's time, the so-called outer body and inner soul/mind were considered interwoven as a real microcosm and supposed to operate in an integrated and mutually affecting way. More importantly, as Furnish also notes, Paul's meaning here must be determined according to the immediate context, that is, the metaphor and the blend in 4:7–11.[31] Paul does not contrast our mortal flesh with "our immortal soul." The word "soul" does not even occur in the context (only

---

[27] Tappenden, *Resurrection in Paul*, 201.
[28] As T. Engberg-Pedersen notes, for Paul, the resurrection was operated by the Spirit (Rom 1:4). He indicates that "Paul has the pneuma, presumably as part of the 'treasure' that he has in his 'clay jars', that is, in his body of flesh and blood." See his *Cosmology and Self in the Apostle Paul: The Material Spirit* (Oxford: Oxford University Press, 2010), 47.
[29] Martin, *2 Corinthians*, 237.
[30] Furnish, *II Corinthians*, 261, 289.
[31] Ibid., 289.

1:23 and 12:15 in 2 Corinthians).[32] Instead, Paul contrasts "us" (who are "mortal flesh" in nature) with the treasure that was originally outside of us—God's power, the life of Jesus, or the light of divine glory. It was God who has shone in our hearts "the light of the knowledge of divine glory in the face of Christ" (4:6), and it is this glory that is transforming us into "the image of the Lord, who is the Spirit" (3:18). Thus, Paul delineates a contrast between a mortal person and the treasure given from the outside into the person, and consequently a renewal induced by that given treasure. Troels Enberg-Pedersen describes this renewal accurately when he recognizes the Spirit as part of the treasure: "The Spirit that [Paul] has received gradually fills out more and more of that body."[33] What is withering away from the outward is Paul himself, a mortal person with flesh and blood, and what is renewed day by day is the Spirit or the life of Jesus given in Paul that transforms Paul from within.[34] Thus, the inner renewal in 4:16 appears to be a clarification of the ongoing transformation in 3:18. Facing the visible reality of the decay of the outer body, Paul has to reiterate that the transformation is now only happening invisibly in the inner and cannot totally reach the outer.

Moreover, continuing the conceptual structure of the blended image, Paul does not stop at simply distinguishing the inner and the outer but goes further to describe their paradoxical relationship and mutual affect. In 4:17, Paul pushes the "regardless" perspective on the outer decay (4:16) to a "productive" perspective. As Murray J. Harris notes, the γὰρ in the beginning links back to 4:16 and offers another reason for "we do not despair."[35] Paul's reason is that our momentary suffering "is producing for us an eternal weight of glory" (αἰώνιον βάρος δόξης κατεργάζεται ἡμῖν). That is, the suffering of decay is not only a necessary contrast for manifestation but in fact beneficial to the glory. Paul thus picks up the logic of paradoxical contrast in the blended image. There, Paul's suffering represents the dying of Jesus and so is somehow associated with the treasure itself. Paul is willing to carry the suffering/Jesus's dying, which shows his frailty yet leads to the life of Jesus in his frail body. Following this logic, Paul claims in 4:17 that the suffering or the decay is producing the eternal glory that is currently inward. Note that this paradoxical production is an ongoing process in the present—both the decay of the outer and the creation of the glory. As Thrall indicates, while the coming age is endless, "it does not logically follow that what is eternal must be wholly future." In 4:17, Paul does not contrast "future" with "present" but "permanent" (αἰώνιον) with "transient" (παραυτίκα).[36] The present tense of κατεργάζεται also indicates that Paul has in mind some fruits of the eternal glory produced in the present.[37] Regarding this producing process, Tappenden astutely observes the ongoing, "mutual affective interplay" of the somatic inner and outer: the suffering of the outer is enacting the inner transformation (4:17), which not only manifests outwardly in the present but also, as Paul continues delineating in ch. 5, will culminate at a decisive event of the outer transformation of the body.[38]

---

[32] Ibid., 279.
[33] Engberg-Pedersen, *Cosmology*, 48. I have to emphasize that, according to Paul's idea in this passage, this "filling out" is never complete in the present.
[34] Ibid.
[35] Harris, *Second Corinthians*, 361.
[36] Thrall, *Second Corinthians*, 353.
[37] Ibid., 353–4.
[38] Tappenden, *Resurrection in Paul*, 199–201.

However, for Paul, the "in-out affectivity"[39] is still limited, and the transformation is still confined in the inner even though it might be manifested already. The blended image emphasizes that the outward manifestation of eternal life must remain in a paradoxical tension with the decaying body. In this regard, Tappenden appears less nuanced in arguing that the inner transformation is already enacting "life on the *somatic exterior*: both for the individual apostle (4:10–11) and the Corinthian ἐκκλησία (4:12)."[40] That is, Tappenden considers Paul's statement in 4:10 as mapping "both death and life to the somatic exterior," the outer body.[41] This interpretation does not fit the body-as-container schema in the blended image in 4:10 (ἐν τῷ σώματι), in which the treasure should be mapped to the interior. His interpretation reduces the paradoxical tension emphasized in the metaphor. Indeed, in 4:11, Paul immediately states that our current form of body, like a clay jar, is subject to death. Projected from the metaphor, it is exactly the mortality of this body in the present that manifests the life/treasure in the body. Thus, organized by the metaphor and the blend in 4:7–11, there is no room in ch. 4 to doubt that the real transformation of the outer still lies in the future. In fact, Paul changes to another set of metaphors in ch. 5 in order to talk about the future transformation of the outer.

5.1.3 Still in the Future

While continuing the in-out contrast schema dominant throughout 2 Cor 4, Paul employs a new set of metaphors in 5:1–4 to offer additional conceptual structures that are crucial for another conceptual blend. Based on this new blend, Paul delineates the future transformation of the body and its relationship with the ongoing transformation. The first metaphor in the set that contributes to the blend is the metaphor of earthly and heavenly dwellings (5:1–2), and the second is the metaphor of clothing (5:2–3). The way in which Paul delivers these two metaphors clearly shows that they are intended to be blended with each other: "[We are] longing to be clothed with our heavenly dwelling" (5:2). With conceptual blending analysis, I will demonstrate that the first metaphor provides a vertical contrast schema to frame the idea of two distinct bodily existences, and the second metaphor relies on the in-out schema yet uses the schema differently from Chapter 4 to provide the transforming mechanism between these two distinct bodies. Thus, as shown in Figure 5.2, three input spaces are involved in this blending network: the opposition of the earthly and heavenly dwellings (I_1), the idea of two distinct bodily existences (I_2), and the clothing metaphor (I_3). Again, all three inputs in this network cross-map with each other simultaneously.

---

[39] Ibid.
[40] Ibid., 201 (emphasis added). As for another disagreement concerning the "life" in 4:12, I have argued above that, while it is indeed an outward and visible manifestation of the life of Jesus, it does not denote a transformation of the "somatic exterior" of any individual. My disagreement is not only rooted in my suggestion that Paul has an image of one social body in mind, an image in which the life is at work on some members in the body of Christ, but also because Paul clearly considers the bodily exterior of an individual as mortal and decaying (4:11, 16).
[41] Ibid., 200.

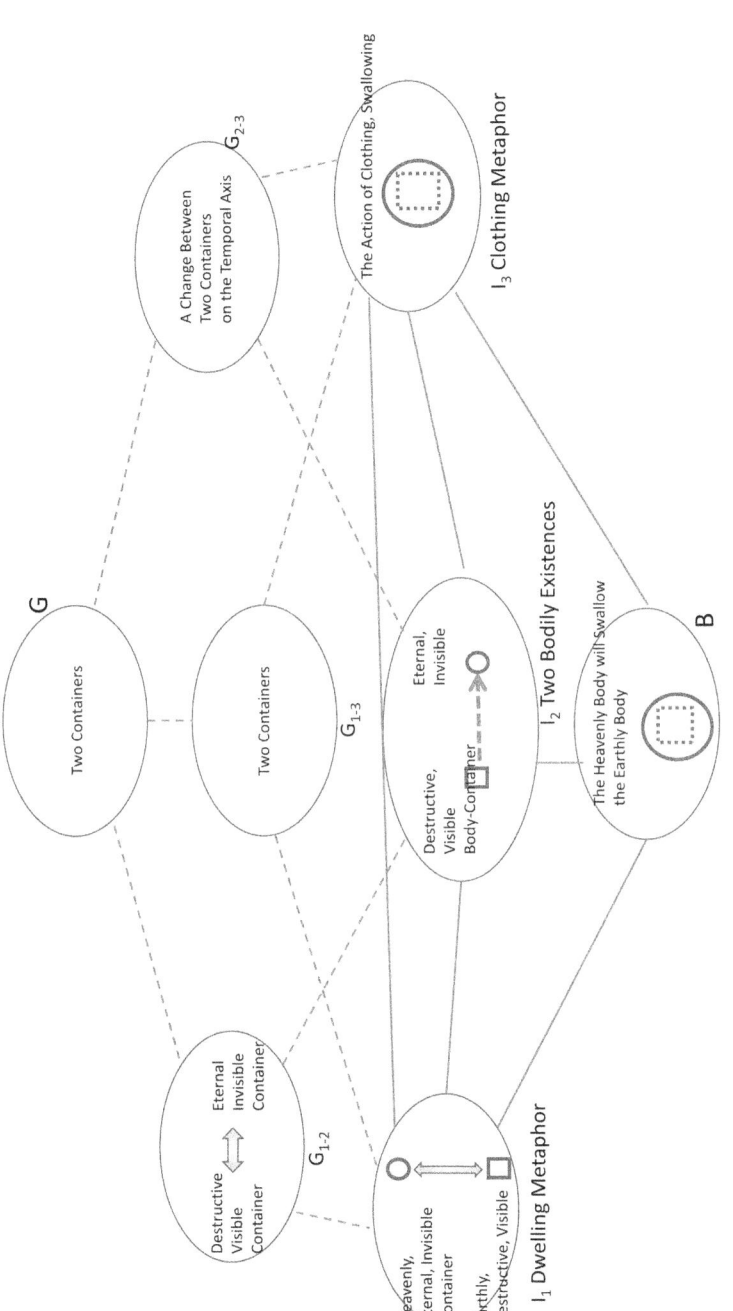

Figure 5.2 The Conceptual Blend Triggered by the Metaphors of Dwellings and Clothing.

Both the first and the second inputs continue some previous themes and conceptual structures that are already delineated in Paul's exposition of the ongoing transformation in Chapter 4. Paul constructs the first input image (I_1) as a sharp contrast between earthly and heavenly dwellings (οἰκία). A dwelling is, of course, a container for people to live in. The earthly dwelling is a disposable tent (σκῆνους), and the heavenly one is an eternal building (οἰκοδομὴν) in heaven. This heavenly building is presently invisible so that people have to long for it by faith (5:2; cf. 5:5, 7). Moreover, both the imageries of σκῆνος and οἰκία are common metaphors for the body in Jewish and Hellenistic literature.[42] It is also clear in the context that Paul's purpose of employing the dwelling metaphor is to speak of two distinct bodily existences: one visible and disposable while another eternal but currently invisible.[43] These two bodily existences constitute I_2. The context also indicates that the container schema is at work in the conceptualization of the body in this passage (4:16; 5:6). Thus, with the dwelling metaphor (I_1) and the idea of two bodies (I_2), Paul is continuing the themes of the visible destruction of the body and the invisible, eternal glory in 4:16–18 and so is providing a very similar set of antitheses between two body-containers—disposable versus eternal and visible versus invisible.[44] Although the current body is disposable, Paul seems to assume that a bodily existence is preferable to a non-bodily existence. As he says, since the disposable body will be "swallowed up" (an action conceptualized through the clothing metaphor; see discussion below) by the eternal one, Paul is not afraid of being naked, that is, being a non-bodily existence (5:3–4).[45] Thus, in I_2, the inevitable destruction of the first body would in time require the existence of the second body, which is still unseen.[46] The relationship between the two bodies in I_2, then, is a necessary change of condition that should happen on the temporal axis. Their detailed relationship and the manner of the change, however, is to be organized by the other two inputs (I_1 and I_3) through conceptual blending.

---

[42] See Isa 38:12; Wis 9:15; and *Corp. Herrn.* 13.12, 15 for σκῆνος; and Job 4:19 and Philo, *Proem.* 120 for οἰκία. Davies argues that Paul's metaphor of σκῆνος is "influenced by the Feast of Tabernacles" in his *Paul and Rabbinic Judaism*, 313–14. Moreover, as John Gillman observes, οἰκία by the imagery itself would suggest a more sturdy and long-standing dwelling than the tent. See his "A Thematic Comparison: 1 Cor 15:50–57 and 2 Cor 5:1–5," *JBL* 107 no. 3 (1988): 451.

[43] As Harris indicates, in view of 4:16, the earthly dwelling in 5:1 undoubtedly refers to the physical body. Therefore, considering the parallelism and contrast of the two parts of 5:1, the second antithetical dwelling should refer to another form of bodily existence. See Harris, *Second Corinthians*, 372.

[44] Thrall notes the Οἴδαμεν γὰρ in 5:1 and καὶ γὰρ in 5:2. She then indicates that these two verses are in parallel and are together clarifying what has been said in 4:18. See Thrall, *Second Corinthians*, 373.

[45] See Harris, *Second Corinthians*, 386; Martin, *2 Corinthians*, 261–2; Gillman, "Thematic Comparison," 447. This preference of bodily existence is also evident in 5:10 where Paul adds the phrase διὰ τοῦ σώματος to the traditional scenario of the final judgment and reward. J. Murphy-O'Connor observes that this phrase is not found "in all other Jewish and Christian statements about final reward." As he argues, "Paul may have added this phrase to a traditional judgement formula precisely in order to refute Corinthian devaluation of the body." See his "Being at Home in the Body We Are in Exile from the Lord (2 Cor. 5:6b)," *RB* 93 no. 2 (1986): 216.

[46] While the verb "have" (ἔχομεν) in 5:1 is in the present tense, it is clear in 5:2 and 5:4–6 that the real possession of the eternal body is an event in the future. Moreover, although the phrase "away from the body" in 5:8 seems to refer to an intermediate state, Gillman rightly notices that Paul is concerned with the two bodily existences "without concentrating on the interval in the between." See Gillman, "Thematic Comparison," 442.

More importantly, in addition to the previous set of antitheses seen in Chapter 4, the dwelling metaphor (I_1) further provides a vertical contrast of earthly versus heavenly. This new contrast that appears in 5:1 is crucial to the blend and leads the passage to the theme of eschatological transformation. In fact, the repetition of "heavenly" in 2 Cor 5:2 suggests that the earthly-heavenly contrast is the organizing schema of the dwelling metaphor. Thus, unlike in Chapter 4 where the in-out contrast organizes other antitheses, here in the dwelling metaphor (I_1) Paul maps the previous set of antitheses onto the vertical contrast of earthly versus heavenly. Now there are two containers on the vertical axis, and all the oppositions are associated not with the in-out axis of a container itself but with the vertical axis, with the two containers at the poles. Consequently, through blending, the two bodily existences in opposition in I_2 will be organized in the blend (B) as an earthly body versus a heavenly body. This contrast recalls the topic of earthly body and heavenly body in 1 Cor 15:39–41 where Paul talks about eschatological transformation, and likely has created an expectation for a discussion of transformation here as well.

This parallelism between 1 Cor 15 and 2 Cor 5 leads our analysis to the third input (I_3) in the blend in 2 Cor 5:1–4, the clothing metaphor that also appears in Paul's exposition of transformation in 1 Cor 15. John Gillman has noticed the close association between 1 Cor 15 and 2 Cor 5. As he demonstrates, Paul's arguments in both passages unfold from the opposition between earthly and heavenly bodies (1 Cor 15:39–41, 50; 2 Cor 5:1) to bodily transformation as the resolution of this opposition (1 Cor 15:52; 2 Cor 5:2a). Moreover, in both passages, Paul then employs the clothing metaphor in order to further describe bodily transformation (1 Cor 15:53; 2 Cor 5:2b) and to proclaim that it is the fulfillment of Isa 25:8 (1 Cor 15:54; 2 Cor 5:4).[47] The same pattern of argument would suggest that, in 2 Cor 5, Paul is recalling his previous teaching about the future transformation right after he has talked about the ongoing transformation of the inner in 4:16–18. He places these two transformations side by side to clarify the similarities and the differences. For this purpose, the clothing metaphor plays a more significant role in 2 Cor 5 than in 1 Cor 15. Paul's emphasis in his teaching about transformation in 1 Cor 15 is on the sowing metaphor and its reversal schema because he attempts to show that the downwards movement of the body can be reversed by God. There, the clothing metaphor is employed not to illustrate transformation but to show God's victory over death—what is said to be swallowed up after introducing this metaphor is "death" (1 Cor 15:53–54). Nevertheless, here in 2 Cor 5:4, what is swallowed up is "the mortal [body]" (τὸ θνητὸν). The clothing metaphor contributes more directly to Paul's imagination of bodily transformation in 2 Cor 5. Thus, I argue that Paul utilizes the clothing metaphor more profoundly here, and, in so doing, he picks up and further develops the idea of eschatological transformation that he already built with the sowing metaphor in 1 Cor 15.[48] He refurbishes this old idea to be compatible with

---

[47] Ibid., 449–50.
[48] I focus on the physical pattern of the act of clothing. For cultural understanding of clothing as symbolizing social status, see J. H. Kim, *The Significance of Clothing Imagery in the Pauline Corpus* (JSNTSup 268; London: T&T Clark, 2004); A. J. Batten, "Clothing and Adornment," *BTB* 40 no. 3 (2010): 148–59; D. Neufeld, "Under the Cover of Clothing: Scripted Clothing Performances in the Apocalypse of John," *BTB* 35 no. 2 (2005): 67–76.

and distinguishable from the idea of ongoing transformation that he has just explicated in 2 Cor 4:16–18.

With the blended image (B), Paul tries to clarify the relationship between the two aspects of transformation. All three inputs in the network contribute significant elements to this image. As mentioned, Paul frames the two bodies in I_2 by the vertical contrast (and so a set of antitheses associated with this vertical contrast) projected from the dwelling metaphor (I_1). The clothing metaphor (I_3) then provides the transforming mechanism to explain the change from the earthly body to the heavenly body.[49] First, like the action of clothing, the transformation happens not on the vertical axis but on the temporal axis as the manner in which it is supposed to happen in the idea of two distinct bodily existences in I_2 (hence $G_{2\text{-}3}$). Second, it happens through the in-out schema: the outer encompasses the inner. Thus, in the blended (B), the verbs of clothing are directly applied to the dwellings-as-bodies. Paul indicates that people are not going to "take off" (ἐκδύσασθαι) the earthly tent but "be clothed" (ἐπενδύσασθαιin) with the heavenly building. In other words, the temporal change through the in-out schema becomes the mechanism to overcome the vertical gap of two distinct bodies. The heavenly body, which is the outer, will swallow the earthly body, which is the inner. This blended image of eschatological transformation is coherent with what Paul says in 1 Cor 15 even though they are illustrated in different ways.[50] Paul thus recalls his previous teaching on the transformation of the earthly body to the heavenly body in 1 Cor 15 and reiterates this event as what will happen from the outer to the inner. Nevertheless, it should be noted that this mechanism is in the opposite direction from the in-out contrast in 2 Cor 4:16–18, in which the inner is being renewed while the outer is decaying. The ongoing transformation in 3:18 and 4:16–18 happens from the inner even though it might be manifested on the outer. Thus, by forming the blend of the two metaphors in ch. 5, Paul is able to avoid contradictions. He maintains that the two aspects of transformation are distinct in the way that they actually happen through opposite directions on the in-out axis (see the opposite icons in B in Figure 5.1 and B in Figure 5.2). While the ongoing transformation of the inner can be seen as the guarantee of the futuristic transformation of the outer (5:5), only the future transformation can overcome the gap between heaven and earth and solve the problem of outer frailty.

Before looking at the next stage of Paul's development, we may briefly summarize our results so far. As analyzed in the previous chapter, the conceptual blend in 1 Cor 12:13 encourages the idea of ongoing transformation that starts from initiatory experiences. Paul develops this idea in 2 Cor 4 as limited in the inner in order to defend his visible frailty in inglorious sufferings. In 2 Cor 5, Paul then reiterates his idea of eschatological

---

[49] In addition, as Gillman observes, the imagery of a heavenly building conveys the sense of a permanent body-container and the clothing imagery makes this body-container more integral to the person. Gillman does not analyze this passage with conceptual blending theory, but he notes that its rhetorical effect relies on the contribution from both metaphors. See his "Thematic Comparison," 453.

[50] In both passages, Paul maintains that the earthly body will not be abandoned but resurrected and transformed. For this purpose, in 1 Cor 15, Paul illustrates the continuity between two bodies with the continuity between a seed and a plant. In 2 Cor 5, he employs the clothing image and indicates that the previous garment is not to be taken off.

transformation that he has already constructed in 1 Cor 15. Paul's teachings about the two aspects of transformation in 2 Cor 4 and 5, respectively, are based on two distinct conceptual blends enacted by two distinct sets of metaphors. In so doing, he clearly attempts to distinguish these two aspects and to clarify their relationship.

However, the conceptual blend in 2 Cor 5 seems to be a loose one because it has very limited common ground with the dwelling metaphor (I_1) and the clothing metaphor (I_3). We can see this looseness in Figure 5.2 in the rather weak generic space of these two metaphors (G_{1-3}) and, consequently, the weak overall generic space (G). These two generic spaces do not provide any clear image or coherent logic. Thus, the degree to which the two metaphors can be conceptually linked and blended is weakened. In fact, to say that one will be clothed with a heavenly dwelling does not provide a human scale. This does not mean that Paul's message delivered with the blended image is not clear in this passage. His idea is unequivocal when he applies the verbs of clothing to the bodies-as-dwellings. However, the conceptual effect of applying the clothing verbs to the dwellings is still questionable due to the weak generic space and the failure of providing human scale. This might be one of the reasons that the blended image in Figure 5.2 did not contribute effectively to Paul's later thought-development as other blended images did. On a conceptual level, the distinction between the two aspects of transformation might not be drawn as clear as Paul intends by forming the two conceptual blends in 2 Cor 4 and 5, respectively. As we will see, the two aspects of transformation were eventually blurred.

5.2 An Unexpected Convergence Here and Now in Baptism

Ritual activities can provide constant experiential and material bases for conceptual blending and so contribute to thought-development. In this way, the clear distinction between two aspects of transformation eventually began to be obscured by the repeated baptismal practices of the early Christian communities. This change was assisted in part by the kind of conceptual blend that we see in Rom 6:3–4, where Paul is arguing for a baptizand's new status and relationship with the law. It is not surprising that Paul associates his argument about a new lifestyle with a boundary-crossing rite that, as we have seen in 1 Cor 12:13, inaugurates the ongoing transformation of a new member.[51] Nevertheless, the conceptual blend in Rom 6:3–4 makes the meaning of baptism richer than that in the previous passages. In the blended, a new member is buried with Christ through baptism into death (συνετάφημεν οὖν αὐτῷ διὰ τοῦ βαπτίσματος εἰς τὸν θάνατο) and is supposed to live a new life afterward just as Christ was resurrected. The conjoined death and the analogical resurrection are noticeable new elements in Paul's description of baptism. Moreover, while the pattern of Christ is only the first fruit of the eschatological resurrection-transformation in 1 Cor 15, the blended image in Romans

---

[51] Through backward projection, the idea of bodily transformation that emerges in the blend in Figure 5.2 is associated with baptism.

seems to map this pattern upon baptismal practices for general members. Thus, in time, the eschatological and ongoing aspects of transformation would converge in the innovative understanding of baptism. As will be illustrated, two input spaces are involved in this conceptual blend: the death-burial-resurrection pattern of Christ (I_1), and the baptism of a new member (I_2). We have analyzed the conceptual structures of these two inputs in Chapters 3 and 4 in this study, respectively, and indicated that each of these two inputs is associated with one aspect of transformation. We have also seen in the previous sections in this chapter that the two aspects of transformation remain distinct in Paul's exposition in 2 Cor 4–5. Thus, the blend in Rom 6:3–4 reveals a significant development in Paul's thought which brings together all we have discussed in this study.

5.2.1 The Conceptual Blend in Romans 6:3-4: Paul's Previous Teachings and His Argument

Both input spaces in this blend recall Paul's previous teachings. As shown in Figure 5.3, the first input (I_1) represents the event of Christ's death, burial, and resurrection. Paul's wording "co-burial" (συνετάφημεν) in Rom 6:4 echoes his description of Christ's pattern in 1 Cor 15:3–4 (ἐτάφη). The -θάπτω words only occur twice in the undisputed Pauline letters, 1 Cor 15:4 (ἐτάφη) and Rom 6:4 (συνετάφημεν).[52] The three components of the Christ event (death, burial, and resurrection) are mentioned in Rom 6:4 in sequence as well as in 1 Cor 15:3–4.

More importantly, the whole event is conceptualized through the structure of "temporal polarity resulting from a reversal transformation"—a structure that appears in 1 Cor 15, as I have shown in Chapter 3. In 1 Cor 15:35–44a, this structure emerges from a conceptual blend enacted by the sowing metaphor (illustrated in Figures 3.2 and 3.3), and it is the structure that Paul uses there to conceptualize both the general resurrection and the prototype pattern of Christ.[53] The key feature of this structure is the transformation occurring at the turning point of a reversal movement, which is a crucial feature for the blend and argument in Rom 5–8. As illustrated in I_1 in Figure 5.3, Jesus underwent a reversal pattern of transformation that consists of a downward movement and an upward movement. This transformation then results in a polarity of two distinct statuses before and after transformation. The difference between two statuses emphasized in Paul's previous teaching in 1 Cor 15 is the radical change in

---

[52] In Col 2:12, συνθάπτω is also used for the same topic of dying together with Christ in baptism.
[53] In 1 Cor 15, this structure of polarity and reversal is constructed for the purpose of framing general resurrection and transformation (15:42–44a). Although Paul regards the pattern of Christ as the prototype of general resurrection (15:20), he has to employ the sowing metaphor to deal with the problem of body-decomposition in death rites, a problem from which Christ seems to be immune. With the sowing metaphor, Paul can solve the problem and describe general resurrection in the pattern of Christ. Thus, this structure that emerges in 1 Cor 15 can also apply to the pattern of Christ Jesus. In fact, in dealing with the decomposition problem, Paul enriches his teachings about the pattern of Christ. Regarding the decomposition problem and Christ, see B. R. McCane, *Roll Back the Stone: Death and Burial in the World of Jesus* (Harrisburg, PA: Trinity Press International, 2003), 111. He indicates that body-decomposition was usually understood as starting at the fourth day after death (cf. John 11:39). Thus, this is not a problem to be solved in Christ's pattern.

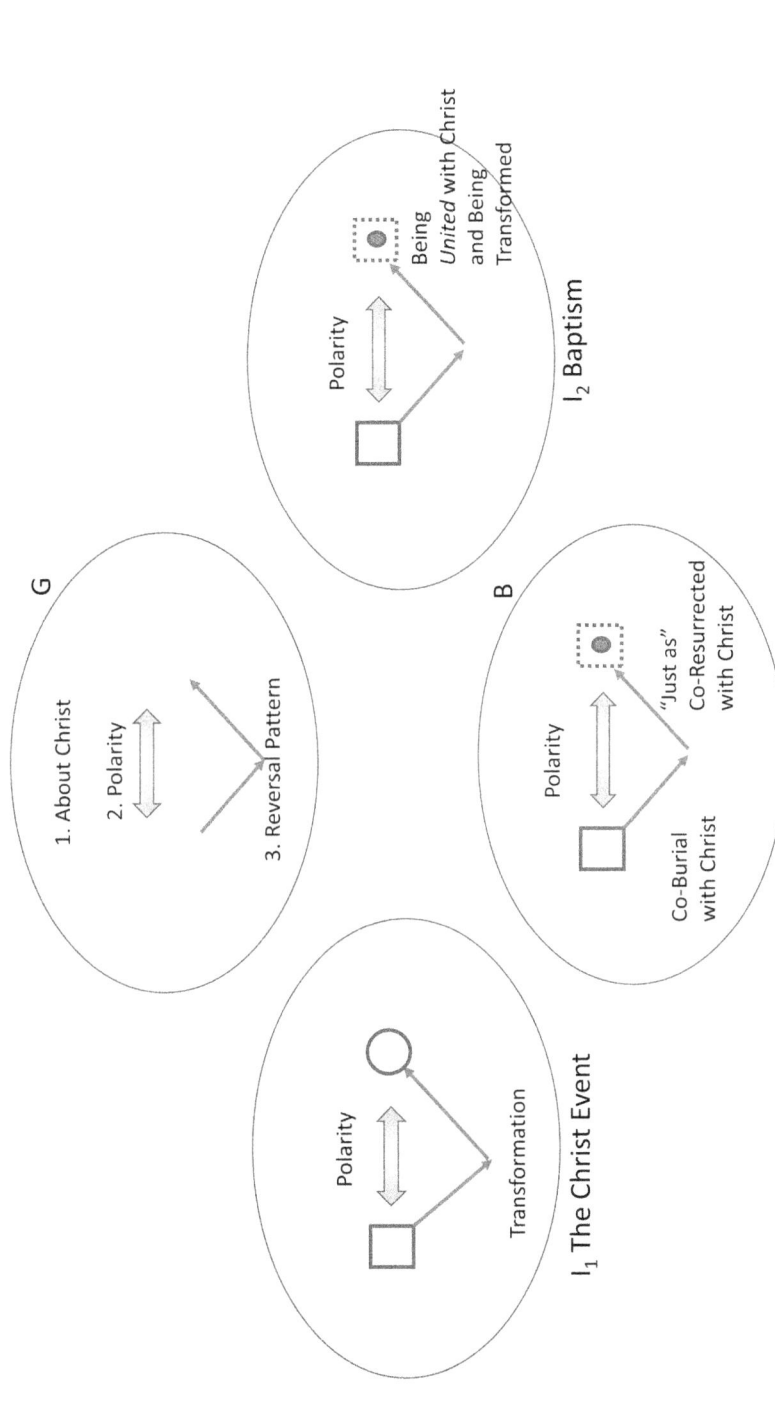

Figure 5.3 The Conceptual Blend between the Christ Event and Baptism.

bodily conditions. That is, Jesus supposedly has a mortal body that is able to die before the turning point, and then he has a heavenly, immortal body after that point. While this kind of transformation should happen to people only in the eschatological event, Jesus has already gone through the transformation and changed his bodily condition. Similarly, as I will indicate soon, I_1 (the pattern of Christ event) in Rom 6:3–4 presents Jesus as the only one who has been completely transformed and overcome the temporal, eschatological polarity. Based on the structure in I_1, Paul attempts to draw out implications from the similar reversal movement of the baptizand's body in baptism (the second input) and argue for a radical change in members' relationship with the law.[54] The bodily aspect of transformation as emphasized in 1 Cor 15 is also prominent here since Paul's argument involves bodily union with Christ and bodily experience in baptism.

The second input (I_2) is a specific understanding of the boundary-crossing rite, baptism. Three essential elements constitute the whole structure of this input image and make its blend with the pattern of the Christ event (I_1) effective. The first element is the reversal pattern of being physically immersed into water and then raised up from water.[55] This movement of the body matches the reversal structure of the Christ event (I_1) and provides a vivid and experiential pattern for the imagination of participating in the event. The second element is the idea of ongoing transformation that results in a temporal polarity. By definition, a boundary-crossing rite marks the group boundary and suggests the polar difference before and after crossing. This polar difference also matches the Christ event (I_1) to an extent. While I_1 represents the eschatological aspect of transformation rather than the ongoing aspect in baptism (I_2), these two inputs share a similar structure of temporal polarity. Nevertheless, as discussed in Chapter 4,

---

[54] Wayne A. Meeks has emphasized the V-shaped pattern of the descending and ascending actions in baptism. Relying on anthropologist Arnold van Gennep (whose model is further developed by Victor M. Turner), Meeks also treats baptism as a "rite of passage." Thus, Meeks considers this V-patterned gesture as corresponding not only to the dying and rising of Christ but also "to the phases of every initiation or rite of passage: separation, transition, and reaggregation." See W. A. Meeks, *The First Urban Christians: The Social World of the Apostle Paul* (New Haven, CT: Yale University Press, 1983), 156–57. Cf. A. van Gennep, *The Rites of Passage* (trans. M. Vizedom and G. Caffee; Chicago, IL: University of Chicago Press, 1960), 10–11; V. M. Turner, *The Ritual Process: Structure and Anti-Structure* (Chicago, IL: Aldine Publishing Company, 1969), 94. However, the correspondence between the model of "rite of passage" and Paul's statements about baptism has been challenged. As John Ashton indicates, baptism in either the first century or later periods "is clearly no more than a token gesture when placed beside the lengthy 'rites of passage' practiced in other societies," the societies that Turner's analysis depends on. More importantly, Agnes Choi astutely indicates that Paul's baptismal themes are mostly arranged in pair and so show a *binary structure* rather than van Gennep's three-stage model of rite of passage. See J. Ashton, *The Religion of Paul the Apostle* (New Haven, CT: Yale University Press, 2000), 153; A. Choi, "Boundary-Crossing in Christian Baptism" in *Early Christian Ritual Life* (ed. R. E. DeMaris, J. T. Lamoreaux, and S. C. Muir; New York: Routledge, 2018), 77. Cf. R. E. DeMaris, *The New Testament in Its Ritual World* (London: Routledge, 2008), 18–21.

[55] As Tappenden indicates, the general usage of βαπτίζω implies downward movements. According to the extant narrative descriptions of early Christian baptismal practices, it appears reasonable that baptism involved some form of down-up movement of the baptizand's body (cf. Barn. 11:11; Shepherd of Herm. Mand. 4.3; Sim. 9.16). Didache 7:1–4 is not really a counterexample. Although Didache speaks of the act of pouring water over the head in the absence of "living water," this passage prefers baptism in living water (yet no practice is described for baptism in living water). See Tappenden, *Resurrection in Paul*, 140–41.

Paul's understanding of a baptizand's radical change is always linked with participation in the body of Christ—the third essential element of baptism in I_2.[56]

The third element, the idea of bodily union with Christ, is at heart of the conceptual blend in Rom 6:3–4 and, as I will argue, is necessary for Paul's overall argument about the law. It appears that the connection between this key idea and baptism emerges from Paul's previous teachings. In 1 Cor 12:13, in order to appeal to the unity of a social body, Paul has employed the image of baptism to form a conceptual blend (illustrated in Figure 4.5) and stated that a baptizand is baptized in the Spirit "into the body of Christ." That blend in 1 Cor 12:13 seems to be a significant development in Paul's ideas. Through backward projection and the blending operation itself, baptism is associated with both the experience of receiving the Spirit and entrance into the "body of Christ."[57] The structure of body-as-container is prominent in that emergent perception of baptism. A baptizand comes to possess the indwelling Spirit in the baptizand's body-container and at the same time is immersed into another body-container of Christ, which is filled with the Spirit (cf. 2 Cor 3:17). Two body-containers are intertwined. Thus, in that blend, the boundary-crossing rite of baptism becomes more than the change of identity. Rather, it is also in the sense of bodily union that baptism marks the initiatory point of belonging to Christ. Accordingly, as suggested in the blend in 1 Cor 12:13, the transformation of a baptizand resulting in polarity is not only about the change of lifestyle that follows the change of identity. Rather, the transformation is also conceptualized in a bodily sense even though it is only an inauguration of the ongoing transformation. As Paul later states in 2 Cor 3:18, a member in Christ is being transformed into the form of the Spirit of the Lord. Thus, here in Romans, I_2 presents baptism as associated with the ideas of bodily union with Christ and the inauguration of bodily transformation, as the blend in Rom 6:3–4 and the overall argument would require.

Now we may look at the blending network in Figure 5.3. A couple of innovative ideas emerge when both the Christ event (I_1) and baptism as a boundary-crossing rite (I_2) contribute significantly to the structure of the blended space. While the reversal pattern and the idea of polarity constitute the common ground between I_1 and I_2 (hence the generic space G), the idea of bodily union with Christ projected from baptism (I_2) provides the necessary mechanism for a baptizand to participate in the Christ event (I_1). With this key idea, the downward movement and the immersion of the body in baptism is conceptualized in the blended space (B) as being baptized into Christ's death and as co-buried (συνετάφημεν) with Christ (Rom 6:3–4). This innovative idea does not exist either in the Christ event (I_1, where only Christ is buried) or in baptism as a boundary-crossing rite (I_2, where a member does not die

---

[56] I conclude in Chapter 4 that Paul has imagined a special realm, the body of Christ. This special realm is marked by religious experience (spirit-possession), a boundary-crossing rite (baptism), and ethical instructions, and thus shows a clear distinction with the cosmos.

[57] In addition to the connection with the body of Christ, as A. J. M. Wedderburn indicates, the connection of baptism with the possession of the Spirit is also "unparalleled in any of the rites of washing" in Paul's time. See his *Baptism and Resurrection: Studies in Pauline Theology against Its Greco-Roman Background* (Wissenschaftliche Untersuchungen zum Neuen Testament 44; Tübingen: Mohr, 1987), 62.

and is not buried). While the general idea of dying with Christ might not originate from this blend (cf. Gal 2:19; 6:14), I will indicate in the next section the effect of this more specific idea of being co-buried with Christ through baptism. Moreover, the second innovation concerns the second half of the reversal pattern shared by both inputs. In B, Paul conceptualizes the body's upward movement of emerging from water as analogical to Christ's resurrection (6:4). The idea of transformation resulting in polarity in both inputs is also projected to B and contributes to the conception of the upward movement in B. Thus, Paul indicates that the co-burial in baptism is to make the new members live "in newness of life ... just as" (ὥσπερ) Christ was raised up (6:4). In other words, the baptizand's status after the upward movement is supposed to be in polar opposition to the status before the downward movement. Relying on this polarity, Paul will argue for a new lifestyle specifically concerning submission to the law.

Is this conceptual blend rhetorically effective? In order to understand how these two ideas emerged from the blend function in Paul's overall argument, we must look at the broader context. In the larger argument about the law in Rom 5–8, the polarity between two bodily existences in the Christ event (I_1) symbolizes the polarity of two opposite realms, and the triumph of Christ over the polarity denotes the only way for traversing from one realm to another.[58] This symbolism is observable in the parallelism between the argument in Rom 5–8 and Paul's previous teaching in 1 Cor 15. According to 1 Cor 15:44b–45, the mortal body before the general resurrection is σῶμα ψυχικόν is represented by Adam, while Jesus Christ on earth is also supposed to have a mortal body that is able to die. The immortal body is σῶμα πνευματικόν represented by the resurrected Christ, the ἔσχατος Ἀδάμ. In this way, Paul maps the polarity of bodily conditions onto the framework of an eschatological drama. Similarly, in Rom 5–8 Paul is making his argument on the basis of this eschatological antithesis of Adam versus Christ. As Paul says, death reigned because people died through the transgression of Adam (5:14–15), but grace might reign into eternal life through Jesus Christ (5:21). Paul thus expands the initial idea into two opposite realms in temporal sequence. The first realm is featured by Adam, sin, and death, and the second is featured by Christ, grace, and life (cf. 6:23). Paul's rhetorical strategy is to ascribe the law to the first realm of the polarity and the Spirit to the second realm (Rom 7:6). Thus, with the idea of bodily union, Paul argues that if one has the Spirit and so belongs to Christ (8:9), one must belong to the second realm and is no longer under the power of anything in the first realm—sin, death, and, of course, the law.[59]

---

[58] Of course, this symbolization is yet another conceptual blend in which the polarity between Adam and Christ is blended with the eschatological drama of two opposite sovereignties. Thus, through conceptual blending, the transformation of Jesus Christ becomes not only about bodily condition but also about the change from one realm to another. My focus here, however, is on the blend in Rom 6:3–4 that involves ritual activity—baptism. My purpose in this paragraph is to locate my focused blend in the whole argument and, as seen below, to emphasize the function of "dying with Christ" (an idea that emerges from the blend in Rom 6:3–4) in the whole argument.

[59] As discussed, the experience of the Spirit is one of the most important common grounds among the early Christian congregations. Moreover, I will discuss in §5.2.2 the specific relation between the ideas of possessing the Spirit and being united with Christ.

Nevertheless, in Paul's argument, death is not only descent and destruction but also the mechanism by which one can be freed from the powers of the first realm (6:2, 7; 7:6; 8:10), and this mechanism requires bodily participation. Paul also offers the same mechanism of death in Gal 2:19 when he argues for not observing the law. In Romans, he first mentions this mechanism in the immediate context of the baptismal blend (6:2) and later illustrates the logic of this mechanism with the metaphor of marriage. That is, like in a marriage, death can end the validity and lordship of the law (7:2–3). This invalidation is a clear and inevitable effect of a real death on a legal relationship. To achieve the invalidation, Paul's analogical argument requires the "death to the law" to be more than merely metaphorical or symbolic. Indeed, Paul resorts to the language of participation in Christ to convince the members that they already died to the first realm because Christ is the only one who has really gone through death and traversed to another end of the eschatological polarity.[60] As Paul states, it is "through the body of Christ" that one can die to the law and come to belong to another lordship of the second realm (7:4). In other words, Paul's argument about being dead to the law relies on the key idea of bodily participation, an idea that is vividly portrayed in 6:3–4 and represented in baptism as a boundary-crossing rite (I_2). It is through bodily union with Christ that members have participated in the Christ event as delineated in I_1. Thus, through conceptual blending as illustrated in Figure 5.3, Paul can argue that all members who are baptized into the body of Christ have already died to the law and gone through the reversal transformation together with Christ into a status of newness. Since the bodily polarity in the Christ event (I_1) symbolizes two opposite realms, the structures of body-container and cosmos-container are intertwined in this symbolization. Those who possess the Spirit and participate in the body of Christ are now in the power of the second realm. As Paul states, they are no longer living "in sin" (ἐν αὐτῇ, 6:2) but walking "in newness of life" (ἐν καινότητι ζωῆς, 6:4). The blend in Rom 6:3–4 appears to effectively deliver the image of bodily dying together with Christ and thus being freed from previous lordships.

5.2.2 "You Were Also Raised with Him": An Unexpected Convergence in Baptism

A primary goal of this study is to explore the embodied influences of rituals on Paul's thought. Thus, after illustrating the network and rhetorical function of the conceptual blend in Rom 6:3–4, I now turn to the contributions of the bodily experience in baptism to the two ideas emerging from this blend. I will discuss the contributions to the two ideas in turn. The first idea influenced by baptism is, of course, dying together with Christ. I will argue that, in Rom 6:3–4, Paul only attempts to strengthen this first

---

[60] Paul assumes the same logic that death can end the validity of the law when he resorts to another mechanism of participating in Christ's death, that is, co-crucifixion with Christ (Gal 2:19; Rom 6:6). Nevertheless, Paul emphasizes the bodily aspect of participation in Romans by employing the common bodily experience of baptism. I will discuss the difference between the co-crucifixion image and the baptismal image in the next section in terms of effectiveness and theological implications.

idea in order to solidify his argument about the law, yet the second idea—being (not analogically but literally) resurrected together with Christ—is naturally implied in the blended image itself. It is the second idea that leads to the unintended convergence of two aspects of transformations.

As analyzed below, the first idea did not originate from baptism and was not completely new in itself (cf. Gal 2:19; 6:14). However, the theme of bodily union that is central to this idea becomes much more vivid, material, and experiential in Rom 6:3–4 when this idea emerges from the blend and is thereby associated with baptism: a baptizand can experience burial with Christ through the physical performance of baptism. In order to fully recognize how baptism has strengthened the first idea, we have to look at two traditional elements relating to this baptismal articulation of participation in Christ's death: (1) the idea of metaphorical death as the initiation of a new identity, status, and lifestyle, and (2) the material understanding of participating in the action and fate of a representative figure. Both elements are embodied ideas arising from common human experiences and are consonant with certain traditions. As for the first element, A. J. M. Wedderburn indicates that the theme of "life through death" is characteristic of all passage rites.[61] After all, being born and dying is one of the most universal and observed human experiences. It is not surprising that dying and being restored to life (or being born again) has become a metaphor for radical transitions and boundary-crossings, and this metaphor has been frequently used in initiatory rites and other rites of passage in various cultures. We have noticed in Chapter 3 that death and death rites in the ancient Mediterranean world could symbolize other transitional moments in various types of boundary-crossing.[62] This phenomenon was also common in the ancient Greek world and the Greco-Roman world.[63] For example, as Niklaus Gäumann observes, Lucius's "voluntary death" in his initiation to Isis (Apuleius, Met. 11.21) shows that "the idea of a death that takes place in the cult and a subsequent renewal is thoroughly at home in Hellenistic religious experience."[64] Paul's argument of death in baptism thus reflects this common initiatory structure.[65]

Nevertheless, the indwelling of the Spirit and bodily union with Christ are the remarkable aspects in Paul's understanding of the connection between initiation and death. Emphasizing these aspects, Wedderburn maintains that "Paul's language of dying with Christ is probably his own."[66] As he argues, for Paul, "it is not just any [death and] burial, but burial *with Christ*" into his death.[67] This co-burial language

---

[61] Wedderburn, *Baptism and Resurrection*, 381.
[62] See DeMaris, *Ritual World*, 57–63. He refers to transitions such as weddings and "all sorts of separations, from departure of the evening to retirement."
[63] Wedderburn, *Baptism and Resurrection*, 371–92.
[64] See N. Gäumann, *Taufe und Ethik: Studien zu Römer 6* (BEvTh47; München: Kaiser, 1967), 43–4. However, H. Ridderbos reminds that it is not the case in their washing rites and baptisms. See his *Paul: An Outline of His Theology* (trans. J. R. de Witt; Grand Rapids, MI: W. B. Eerdmans, 1975), 24. For other examples of the theme of "life through death," see Wedderburn, *Baptism and Resurrection*, 373–7.
[65] Wedderburn, *Baptism and Resurrection*, 380.
[66] Ibid., 356.
[67] Ibid., 391 (original emphasis).

leads to the second traditional element that Paul likely inherited from traditions—the underlying idea of participating in the action and fate of a figure. In fact, except for Paul's emphasis on the indwelling Spirit, this underlying idea is very much in line with the tradition from Israel that reflects a sense of unity with representative figures, such as Adam and Abraham. Later generations to an extent align with the actions of these figures and depend on those figures' destinies.[68] Moreover, Caroline Johnson Hodge recognizes the prominent schema of body-as-container in this tradition and introduces the ancient "ideology of patrilineal descent" to explain the idea of oneness with ancestral figures.[69] At the heart of this ideology is a concept of containment that ancestors contain in their bodies the material "stuff" of the descendants: "Descendants are contained 'in' their ancestors, whether in their seed or womb or in some other way."[70] It is in this material logic that Abraham becomes an ethnos (Gen 12:1–3): the material stuff in his body transfers to his descendants who become a whole people. Also in this logic, Paul states that gentiles are blessed "in Abraham" when they participate in Christ and so become included in the σπέρμα of Abraham (Gal 3:16–18).[71] More importantly, Stanley K. Stowers insightfully extends Johnson Hodge's work on the "patrilineal descent" ideology to the material understanding of the indwelling Spirit, a crucial point of Paul's gospel. As Stowers observes, it is precisely on the basis of possessing the material πνεῦμα in their bodies that Paul claims that gentiles in Christ are included in Abraham's seed: "Gentiles who come to share the pneuma of Christ in baptism share in this contiguity back to Abraham and are thus seed of Abraham and coheirs as they participate in the stuff of Christ.... Those in Christ are literally of the same stuff."[72] Thus, the peculiarity of Paul's language of dying with Christ seems to rely on his emphasis on the indwelling Spirit. Paul proclaims that Christians are bodily united with Christ and with Christ's death by sharing the same stuff in their bodies.

It is noteworthy that Paul also closely associates this material logic of sharing the same Spirit of Christ with his language of being crucified with Christ. In addition to baptism, co-crucifixion is another image that Paul employs to speak of the participation in Christ's death and to argue for his position of not enforcing circumcision and the law in general (Gal 2:19; Rom 6:6). In Galatians, Paul also mentions the idea of the indwelling Spirit and bodily union when he talks about co-crucifixion: "I have been crucified with Christ; yet I live, no longer I, but Christ lives in me" (Gal 2:19–20). Immediately following this statement, Paul then reaffirms the fact that the Galatians have received the Spirit (3:1–5) and so participated in Christ as heirs (3:6–4:7). The image of co-crucifixion is effective for reminding them of the core message of the gospel, the death of Christ (3:1), and the radical change after initiation (6:14) that Paul consistently emphasizes, especially when talking about circumcision and the law.

---

[68] Ibid., 342–56.
[69] C. J. Hodge, *If Sons, Then Heirs: A Study of Kinship and Ethnicity in the Letters of Paul* (Oxford: Oxford University Press, 2007), 93.
[70] Ibid., 94–7 (quote from 94).
[71] Ibid., 98.
[72] S. Stowers, "What Is 'Pauline Participation in Christ'?" in *Redefining First-Century Jewish and Christian Identities: Essays in Honor of Ed Parish Sanders* (ed. F. E. Udoh; Notre Dame: University of Notre Dame Press, 2008), 360. See also Tappenden, *Resurrection in Paul*, 216–17.

Indeed, Paul uses this image again in Rom 6:6. Nevertheless, in Romans, Paul constructs the image of co-burial in baptism (6:3–4) right before his use of co-crucifixion image. The baptismal image strengthens his argument by making the connection with the Spirit much clearer and more experiential since baptism as a boundary-crossing rite has been associated with the reception (drinking) of the Spirit. This connection has been particularly emphasized in the conceptual blend in 1 Cor 12:13. The bodily experience of baptism also highlights the bodily aspect of a member's participation in death in addition to a symbolic understanding of the change in one's identity and legal status as in the co-crucifixion image. As Paul adds to the co-crucifixion language in Rom 6:6 after the baptismal blend in 6:3–4, our "body of sin (τὸ σῶμα τῆς ἁμαρτίας) would no longer dominate us." This statement that emphasizes the bodily aspect does not occur in Gal 2:19–20. According to embodied cognition theory, the baptismal image would be more effective than the co-crucifixion image in terms of the imaginative perception of one's own death and material arguments about bodily union. Unlike being crucified, baptism is a ritual activity that people practice from time to time. Members in the Christian groups should all have bodily experienced baptism on their own and repeatedly witnessed this ritual practice by other baptizands. The repeated experience would provide constant material basis for strengthening the material conceptualization of participation in Christ's death and burial.

The embodied effect of rituals leads us to the second idea fostered by baptism—being resurrected together with Christ. I have been emphasizing that the constant material basis provided by rituals can do more than symbolize or strengthen ideas: it can contribute to the generation of new ideas through conceptual blending. In this blend in Rom 6:3–4, the idea of conjoined resurrection is implied in the upward movement of the reversal pattern and is symmetrical to the downward movement. On the emergence of this idea, Tappenden recognizes the conceptual effect of the blended image in Rom 6:3–4: once the immersion of the body into water is conceptualized in the blend as death and burial, the departure from water would "naturally entail" a new life.[73] The symmetrical pattern of bodily movement seems to lead to the symmetrical statement in Col 2:12: "You were buried together with (συνταφέντες) him in baptism, in which (ἐν ᾧ) you were also raised together with (συνηγέρθητ) him" (cf. 3:1).[74] Conjoined resurrection naturally and immediately follows the conjoined

---

[73] Tappenden, *Resurrection in Paul*, 143.
[74] I follow Everett Ferguson in taking the pronoun ᾧ as referring to the immediately antecedent noun, τῷ βαπτισμῷ. Nevertheless, another possible translation of ἐν ᾧ in 2:12 is "in whom," and the translation of 2:11–12 would be "In him [Christ] you were also circumcised … when you were buried with him in baptism, in whom you were also raised with him." In this case, the author of Colossians still explicitly states the idea of conjoined resurrection (with Christ) as a past event, and the author states this idea immediately after talking about the conjoined burial in baptism. As I argue below, this idea of resurrection is not seen in Romans. And, presumably, this realized and conjoined resurrection happens at baptism because, in Col 2:11–12, baptism has replaced circumcision and become the initiation of the new life for Christians. Thus, while being fully aware of the later translation, Ferguson still maintains that one is raised together with Christ in baptism according to 2:12. See his *Baptism in the Early Church: History, Theology, and Liturgy in the First Five Centuries* (Grand Rapids, MI: W. B. Eerdmans, 2009), 159. For similar translations (taking ᾧ as referring to baptism), see F. F. Bruce, *The Epistles to the Colossians, to Philemon, and to the Ephesians* (Grand Rapids, MI: W. B. Eerdmans, 1984), 105; D. J. Moo, *The Letters to the Colossians*

death in baptism. It is noteworthy that the word συνθάπτω only occurs twice in the New Testament, Rom 6:4 and Col 2:12. Most scholars regard the statement in Col 2:12 as a later development from Rom 6:3–4 or elaboration upon it, whether by Paul or his followers.[75] As Tappenden accurately concludes, "conceptually speaking, because baptismal death has happened, so has baptismal resurrection."[76] The development between Rom 6:3–4 and Col 2:12 is a good example of how conceptual blend might generate new ideas.

However, in Romans itself, it appears that Paul does not intend to deliver the idea of baptismal resurrection in its fullest sense. Rather, Paul seems to be maintaining his understanding of the paradoxical association between the dying of Christ and the life of Christ, which he has argued by employing the treasure metaphor in 2 Cor 4 (see Figure 5.1). That is, as I argued above, the dying and the resurrected life of Christ are two sides of a coin for a believer and are carried simultaneously in Paul's body-container. Similarly, here in Romans, Paul does not intend to describe a new life after baptism that is really beyond death as the gesture of departing water might suggest. In Wedderburn's term, what Paul describes is rather a new lifestyle "within death" (cf. 8:10–13; 12:1).[77] As James D. G. Dunn and Wedderburn observe, although the baptismal image is symmetrical, Paul does not treat a baptizand's participation in Christ's death and resurrection in a symmetrical way.[78] Dunn notices that Paul does not directly speak of participation in Christ's resurrection as he does for Christ's death and burial (6:4) but in fact deliberately "sets up a tension" between "the degree of self-identification with Christ's death" and that with resurrection.[79] This tension is evident in Paul's choices of verb tense. On the one hand, Paul consistently describes the general resurrection or the union with Christ's resurrection only in the future tense (τῆς ἀναστάσεως ἐσόμεθα, 6:5; see also 6:8; 8:11, 13). Of course, this future understanding is in line with Paul's previous teachings about eschatological resurrection in 1 Cor 15 and complete transformation in 2 Cor 5. Paul believes that these things are still in the future. On the other hand, Paul describes the union with Christ's death in the perfect tense: we have become united (σύμφυτοι γεγόναμεν) with him in the form of his death. As Dunn indicates, a baptizand "has been and

---

and to Philemon (Grand Rapids, MI: W. B. Eerdmans, 2008), 203; M. Y. MacDonald, *Colossians and Ephesians* (Collegeville, MN: Liturgical Press, 2008), 100; and S. McKnight, *The Letter to the Colossians* (Grand Rapids, MI: W. B. Eerdmans, 2018), 239–43. For the second kind of translations (taking ᾧ as referring to Christ), see E. Lohse, *Colossians and Philemon* (trans. W. R. Poehlmann and R. J. Karris; ed. H. Koester; Philadelphia: Fortress Press, 1971), 104–5; J. D. G. Dunn, *The Epistles to the Colossians and to Philemon* (Grand Rapids, MI: W. B. Eerdmans, 1996), 160–61; U. Luz, "Der Brief an die Kolosser," in *Die Briefe an die Galater, Epheser und Kolosser* (ed. J. Becker and U. Luz; Göttingen: Vandenhoeck & Ruprecht, 1998), 213; and P. Foster, *Colossians* (London: Bloomsbury T&T Clark, 2016), 267.

[75] Wedderburn, *Baptism and Resurrection*, 72. E.g., E. P. Sanders, "Literary Dependence in Colossians," *JBL* 85 no. 1 (1966): 40–41; J. D. G. Dunn, *The Epistles to the Colossians and to Philemon: A Commentary on the Greek Text* (Philadelphia: Fortress Press, 1971), 158–59; McKnight, *The Letter to the Colossians*, 239–43.

[76] Tappenden, *Resurrection in Paul*, 143.

[77] Wedderburn, *Baptism and Resurrection*, 381–90 (his term "life in death" in page 381).

[78] J. D. G. Dunn, *Romans 1–8* (WBC 38; Dallas: Word Books, 1988), 329–33.

[79] Ibid., 330.

still is bonded together with" Christ's death.[80] It seems that Paul does not attempt to regard the emergence from water as a departure from the death into which the baptizands have been immersed. Rather, they are still living in death. In fact, through the body-container schema, Paul explicitly states the paradoxical coexistence of death and life as a member's current condition: "if Christ is in you, the body is dead, and the Spirit is life" (8:10). The part of a person that is already renewed or resurrected is the inner body, the indwelling Spirit (cf. 2 Cor 4:16). It seems that, in Romans, the transformation that one can go through in baptism is just like the transformation that Paul describes in 2 Cor 4—an incomplete, inner transformation. The change of the "inner" is already enough for Paul's argument about not observing the law. A member should live by the indwelling Spirit and kill the deeds of the body (8:10-13). The redemption of the outer body still lies in the future (Rom 8:11, 23-27). In short, by forming a blend in 6:3-4, Paul attempts to strengthen the idea of dying with Christ for his argument about the law without inventing the idea of being resurrected with Christ, even though the blend would suggest both.

I suggest that, in addition to Paul's previous teachings, the common experience that the physical body is wearing away is another reason that Paul applies the symmetrical image of baptism in an asymmetrical way. In fact, the weakness of the body is not only a common experience for Paul but also a constant problem and challenge that he struggles with when he proclaims his somatically oriented gospel and when he ingloriously suffers for it. Taking the weakness of the body into account, Wedderburn seems correct in indicating that the hope of resurrection is "far too physical" for Paul to conceive of full and literal participation in the present.[81] Admittedly, as Tappenden argues against Wedderburn, participation in Christ's death also requires a literal and physical understanding.[82] I have also argued above that the literal sense of death is the reason that the idea of bodily union with the one who literally and physically died (Christ) is so important to this blend. Nevertheless, the daily wearing of the body can help a baptizand to fully identify with the downward movement in the blended image of baptism. Tappenden is certainly right in indicating that it would "obscure the logic of the baptismal metaphor" to conceive that the baptizands only participate in a kind of new life that is different from the eschatological resurrection life.[83] However, it appears that Paul himself is the one who deliberately maintains the paradoxical idea of "life in death"[84] for his own argument in Romans and does not apply the logic of the blended image in Rom 6:3-4 to its full sense.

In time, however, the symmetrical logic of the blended image would lead to the idea of conjoined resurrection occurring immediately after the conjoined death in baptism, as seen in Col 2:12-13. Moreover, Paul has been assuming and teaching that the complete transformation happens at resurrection since he constructs the reversal schema in 1 Cor 15 with the sowing metaphor. Thus, although in Romans Paul intends

---

[80] Ibid., 331 (original emphasis).
[81] Wedderburn, *Baptism and Resurrection*, 395, 160-232.
[82] Tappenden, *Resurrection in Paul*, 145.
[83] Ibid.
[84] Wedderburn, *Baptism and Resurrection*, 381.

to describe the transformation of a baptizand as only into a condition analogical to Christ's resurrected life, a literal and overall sense of transformation would naturally follow the idea of conjoined resurrection in baptism. This development could be further encouraged by the bodily experience of the Spirit that has been associated with baptism. With the idea of conjoined resurrection, the repeated ecstatic experience of limitless and boundary-blurring could be considered as the ongoing transformation of not only the inner but the whole person. It is intriguing that the eschatological transformation is not even mentioned in Colossians. What is claimed in this book to happen at the Parousia is not resurrection (1 Thess 4:16) or resurrection with transformation (1 Cor 15:15; Phil 3:21) but the appearance of the life that is already in existence yet concealed with Christ in God (Col 3:4).[85] Resurrection has happened (3:1) in baptism and the life after baptism is put in opposition to the baptizand's previous death in "flesh" (τῆς σαρκὸς). Nevertheless, this does not mean that the transformation in baptism is considered complete in Colossians. Although the members have already "put off the old person," the new person is still being renewed (ἀνακαινούμενον) in an ongoing process (3:9–10; cf. 3:5).[86] In other words, the ongoing aspect of transformation is still seen in Colossians. Thus, Colossians seems to indicate the convergence of the ongoing aspect and the eschatological aspect of bodily transformation in baptism, a convergence that is largely enacted by the conceptual blend in Rom 6:3–4.

5.3 Conclusion

Bodily experience plays a significant role in the development of Paul's ideas. This is particularly evident in the development of his ideas about resurrection and transformation, which are somatically oriented in themselves. These Pauline ideas always include the expectation of the redemption and glorious transformation of the body, either in the present or future. Thus, in order to construct and proclaim these somatic ideas, Paul constantly struggles with the experience of the weakness and wearing of the body. In this chapter, we have seen that Paul distinguishes the present, ongoing transformation from the future, complete transformation by indicating that the former is happening in the inside (2 Cor 4:16) while the latter will happen with a new body swallowing the old body from the outside (5:4). Paul also delineates a paradoxical condition of the current body by employing the metaphor of treasure in clay jars. In his exposition, the dying and the life of Christ are closely linked and simultaneously carried in the body-container. This exposition in 2 Corinthians is consistent with Paul's previous teachings. Nevertheless, in addition to common experience, ritual practice and religious experience also provide concrete and vivid bodily experience that can influence thought-development. As we have analyzed Rom 6:3–4 with conceptual blending theory, the physical performance of baptism matches the reversal pattern

---

[85] For similar observation see Lohse, *Colossians and Philemon*, 104.
[86] This idea never occurs in the clothing metaphors in either 1 Cor 15 or 2 Cor 5. Paul explicitly states in 2 Cor 5:4 that the old one is not to be put off. Rather, it is to be swallowed by the new one *in the future*.

of Christ's death-burial-resurrection event and, as a boundary-crossing rite, also denotes a polar structure. Thus, when baptism is further associated with the ecstatic experience of receiving the Spirit and bodily union with Christ, it delivers a powerful conceptual image that allows a baptizand to identify with the Christ event—including the upward movement—regardless of the incompatibility between this movement and physical weakness. In other words, bodily experiences in baptism and in ecstasy provide the alternative physical basis to conceptualize what is still not available in our current body. Once a baptizand identifies with the upward movement of Christ event through baptism (that is, resurrection with Christ in baptism), the distinction between two aspects of transformation is blurred. Moreover, before writing Romans, Paul has indicated the paradox that the decay of the outer is producing the eternal glory that is currently only in the inner (2 Cor 4:17). This idea might have helped to reconcile the common experience of physical weakness and the religious experiences in baptism and ecstasy, and so encouraged the convergence of the two aspects of transformation.

6

Conclusion

Applying cognitive linguistic tools to Paul's resurrection thought, this study has demonstrated a promising method to explore the interplay between text and idea on the one hand and somatic experience on the other. In so doing, I have emphasized the contribution of experience to Paul's resurrection thought without downplaying his intellectual activities. Rather, this exploration shows that there were reciprocal interactions between Paul's thinking and experience. Somatic experiences not only generated the practical and circumstantial issues that Paul had to deal with by analytic reasoning but also, in a more fundamental way, provided the embodied basis for his complex and abstract thought. This study has touched on a variety of experiences that influenced Paul's resurrection thought. These include common experiences in daily life, such as traversing a path and observing the growth of a sown seed, and two kinds of religious experiences. I have considered intense religious experiences, such as altered states of consciousness and the phenomenon of body-bewilderment in spirit-possession, and the repeated experiences of ritual practices, such as the reversal pattern in baptism and observing the downward movement of decomposing corpses in most Greco-Roman death rites. Without delineating a neat, evolving process of Paul's resurrection thought, I have indicated three significant and related developments in Paul's ideas in which these somatic experiences played either fundamental or supporting roles.

With the three major findings, my study contributes to the scholarly debate concerning Paul's thought-development. In the first chapter, I have pointed out two crucial questions in the debate: (1) whether the idea of bodily transformation is absent in 1 Thess 4 and is Paul's innovation in 1 Cor 15; and (2) whether the idea of experienced resurrection occurring at baptism can be found in undisputed Pauline letters. I have answered the first question positively. As I have demonstrated by using image schema, before the three developments that I identified, Paul's resurrection thought as reflected in 1 Thess 4:13–17 agrees with Jewish resurrection texts in terms of the key idea of bodily transformation. In these traditions (including 1 Thess 4:13–17), bodily transformation is not directly linked with resurrection but with the ascent or exaltation of the resurrected because ascent and exaltation require the resurrected to traverse the polarity of the celestial and the terrestrial realms. Resurrection itself, however, is generally considered as the restoration of life. Although both resurrection and ascent are conceptualized with the verticality schema as upward movements, they are consistently distinguished in traditions as two distinct and sequential events. In other words, bodily transformation is supposed to be temporally later than resurrection even though the two are certainly associated.

The first significant development identified in my study is that Paul begins to use an alternative image schema, the reversal schema, to conceptualize resurrection and bodily transformation as seen in 1 Cor 15:35–58. This reversal schema emerges from the common experience of sowing seeds and observing their growth. It is different from, yet is not contradictory to, the traditional image schemas that are found in Jewish resurrection texts and Paul's earlier teaching in 1 Thess 4:13–17. Central to traditional schemas is an upward movement of the resurrected, while a preceding downward movement of the dead is only assumed but not addressed. Paul's reversal schema, however, highlights the downward movement and the point of transformation. Thus, it allows him to address the experiential issue of the decomposition of the corpse and defend against the Gentile challenge to resurrection. In everyday life, particularly in ancient times, the vivid observation that the body reduces into dust and goes down into the earth suggests that it would never, even if it is restored, move upwards to partake in the afterlife in the heavenly realm. In other words, in the case of 1 Cor 15:35–58, both the issue that Paul has to deal with and the somatic basis for his thinking arise from experience. With the reversal schema, Paul locates bodily transformation at resurrection (which happens at the Parousia) instead of the traditional timing that is after both resurrection and ascent/exaltation. This change of timing cannot be explained by merely resorting to intellectual backgrounds of cosmology in Hellenistic philosophies.

The reversal schema is not only a contingent solution to the Corinthian issue but becomes a crucial framework for Paul's resurrection thinking. This new framework fuels the progression of Paul's resurrection ideas and prompts him to build on it. I have shown that the reversal schema contributes to Paul's later thought in two important aspects. First, with this schema and the conjoined timing of resurrection and transformation, transformation becomes less about cosmic polarity and vertical ascent. Rather, it comes to denote a dualistic relationship between two statuses on the temporal dimension—what I call "temporal polarity." As suggested by the schema, a person will experience a transforming moment and will emerge into a radically different existence. Second, the reversal schema coincides with the pattern of the physical gesture in baptismal practice: being immersed into water and then raised up from water. In addition, as a boundary-crossing rite, baptism also denotes a radical change of status after the reversal gesture in the rite. Thus, the similar baptismal pattern of "a reversal movement that makes a change" opens a door for the ritualization of the eschatological resurrection hope into what can be practiced here and now. The continuing influences of these two aspects of the reversal schema on Paul's thought is most evident in Rom 6:3–4, where Paul argues that believers have died and been buried together with Christ in the baptismal practice and have undergone a radical change. Paul then says that the baptized should live like they are resurrected and are no longer under the power of the law. In other words, Paul claims that a kind of radical transformation happens in a believer's baptism and that this transformation is analogical to the pattern of Christ's resurrection that would only happen to believers at the Parousia.

Nevertheless, as I have argued, it still requires the idea of being bodily united with Christ in baptism to constitute the conceptual blend that generates Paul's argument in Rom 6:3–4. This then leads to the second significant development in Paul identified in this study—the link between baptism and the reception of the Spirit, as seen in 1 Cor 12:13. Again, Paul makes this link in order to deal with an experiential issue, and the basis that he relies on is a kind of experience as well. According to 1 Cor 12, one of the reasons that has caused the problem of divisions in Corinth is the variety of pneumatic phenomena that believers manifest. Addressing this issue, Paul's strategy is to apply a political metaphor of the body common in his time, and in v. 13 he integrates the body metaphor and the pneumatic phenomena by employing the experiential image of being immersed into water. In so doing, Paul creates an image with two body-containers; when one receives the Spirit into one's body-container, one is simultaneously immersed into another body-container, the body of Christ, in which the Spirit also dwells. This innovative image not only bolsters Paul's rhetorical thesis that every member receives the same Spirit but also enriches baptism with the idea of being bodily united with Christ by being surrounded and pervaded by the Spirit. This understanding of baptism is another development in Paul that clearly contributes to his expression in Rom 6:3–4. I have further suggested that, based on the ancient idea of the "porous body," this image of simultaneously "containing" and being immersed in the Spirit would encourage the idea of bodily transformation into the form of the Spirit, an idea that is found in 2 Cor 3:18.

Thus, the third significant development is what I have already mentioned above regarding Rom 6:3–4: the idea of dying and being buried together with Christ in baptism and the consequent transformation analogous to Christ's resurrection. Baptism plays a pivotal role in the emergence of this idea because, on the one hand, it coincides with the reversal pattern of death and resurrection, and, on the other hand, it has been associated with the reception of the Spirit and the idea of being bodily united with Christ. The repeated practice of baptism as a boundary-crossing rite in Christian groups provides a constant physical and material basis for community members to reflect on. It is then fair to say that experience, including ritual and intense religious experience, directly contributes to Paul's resurrection thought to a considerable extent.

In addition, in the Pauline communities, ritual and religious experiences seem to provide alternative physical grounds to reconceptualize daily experiences through the lens of the reversal conceptualization of resurrection. This is another aspect of interplay between experience and resurrection ideas found in this study. We have seen that Paul constantly struggles with the mortal nature of the human body when he articulates and elaborates his resurrection ideas. After all, resurrection is a hope about the body in conflict with daily experience. Thus, when Paul defends the resurrection hope against the Corinthian denial in 1 Cor 15, he deals with the issue of corpse-decomposition. When he elaborates the idea of experienced transformation in 2 Cor 3–5, he deals with the weakness and wearing of the body and claims that only the inner person is transformed. When he claims a radical transformation in baptism in Rom 6:3–4 in order to abrogate the authority of the law, he still reserves the idea of conjoined resurrection and says that the transformation of a baptizand is only analogous to Christ's resurrected life. However, as Paul claims, dying with Christ and the life in Christ are two sides of a coin, and the former is paradoxically producing the latter. This claim provides a meaningful basis to reconceptualize the common experience of wearing, and some experiences can support this kind of reconceptualization. Particularly, the link that is made in baptism between the reversal pattern of the anticipated resurrection and the initiation of the pneumatic, ecstatic, and even transforming experience provides the recurrent physical basis for the Pauline communities to practice and experience what is still not available in the current body. While the current body is gradually wearing away and can only be reasonably identified with the downward stage of the reversal pattern, the upward stage is repeatedly practiced through the baptismal gesture and might be experienced to an extent in pneumatic ecstasy. In this way, it is possible to reinterpret the daily downward experience as constantly leading to the upward movement because the upward is also repeatedly experienced in these Pauline communities. Such reinterpretation of daily experience appears to encourage a fuller sense of the reversal pattern experienced in the present in the community, as seen in the idea of conjoined resurrection in Col 2:12. Thus, regarding the second crucial question in the debate concerning Paul's development, my conclusion is that the idea of experienced resurrection occurring at baptism is not found in undisputed Pauline letters, but it is already implied in the conceptual blend of baptism and resurrection in Rom 6:3–4. It is not surprising that later Christian works would continue this direction of development.

Social formation has also been an important aspect in this study's exploration of the interplay between religious experience and idea development. The role of social formation is evident in the way that the feeling of being privileged to experience upward movement has helped Paul in building communities. Ritual/religious experiences and Paul's idea of being physically united within the "body of Christ" together create a special realm on earth for community members to reinterpret daily experience on earth. This realm is marked not only by the confessional belief of God's reversing power but also by a boundary-crossing rite with the reversal pattern and the experience that follows the rite. Thus, both ideas and religious experiences mark community boundaries. We have also seen that there are experiential issues in this special realm, and Paul relies on experiential basis to deal with those issues. In this way, ideas were formed largely in response to the community-building process, and ritual experience directly contributed to the idea-formation in this social process. My results are consonant with both the currents of social-scientific approaches in the field of New Testament studies and recent developments in ritual theories. While recent ritual theories emphasize the role of ritual practices in social formation and maintaining, social approaches to understanding early Christianity have been considering the formation of religious ideas in terms of their social function. This study, then, has proceeded with the insights and assumptions of both to see how the interplay between resurrection ideas and experiences enhances social formation. Thus, this study contributes to a fuller picture of the early Christian movement by exploring this interplay.

As someone who is writing at a school of theology that is very much embedded in faith communities, I think the findings in my study are helpful for reflecting on the nature of divine revelation. Instead of considering Paul as a robot-like recipient of a once-for-all revelation, my study has depicted Paul as "a full-blooded human agent" who thinks and grows within his body, his communities, and the larger contexts of his time.[1] This study does not find Paul forsaking the hope of bodily resurrection through his intense contextual interactions or conceiving a version of resurrection that contradicted his Jewish heritage. Rather, Paul developed his theology of resurrection into a more elaborate form, by which he could deal with the issues arising from reality and his faith in Christ and could facilitate the growth of faith communities. It seems to me that carrying his faith in Christ and struggling with it was the way that Paul received revelation. As already shown in the way God reveals himself in Christ, revelation is supposed to be fully divine and at the same time fully human. However, the human aspect of revelation is usually downplayed in Christian traditions. Applying cognitive linguistics, my study explores the human aspect of revelation to a fuller extent. Also, my study emphasizes an understanding of God as creative and active among faith communities. To me, God knows his creatures and communicates with people according to their designed nature. God also reveals himself through the interactions between members of faith communities and between faith communities and their environments. While the Christ event, his death and resurrection, is not a part of the current natural order, his believers can grasp this divine and supernatural revelation through conceptual blends (which is our significant cognitive phenomenon) of various experiences in community, in ritual, and in daily life.

My approach might be applied to another set of Pauline ideas: justification by faith. As we have seen, the hope of resurrection arises in Jewish traditions as the precondition of divine judgment and justification for the righteous. The whole set of these related ideas is traditionally conceptualized through images of vertical paths. As for Paul, the three significant developments that I identified in his resurrection thought appear to be important resources for him to illustrate his idea of justification by faith in Rom 5–7. First, the Adam-Christ typology that Paul first introduces in 1 Cor 15 elaborates the reversal pattern of resurrection into a dualistic sense. In Romans, Paul uses this typology to explain how one man's transgression leads to condemnation and how grace in one man leads to justification (Rom 5:15–16). A reversal pattern seems to reflect in Paul's description that many were made sinners by one man's disobedience and will be made righteous by one man's obedience (5:19). Second, we have also seen that the ideas of being physically united with Christ and dying together with him provide the crucial logic in Rom 7:1–6 to abrogate the authority of the law, and that baptism is the event in which the conjoined death happens (6:3–4). The same logic of the connection between physical union and justification seems to apply even to wife, husband, and children (1 Cor 7:14). Further research might consider the fuller range of experiential grounds of Paul's justification thought, such as the image schemas of verticality and reversal that I have mentioned, purification and pneumatic experience (1 Cor 6:11), sexual union (6:11–19), and the rite of expiation (Rom 3:25).

Setting suggestions of future studies aside, what this study has offered is a rigorous and testable method to identify developments in Paul's thinking and to distinguish them from merely contextual differences in his letters. This method comes from improving

---

[1] Colleen Shantz's phrase in *Paul in Ecstasy: The Neurobiology of the Apostle's Life and Thought* (Cambridge: Cambridge University Press, 2009), 2.

Jeffery R. Asher's approach by using cognitive linguistic tools.[2] While Asher looks for Paul's contextual reason (primarily intellectual) for inventing a certain idea in a letter and then pays attention to the continuing effects of that identified idea, I have further analyzed Paul's ideas in terms of experiential patterns and conceptual structures. Thus, by recognizing the reversal schema as the most fundamental innovation behind Paul's new idea of "transformation at resurrection," I have explored Paul's contextual reason for this innovation more thoroughly and identified the continuing effects of this innovation more clearly and extensively than prior scholarship. Indeed, the logic inherent in the reversal schema explains the emergences of several key ideas in the progression of Paul's development—the timing of transformation as at resurrection, the detachment of transformation from ascent, and the experiential aspect or the ritualization of transformation and resurrection. Thus, I have depicted the progression of Paul's resurrection theology from 1 Thessalonians to Romans as a process largely driven by the logic of the experiential pattern of reversal. My exploration then provides a profound case study of the integration of the body and the mind. Bodily experience contributes significantly to the way we think.

---

[2] J. R. Asher, *Polarity and Change in 1 Corinthians 15: A Study of Metaphysics, Rhetoric, and Resurrection* (Tübingen: Mohr Siebeck, 2000).

Bibliography

Achtemeier, Paul J. "Finding the Way to Paul's Theology: A Response to J. Christiaan Beker and J. Paul Sampley." Pages 25–36 in *Pauline Theology Volume 1: Thessalonians, Philippians, Galatians, Philemon*. Edited by Jouette M. Bassler. Minneapolis, MN: Fortress Press, 1991.

Ascough, Richard S. "Paul's 'Apocalypticism' and the Jesus Associations at Thessalonica and Corinth." Pages 151–86 in *Redescribing Paul and the Corinthians*. Edited by Ron Cameron and Merrill P. Miller. Atlanta: Society of Biblical Literature, 2011.

Asher, Jeffrey R. *Polarity and Change in 1 Corinthians 15: A Study of Metaphysics, Rhetoric, and Resurrection*. Tübingen: Mohr Siebeck, 2000.

Ashton, John. *The Religion of Paul the Apostle*. New Haven, CT: Yale University Press, 2000.

Barclay, John M. G. "'That you may not grieve, like the rest who have no hope' (1 Thess 4.13) Death and Early Christian Identity." Pages 217–35 in *Pauline Churches and Diaspora Jews*. Edited by John M. G. Barclay. Tübingen: Mohr Siebeck, 2011.

Barclay, John M. G. "Thessalonica and Corinth: Social Contrasts in Pauline Christianity." Pages 181–203 in *Pauline Churches and Diaspora Jews*. Edited by John M. G. Barclay. Tübingen: Mohr Siebeck, 2011.

Bassler, Jouette M. "Paul's Theology: Whence and Whither?" Pages 3–17 in *Pauline Theology Volume II: 1 & 2 Corinthians*. Edited by David M. Hay. Minneapolis, MN: Fortress Press, 1991.

Bassler, Jouette M. "Preface." Pages ix–xi in *Pauline Theology Volume 1: Thessalonians, Philippians, Galatians, Philemon*. Edited by Jouette M. Bassler. Minneapolis, MN: Fortress Press, 1991.

Batten, Alicia J. "Clothing and Adornment." *Biblical Theology Bulletin* 40, no. 3 (2010): 148–59.

Beasley-Murray, George R. *Baptism in the New Testament*. London: Macmillan, 1963.

Beker, J. Christiaan. *Paul the Apostle: The Triumph of God in Life and Thought*. Philadelphia: Fortress Press, 1980.

Beker, J. Christiaan. "Recasting Pauline Theology: The Coherence-Contigency Schema as Interpretive Model." Pages 15–24 in *Pauline Theology Volume 1: Thessalonians, Philippians, Galatians, Philemon*. Edited by Jouette M. Bassler. Minneapolis, MN: Fortress Press, 1991.

Betz, Hans Dieter. "Spirit, Freedom, Law: Paul's Message to the Galatian Churches." *Svensk Exegetisk Årsbok* 39 (1974): 145–60.

Betz, Hans Dieter. *Galatians: A Commentary on Paul's Letter to the Churches in Galatia*. Hermeneia. Minneapolis, MN: Fortress Press, 1979.

Bonneau, Normand. "The Logic of Paul's Argument on the Resurrection Body in 1 Cor 15:35-44a." *Science et Esprit* XL V/1 (1993): 79–92.

Bourguignon, Erika. *Psychological Anthropology: An Introduction to Human Nature and Cultural Differences*. New York: Holt, Rinehart & Winston, 1979.

Brazis, Paul W., Joseph C. Masdeu, and José Biller. *Localization in Clinical Neurology*. 3rd edition. Boston: Little, Brown, 1996.
Bruce, F. F. *The Epistle of Paul to the Galatians: A Commentary on the Greek Text*. Exeter: Paternoster Press, 1982.
Bruce, F. F. *The Epistles to the Colossians, to Philemon, and to the Ephesians*. Grand Rapids, MI: W. B. Eerdmans, 1984.
Buck, Charles, and Greer Taylor. *Saint Paul: A Study of the Development of His Thought*. New York: Scribner, 1969.
Bultmann, Rudolf. *The Theology of the New Testament*. New York: Charles Scribner's Sons, 1951.
Bultmann, Rudolf. "νεκρός, νεκρόω, νέκρωσις." Pages 892–95 in vol. 4 of *Theological Dictionary of the New Testament*. Edited by Gerhard Kittel. Translated and Edited by Geoffrey W. Bromiley. Grand Rapids, MI: W. B. Eerdmans, 1967.
Burchard, Christoph. "1 Korinther 15:39–41." *ZNW* 75 (1984): 233–58.
Choi, Agnes. "Boundary-Crossing in Christian Baptism." Pages 75–91 in *Early Christian Ritual Life*. Edited by Richard E. DeMaris, Jason T. Lamoreaux, and Steven C. Muir. New York: Routledge, 2018.
Chow, John K. "The Rich Patron." Pages 197–206 in *Christianity at Corinth: The Quest for the Pauline Church*. Edited by Edward Adams and David G. Horrell. Louisville, KY: Westminster John Knox Press, 2004.
Collins, John J. *The Apocalyptic Imagination: An Introduction to Jewish Apocalyptic Literature*. Grand Rapids, MI: W. B. Eerdmans, 1998.
Conzelmann, Hans. *1 Corinthians: A Commentary on the First Epistle to the Corinthians*. Translated by James W. Leitch. Bibliography and references by James W. Dunkly. Edited by George W. MacRae. Philadelphia: Fortress Press, 1975.
Cross, Anthony R. "Spirit- and Water-Baptism in 1 Corinthians 12.13." Pages 120–48 in *Dimensions of Baptism: Biblical and Theological Studies*. Edited by Stanley E. Porter and Anthony R. Cross. London: Sheffield Academic Press, 2002.
Cumont, Franz. *After Life in Roman Paganism: Lectures Delivered at Yale University on the Silliman Foundation*. New Haven, CT: Yale University Press, 1922.
Cuming, G. J. "Ἐποτίσθημεν (I Corinthians 12.13)." *NTS* 27 no. 2 (1981): 283–5.
Damasio, Antonio R. *The Feeling of What Happens: Body and Emotion in the Making of Consciousness*. New York: Harcourt, 1999.
D'Aquili Eugene G., and Andrew B. Newberg. *The Mystical Mind: Probing the Biology of Religious Experience Theology and the Sciences*. Minneapolis, MN: Fortress Press, 1999.
Davies, William D. *Paul and Rabbinic Judaism: Some Rabbinic Elements in Pauline Theology*. 4th edition. Philadelphia: Fortress Press, 1948.
De Boer, Martinus C. *Galatians: A Commentary*. Louisville, KY: Westminster John Knox Press, 2011.
DeMaris, Richard E. "Corinthian Religion and Baptism for the Dead (1 Corinthians 15:29): Insights from Archaeology and Anthropology." *JBL* 114 no. 4 (1995): 661–82.
DeMaris, Richard E. "Funerals and Baptisms, Ordinary and Otherwise: Ritual Criticism and Corinthian Rites." *Biblical Theology Bulletin* 29 no. 1 (1999): 23–34.
DeMaris, Richard E. "The Baptism of Jesus: A Ritual Critical Approach," Pages 137–58 in *The Social Setting of Jesus and the Gospels*. Edited by Wolfgang Stegemann, Bruce J. Malina, and Gerd Theissen. Minneapolis, MN: Fortress Press, 2002.
DeMaris, Richard E. *The New Testament in Its Ritual World*. London: Routledge, 2008.
DeMaris, Richard E. "Backing Away from Baptism: Early Christian Ambivalence about Its Ritual." *Journal of Ritual Studies* 27 no. 1 (2013): 11–19.

DeSilva, David A. *The Letter to the Galatians*. Grand Rapids, MI: W. B. Eerdmans, 2018.
Dodd, Charles H. "The Mind of St. Paul: A Psychological Approach." *Bulletin of the John Rylands Library* 17 no. 1 (1933): 3–17.
Dodd, Charles H. "The Mind of St. Paul: Change and Development." *Bulletin of the John Rylands Library* 18 no. 1 (1934): 3–44.
Donaldson, Terence L. "Zealot and Convert: The Origin of Paul's Christ-Torah Antithesis." *CBQ* 51 no. 4 (1989): 655–82.
Donaldson, Terence L. *Paul and the Gentiles: Remapping the Apostle's Convictional World*. Minneapolis, MN: Fortress Press, 1997.
Douglas, Mary. *Rules and Meanings: The Anthropology of Everyday Knowledge, Selected Readings*. Harmondsworth: Penguin Education, 1973.
Dunn, James D. G. *Baptism in the Holy Spirit: A Re-Examination of the New Testament Teaching on the Gift of the Spirit in Relation to Pentecostalism Today*. London: S. C. M. Press, 1970.
Dunn, James D. G. *The Epistles to the Colossians and to Philemon: A Commentary on the Greek Text*. Philadelphia: Fortress Press, 1971.
Dunn, James D. G. *Romans 1–8*. WBC 38. Dallas: Word Books, 1988.
Dunn, James D. G. *The Epistles to the Colossians and to Philemon*. Grand Rapids, MI: W. B. Eerdmans, 1996.
Dunn, James D. G. "'Baptized' as Metaphor." Pages 294–310 in *Baptism, the New Testament and the Church: Historical and Contemporary Studies in Honour of R. E. O. White*. Edited by Stanley E. Porter and Anthony R. Cross. Sheffield: Sheffield Academic Press, 1999.
Dunn, James D. G. "The New Perspective on Paul: Paul and the Law." Pages 131–42 in *The New Perspective on Paul: Collected Essays*. Edited by James D. G. Dunn; Tübingen: Mohr Siebeck, 2005.
Eastman, Susan G. *Paul and the Person: Reframing Paul's Anthropology*. Grand Rapids, MI: W. B. Eerdmans, 2017.
Engberg-Pedersen, Troels. *Paul and the Stoics*. Louisville, KY: Westerminster/John Knox, 2000.
Engberg-Pedersen, Troels. *Cosmology & Self in the Apostle Paul: The Material Spirit*. Oxford: Oxford University Press, 2010.
Esler, Philip F. *The First Christians in Their Social Worlds: Social Scientific Approaches to New Testament Interpretation*. New York: Routledge, 1994.
Evans, Elizabeth C. *Physiognomics in the Ancient World*. Philadelphia: American Philosophical Society, 1967.
Evans, Vyvyan, and Melanie Green. *Cognitive Linguistics: An Introduction*. Edinburgh: Edinburgh University, 2006.
Fauconnier, Gilles, and Mark Turner. *The Way We Think: Conceptual Blending and the Mind's Hidden Complexities*. New York: Basic Books, 2002.
Fee, Gordon D. *The First Epistle to the Corinthians*. Revised edition. Grand Rapids, MI: W. B. Eerdmans, 2014.
Ferguson, Everett. *Backgrounds of Early Christianity*. 3rd edition. Grand Rapids, MI: W. B. Eerdmans, 2003.
Ferguson, Everett. *Baptism in the Early Church: History, Theology, and Liturgy in the First Five Centuries*. Grand Rapids, MI: W. B. Eerdmans, 2009.
Fine, Steven. "A Note on Ossuary Burial and the Resurrection of the Dead in the First Century Jerusalem." *Journal of Jewish Studies* 51 no. 1 (2000): 69–76.
Foster, Paul. *Colossians*. London: Bloomsbury T&T Clark, 2016.

Fraser, Peter M. *Rhodian Funerary Monuments*. Oxford: Clarendon Press, 1977.
Furnish, Victor Paul. "Development in Paul's Thought." *Journal of the American Academy of Religion* 38 (1970): 289–303.
Furnish, Victor Paul. *II Corinthians*. 2nd edition. Garden City: Doubleday, 1984.
Garland, Robert. *The Greek Way of Death*. London: Duckworth, 1985.
Gäumann, Niklaus. *Taufe und Ethik: Studien zu Römer 6*. BEvTh47. München: Kaiser, 1967.
Gillman, John. "Signals of Transformation in 1 Thessalonians 4:13–18." *CBQ* 47 no. 2 (1985): 263–81.
Gillman, John. "A Thematic Comparison: 1 Cor 15:50–57 and 2 Cor 5:1–5." *JBL* 107 no. 3 (1988): 439–54.
Glenberg, Arthur M., Jessica K. Witt, and Janet Metcalfe. "From the Revolution to Embodiment: 25 Years of Cognitive Psychology." *Perspectives on Psychological Science* 8 no. 5 (2013): 573–85.
Goodman, Felicitas D. *Speaking in Tongues: A Cross-Cultural Study of Glossolalia*. Chicago, IL: University of Chicago Press, 1972.
Goodman, Felicitas D. *Ecstasy, Ritual, and Alternate Reality: Religion in a Pluralistic World*. Bloomington: Indiana University Press, 1988.
Gordon, R. L. "Mithraism and Roman Society." *Religion* 2 no. 2 (1972): 92–121.
Grady, Joseph, Todd Oakley, and Seana Coulson, "Blending and Metaphor." Pages 101–24 in *Metaphor in Cognitive Linguistics: Selected Papers from the Fifth International Cognitive Linguistics Conference, Amsterdam, July 1997*. Edited by Raymond. W. Gibbs and Gerard Steen. Amsterdam: John Benjamins, 1999.
Grimes, Ronald L. "Defining Nascent Ritual." *Journal of the American Academy of Religion* 50 no. 4 (1982): 539–55.
Grimes, Ronald L. "Research in Ritual Studies: A Programmatic Essay." Pages 1–33 in *Research in Ritual Studies: A Programmatic Essay and Bibliography*. Edited by Ronald L. Grimes. American Theological Library Association Bibliography Series 14. Metuchen, NJ: American Theological Library Association & Scarecrow Press, 1985.
Grimes, Ronald L. *Beginnings in Ritual Studies*. Studies in Comparative Religion, rev. ed. Columbia: University of South Carolina Press, 1995.
Harland, Philip A. *Associations, Synagogues and Congregations: Claiming a Place in Ancient Mediterranean Society*. Minneapolis, MN: Fortress Press, 2003.
Harris, Murray J. *The Second Epistle to the Corinthians: A Commentary on the Greek Text*. Grand Rapids, MI: W. B. Eerdmans, 2005.
Hartman, Lars. *'Into the Name of the Lord Jesus': Baptism in the Early Church*. Edinburgh: T&T Clark, 1997.
Hayward, Nicola. "Early Christian Funerary Ritual." Pages 112–29 in *Early Christian Ritual Life*. Edited by Richard E. DeMaris, Jason T. Lamoreaux, and Steven C. Muir. New York: Routledge, 2018.
Hertz, Robert. *Death and the Right Hand*. Translated by R. Needham and C. Needham. London: Cohen and West, 1960.
Hopkins, Keith. *Death and Renewal*. Sociological Studies in Roman History 2. Cambridge: Cambridge University Press, 1983.
Howe, Bonnie. *Because You Bear This Name: Conceptual Metaphor and the Moral Meaning of 1 Peter*. BibInt 81. Leiden: Brill, 2006.
Hunter, Harold D. *Spirit-Baptism: A Pentecostal Alternative*. Lanham, MD: University Press of America, 1983.
Hurd, John C., Jr. *The Origin of 1 Corinthians*. London: S.P.C.K., 1965.

Jeremias, Joachim. "Flesh and Blood Cannot Inherit the Kingdom of God (1 Cor. XV.50)." *NTS* 2 no. 3 (1956): 151–9.
Jervis, L. Ann. *Galatians*. Grand Rapids, MI: Baker, 2011.
Jewett, Robert. *Paul's Anthropological Terms: A Study of Their Use in Conflict Settings*. Leiden: Brill, 1971.
Jewett, Robert. *A Chronology of Paul's Life*. Philadelphia: Fortress Press, 1979.
Johnson, Mark. *The Body in the Mind: The Bodily Basis of Meaning, Imagination, and Reason*. Chicago, IL: University of Chicago Press, 1987.
Johnson, Mark. *The Meaning of the Body: Aesthetics of Human Understanding*. Chicago, IL: University of Chicago Press, 2007.
Johnson Hodge, Caroline. *If Sons, Then Heirs: A Study of Kinship and Ethnicity in the Letters of Paul*. Oxford: Oxford University Press, 2007.
Johnston, Sarah I. *Restless Dead: Encounters between the Living and the Dead in Ancient Greece*. Berkeley: University of California Press, 1999.
Kazen, Thomas. "The Role of Disgust in Priestly Purity Law: Insights from Conceptual Metaphor and Blending Theories." *Journal of Law, Religion and State* 3 no. 1 (2014): 62–92.
Kearl, Michael C. *Endings: A Sociology of Death and Dying*. New York: Oxford University Press, 1989.
Kim, Jung Hoon. *The Significance of Clothing Imagery in the Pauline Corpus*. JSNTSup 268. London: T&T Clark, 2004.
Kloppenborg, John. "An Analysis of the Pre-Pauline Formula 1 Cor 15:3b-5 in Light of Some Recent Literature." *CBQ* 40 no. 3 (1978): 351–67.
Knox, John. *Chapters in a Life of Paul*. Revised by John Knox. Edited by Douglas R. A. Hare. Macon: Mercer University Press, 1987.
Knox, John. "On the Pauline Chronology: Buck-Taylor-Hurd Revisited." Pages 258–74 in *The Conversation Continues: Studies in Paul & John: In Honor of J. Louis Martyn*. Edited by Robert T. Fortna and Beverly R. Gaventa. Nashville: Abingdon Press, 1990.
Kurtz, Donna C., and John Boardman. *Greek Burial Customs*. Ithaca: Cornell University Press, 1971.
Lakoff, George. *Women, Fire, and Dangerous Things: What Categories Reveal about the Mind*. Chicago, IL: University of Chicago Press, 1987.
Lakoff, George. "The Contemporary Theory of Metaphor." Pages 202–51 in *Metaphor and Thought*. 2nd edition. Edited by Andrew Ortony. Cambridge: Cambridge University Press, 1993.
Lakoff, George, and Mark Johnson. *Metaphors We Live By*. Chicago, IL: University of Chicago Press, 1980.
Lakoff, George, and Mark Johnson. *Philosophy in the Flesh: The Embodied Mind and Its Challenge to Western Thought*. New York: Basic Books, 1999.
Lakoff, George, and Mark Turner. *More than Cool Reason: A Field Guide to Poetic Metaphor*. Chicago, IL: University of Chicago Press, 1989.
Lampe, Geoffrey W. H. *The Seal of the Spirit: A Study in the Doctrine of Baptism and Confirmation in the New Testament and the Fathers*. London: Longmans, Green, 1951.
Lattimore, Richmond. *Themes in Greek and Latin Epitaphs*. Urbana: University of Illinois Press, 1962.
Leach, Edmund R. *Culture and Communication: The Logic by Which Symbols Are Connected: An Introduction to the Use of Structuralist Analysis in Social Anthropology*. Themes in the Social Sciences. New York: Cambridge University Press, 1976.

Lee, Michelle V. *Paul, the Stoics, and the Body of Christ*. Cambridge: Cambridge University Press, 2006.

Lincoln, Andrew T. *Paradise Now and Not Yet: Studies in the Role of the Heavenly Dimension in Paul's Thought with Special Reference to His Eschatology*. Cambridge: Cambridge University Press, 1981.

Lock, Margaret M. *East Asian Medicine in Urban Japan*. Berkeley: University of California, 1980.

Lohse, Eduard. *Colossians and Philemon*. Translated by William R. Poehlmann and Robert J. Karris. Edited by Helmut Koester. Philadelphia: Fortress Press, 1971.

Longenecker, Richard N. *Galatians*. Nashville: Thomas Nelson, 1990.

Longenecker, Richard N. "Is There Development in Paul's Resurrection Thought?" Pages 171–202 in *Life in the Face of Death: The Resurrection Message of the New Testament*. Edited by Richard N. Longenecker. Grand Rapids, MI: W. B. Eerdmans, 1998.

Lowe, John. "An Examination of Attempts to Detect Developments in St. Paul's Theology." *Journal of Theological Studies* 42 (1941): 129–42.

Luck, Georg. "Studia Divina in Vita Humana: On Cicero's 'Dream of Scipio' and Its Place in Greco-Roman Philosophy." *Harvard Theological Review* 49 no. 4 (1956): 207–18.

Lüdemann, Gerd. *Paul, Apostle to the Gentiles: Studies in Chronology*. Translated by F. Stanley Jones. Philadelphia: Fortress Press, 1984.

Lüdemann, Hermann. *Die Anthropologie des Apostels Paulus und ihre Stellung innerhalb seiner Heilslehre: nach den vier Hauptbriefen*. Kiel: Universitätsbuchhandlung, 1872.

Lundhaug, Hugo. "Conceptual Blending in the *Exegesis* of the Soul." Pages 141–60 in *Explaining Christian Origins and Early Judaism: Contributions from Cognitive and Social Science*. Edited by Petri Luomanen, Ilkka Pyysiäinen, and Risto Uro. Leiden: Brill, 2007.

Lundhaug, Hugo. *Images of Rebirth: Cognitive Poetics and Transformational Soteriology in the Gospel of Philip and the Exegesis on the Soul*. NHMS73. Leiden: Brill, 2010.

Luz, Ulrich. "Der Brief an die Kolosser." Pages 181–244 in *Die Briefe an die Galater, Epheser und Kolosser*. Edited by Jürgen Becker and Ulrich Luz. Göttingen: Vandenhoeck & Ruprecht, 1998.

McCane, Byron R. *Roll Back the Stone: Death and Burial in the World of Jesus*. Harrisburg, PA: Trinity Press International, 2003.

MacDonald, Margaret Y. *Colossians and Ephesians*. Collegeville, MM: Liturgical Press, 2008.

MacMullen, Ramsay. *Enemies of the Roman Order: Treason, Unrest, and Alienation in the Empire*. Cambridge, MA: Harvard University Press, 1966.

MacMullen, Ramsay. *Christianizing the Roman Empire: A.D. 100–400*. New Haven, CT: Yale University Press, 1984.

Martin, Dale B. *Slavery as Salvation: The Metaphor of Slavery in Pauline Christianity*. New Haven, CT: Yale University Press, 1990.

Martin, Dale B. "Tongues of Angels and Other Status Indicators." *Journal of the American Academy of Religion* 59 no. 3 (1991): 547–89.

Martin, Dale B. *The Corinthian Body*. New Haven, CT: Yale University Press, 1995.

Martin, Dale B. "Paul and the Judaism/Hellenism Dichotomy: Toward a Social History of the Question." Pages 29–62 in *Paul Beyond the Judaism/Hellenism Divide*. Edited by T. Engberg-Pedersen. Louisville, KY: Westminster John Knox Press, 2000.

Martin, Ralph P. *2 Corinthians*. 2nd edition. Grand Rapids, MI: Zondervan, 2014.

Martyn, J. Louis. *Galatians: A New Translation with Introduction and Commentary*. New York: Doubleday, 1997.

McKnight, Scott. *The Letter to the Colossians*. Grand Rapids, MI: W. B. Eerdmans, 2018.
Mearns, Christopher L. "Early Christian Eschatological Development in Paul: The Evidence of I and II Thessalonians." *New Testament Studies* 27 (1980–1): 137–57.
Mearns, Christopher L. "Early Christian Eschatological Development in Paul: The Evidence of 1 Corinthians." *Journal for the Study of the New Testament* 22 (1984): 19–35.
Meeks, Wayne A. "Image of the Androgyne: Some Uses of a Symbol in Earliest Christianity." *History of Religions* 13 no. 3 (1974): 165–208.
Meeks, Wayne A. *The First Urban Christians: The Social World of the Apostle Paul*. New Haven, CT: Yale University Press, 1983.
Meyer, Ben F. "Did Paul's View of the Resurrection of the Dead Undergo Development?" *Theological Studies* 47 no. 3 (1986): 363–87.
Meyers, Eric M. "Secondary Burial in Palestine." *The Biblical Archaeologist* 33 no. 1 (1970): 2–29.
Mitchell, Margaret M. *Paul and the Rhetoric of Reconciliation: An Exegetical Investigation of the Language and Composition of 1 Corinthians*. Tübingen: Mohr Siebeck, 1991.
Momigliano, Arnaldo. "Camillus and Concord." *The Classic Quarterly* 36 no. 3 (1942): 111–20.
Moo, Douglas J. *The Letters to the Colossians and to Philemon*. Grand Rapids, MI: W. B. Eerdmans, 2008.
Morissette, Rodolphe. "La condition de ressuscité, 1 Cor 15, 35–49: Structure littéraire de la péricope." *Biblica* 53 no. 2 (1972): 208–28.
Murphy-O'Connor, Jerome. "Being at Home in the Body We Are in Exile from the Lord (2 Cor. 5:6b)." *Revue Biblique* 93 no. 2 (1986): 214–21.
Mylonas, George E. *Mycenae and the Mycenaean Age*. Princeton, NJ: Princeton University Press, 1966.
Næss, Åshild. "How Transitive Are Eat and Drink Verbs?" Pages 27–43 in *The Linguistics of Eating and Drinking*. Edited by John Newman. Amsterdam;: John Benjamins, 2009.
Neufeld, Dietmar. "Under the Cover of Clothing: Scripted Clothing Performances in the Apocalypse of John." *Biblical Theology Bulletin* 35 no. 2 (2005): 67–76.
Neyrey, Jerome. *Paul in Other Words: A Cultural Reading of His Letters*. Louisville, KY: Westminster/John Knox Press, 1990.
Newman, John. "Eating and Drinking as Sources of Metaphor in English." *Cuadernos Filología Inglesa* 6 no. 2 (1997): 213–31.
Nickelsburg, George W. E. *Resurrection, Immortality, and Eternal Life in Intertestamental Judaism and Early Christianity*. Cambridge, MA: Harvard University Press for Harvard Theological Studies, 2006.
Nickelsburg, George W. E., and James C. VanderKam. *1 Enoch 2: A Commentary on the Book of 1 Enoch Chapters 37–82*. Minneapolis, MN: Fortress, 2012.
Padel, Ruth. *In and Out of the Mind: Greek Images of the Tragic Self*. Princeton, NJ: Princeton University Press, 1992.
Panagiotidou, Olympia, and Roger Beck. *The Roman Mithras Cult: A Cognitive Approach*. London: Bloomsbury, 2016.
Pfleiderer, Otto. *Paulinism: A Contribution to the History of Primitive Christian Theology*. Translated by Edward Peters. London: Williams and Norgate, 1891.
Pohlenz, Max. *Die Stoa: Geschichte einer geistigen Bewegung*. Göttingen: Vandenhoeck [und] Ruprecht, 1948–1949.
Porter, Stanley E. *Idioms of the Greek New Testament*. 2nd edition. Sheffield: JSOT Press, 1996.

Rebillard, Éric. *The Care of the Dead in Late Antiquity*. Translated by Elizabeth T. Rawlings and Jeanine Routier-Pucci. Ithaca: Cornell University Press, 2009.

Ridderbos, Herman. *Paul: An Outline of His Theology*. Translated by John Richard de Witt. Grand Rapids, MI: W. B. Eerdmans, 1975.

Robbins, Vernon K. "Conceptual Blending and Early Christian Imagination." Pages 161–95 in *Explaining Christian Origins and Early Judaism: Contributions from Cognitive and Social Science*. Edited by Petri Luomanen, Ilkka Pyysiäinen, and Risto Uro. Leiden: Brill, 2007.

Robinson, Betsey A. "Fountains and the Formation of Culture of Water at Roman Corinth." Pages 111–40 in *Urban Religion in Roman Corinth: Interdisciplinary Approaches*. Edited by Daniel N. Schowalter and Steven J. Friesen. HTS 53. Cambridge, MA: Harvard University Press, 2005.

Robertson, Archibald, and Alfred Plummer. *A Critical and Exegetical Commentary on the First Epistle of St Paul to the Corinthians*. 2nd edition. Edinburgh: T&T Clark, 1971.

Roebuck, Carl. *Corinth vol. 14: The Asklepieion and Lerna*. Princeton, NJ: American School of Classical Studies at Athens, 1951.

Rogers, E. R. "Ἐποτίσθημεν Again." *NTS* 29 (1983): 139–42.

Roitto, Rikard. *Behaving as a Christ-Believer: A Cognitive Perspective on Identity and Behavior Norms in Ephesians*. Winona Lake, IN: Eisenbrauns, 2011.

Sabatier, A. *The Apostle Paul: A Sketch of the Development of His Doctrine*. Translated by George G. Findlay. New York: Pott, 1891.

Sanders, Ed Parish. "Literary Dependence in Colossians." *JBL* 85 no. 1 (1966): 28–45.

Sanders, Ed Parish. *Paul and Palestinian Judaism: A Comparison of Patterns of Religion*. Philadelphia: Fortress Press, 1977.

Schnackenburg, Rudolf. *Baptism in the Thought of St. Paul: A Study in Pauline Theology*. Translated by George R. Beasley-Murray. New York: Herder and Herder, 1964.

Schüssler Fiorenza, Elisabeth. *In Memory of Her: A Feminist Theological Reconstruction of Christian Origins*. New York: Crossroad, 1983.

Schweitzer, Albert. *Paul and His Interpreters: A Critical History*. Translated by W. Montgomery. New York: Schocken Books, 1964.

Segal, Alan F. *Paul the Convert: The Apostolate and Apostasy of Saul the Pharisee*. New Haven, CT: Yale University Press, 1990.

Segal, Alan F. *Life after Death: A History of the Afterlife in Western Religion*. New York: Doubleday, 2004.

Shantz, Colleen. *Paul in Ecstasy: The Neurobiology of the Apostle's Life and Thought*. Cambridge: Cambridge University Press, 2009.

Slingerland, Edward. *What Science Offers the Humanities: Integrating Body and Culture*. Cambridge: Cambridge University Press, 2008.

Smith, Morton. *Clement of Alexandria and a Secret Gospel of Mark*. Cambridge, MA: Harvard University Press, 1973.

Squire, Michael. "*Corpus Imperii*: Verbal and Visual Figurations of the Roman 'Body Politic.'" *Word & Image* 31 no. 3 (2015): 305–30.

Stowers, Stanley. "What Is 'Pauline Participation in Christ'?" Pages 352–71 in *Redefining First-Century Jewish and Christian Identities: Essays in Honor of Ed Parish Sanders*. Edited by Fabian E. Udoh. Notre Dame: University of Notre Dame Press, 2008.

Sweetser, Eve. "Blended Spaces and Performativity," *Cognitive Linguistics* 11 no. 3 (2001): 305–33.

Teichmann, Ernst. *Die paulinische Vorstellungen von Auferstehung und Gericht*. Freiburg: Akademische Verlagsbuchhandlung, 1896.
Tambiah, Stanley Jeyaraja. *Culture, Thought, and Social Action: An Anthropological Perspective*. Cambridge: Harvard University Press, 1985.
Tappenden, Frederick S. "Aural-Performance, Conceptual Blending, and Intertextuality: The (Non-)Use of Scripture in Luke 24.45–48." Pages 180–200 in *The Gospel of Luke*. Edited by Thomas R. Hatina; London: T&T Clark, 2010.
Tappenden, Frederick S. "Luke and Paul in Dialogue: Ritual Meals and Risen Bodies as Instances of Conceptual Blending." Pages 203–28 in *Resurrection of the Dead: Biblical Traditions in Dialogue*. Edited by Geert van Oyen and Tom Shepherd; Leuven: Peeters, 2012.
Tappenden, Frederick S. *Resurrection in Paul: Cognition, Metaphor, and Transformation*. Atlanta: Society of Biblical Literature, 2016.
Taylor. Joan E. *The Immerser: John the Baptist within Second Temple Judaism*. Grand Rapids, MI: W. B. Eerdmans, 1997.
Thaden, Robert H von, Jr. *Sex, Christ, and Embodied Cognition: Paul's Wisdom for Corinth*. Dorset, UK: Deo., 2012.
Theissen, Gerd. *The Social Setting of Pauline Christianity: Essays on Corinth*. Translated and edited by John H. Schütz. Philadelphia: Fortress Press, 1982.
Thrall, Margaret E. *A Critical and Exegetical Commentary on the Second Epistle to the Corinthians*. Edinburgh: T&T Clark, 1994.
Thrall, Margaret E. "Paul's Journey to Paradise: Some Exegetical Issues in 2 Cor 12,2-4." Pages 347–63 in *The Corinthian Correspondence*. Edited by Reimund Bieringer; Leuven: Leuven University Press, 1996.
Turner, Victor M. *The Ritual Process: Structure and Anti-Structure*. Chicago, IL: Aldine, 1969.
Toynbee, Jocelyn M. C. *Death and Burial in the Roman World*. Aspects of Greek and Roman Life; London: Thames & Hudson, 1971.
Uro, Risto. *Ritual and Christian Beginnings: A Socio-Cognitive Analysis*. Oxford: Oxford University Press, 2016.
Usami, Kôshi. "'How Are the Dead Raised?' (1 Cor 15,35-58)." *Biblica* 57 no. 4 (1976): 468–93.
Van Gennep, Arnold. *The Rites of Passage*. Translated by Monika Vizedom and Gabrielle Caffee. Chicago, IL: University of Chicago Press, 1960.
Van Nijif, Onno M. *The Civic World of Professional Associations in the Roman East*. Amsterdam: J.C. Gieben, 1997.
Vos, Geerhardus. "Alleged Development in Paul's Teaching on Resurrection." *Princeton Theological Review* 27 (1929): 193–226.
Watson, Duane F. "Paul's Rhetorical Strategy in 1 Corinthians 15." Pages 231–49 in *Rhetoric and the New Testament: Essays from the 1992 Heidelberg Conference*. Edited by Stanley E. Porter and Thomas H. Olbricht. Sheffield: Sheffield Academic Press, 1993.
Wedderburn, A. J. M. *Baptism and Resurrection: Studies in Pauline Theology against Its Greco-Roman Background*. Wissenschafliche Untersuchungen zum Neuen Testament 44. Tübingen: Mohr, 1987.
Weiss, Johannes. *The History of Primitive Christianity*. Completed after the author's death by Rudolf Knopf. Translated and edited by Frederick C. Grant. 2 vols. New York: Wilson-Erickson, 1937.

Westerholm, Stephen. *Perspectives Old and New on Paul: The "Lutheran" Paul and His Critics*. Grand Rapids, MI: W. B. Eerdmans, 2004.

Winkelman, Michael. *Shamans, Priests, and Witches: A Cross-Cultural Study of Magico-Religious Practitioners*. Anthropological Research Papers 44. Tempe: Arizona State University, 1992.

Wright, N. T. *The Resurrection of the Son of God*. Minneapolis, MN: Fortress Press, 2003.

Ancient Source Index

OLD TESTAMENT
Genesis
2:7   67
12:1–3   131
37:35   20

Judges
23:27–31   29

Job
14:10–12   20
14:20   20

Psalms
22:30   19
30:4   20
55:15   20
139:8   20

Proverbs
9:18   20

Isaiah
11:8   20
14:15   20
25:8   121
29:10   99
30:27–28   96
44:3   95

Ezekiel
39:29   95

Daniel
1–3   83
12   27
12:1–3   4, 16, 29
12:2   20, 26
12:2–3   29
12:3   23

Joel
2:28   95

Amos
9:2   20

NEW TESTAMENT
Matthew
3:7   92
3:7–8   91, 96
3:11   96
3:12   96
28:19   96

Mark
1:4   91, 96
1:8   91, 95, 96
10:38–39   94
10:39   92

John
11:39   66
12:24   52

Acts
2:38   96
8:12   96
8:16   96
10:44–48   79
10:47   92
10:47–48   96
19:1–6   79
19:5   96

Romans
1:4   114
3:25   141
4:19   113
5:14–15   128
5:15–16   141
5:19   141

5:21	128	4:10	46
6:2	129	4:12	108
6:3–4	1, 10, 13, 38, 92, 96, 106, 109, 123, 124, 126, 127, 129, 130, 132, 133, 134, 135, 139, 140, 141	4:28	80
		5	13
		5:2	121
		5:5	105
		5:6	104
6:4	94, 124, 133	5:10	45, 104
6:5	133	5:11	104
6:6	131, 132	5:12	108
6:7	129	6:1–5	81
6:8	133	6:2	129
6:23	128	6:3–4	129
7:1–6	141	6:9–11	51
7:6	128, 129	6:10–17	105
8:1	21	6:11	96, 105, 141
8:2	21	6:11–19	141
8:9	128	6:11–20	84
8:10	129, 134	6:12	51
8:10–13	133, 134	6:12–20	86
8:11	133, 134	6:13	51
8:13	133	6:15	86
8:21	106	6:17	76, 86
8:23	8	6:17–19	103
8:23–27	134	6:19	86
8:26	77	7:2–3	129
12:1	133	7:4	129
12:2	12, 104	7:14	141
15:15–19	79	8	47
15:18–19	77	8:1	51
16:1–2	51	8:1–3	88
		8:1–8	84
1 Corinthians		8:4	51
1:10	88	8:7	51
1:11–17	91	8:10	47, 51
1:13–17	92, 95	8:10–13	88
1:13	96	9:1	81
1:15	96	10	47
1:18–19	88	10:2	94
1:26–28	105	10:10	108
2:10–11	81	10:14–22	86
2:10–14	81	10:23	51
2:12	76, 104	10:27	47
2:16	103	11:16–21	108
3:2	99	11:17–26	51
3:6–7	99	11:18–22	88
3:7–18	108	11:18–34	81
4:8	51	11:29	86
4:9–14	46	12	13, 86

12:1–3	89	15:20–27	69
12:1–4	101	15:21–22	69
12:1–11	79, 101	15:22	69
12:2	51	15:23	37
12:6	81	15:24	31
12:7–12	108	15:24–25	31, 69
12:10	108	15:25–26	36, 37, 69, 103, 105
12:12–13	103	15:29	46
12:12–27	88	15:30–31	31
12:13	1, 21, 72, 76, 81, 86, 87, 89, 91, 92, 94, 95, 96, 97, 98, 99, 100, 101, 103, 104, 105, 107, 116, 122, 123, 127, 132, 139	15:35	15, 33, 42, 54, 55, 57, 58, 59, 63, 67
		15:35–44	67, 124
		15:35–50	12, 58
		15:35–54	34, 38
		15:35–57	41, 42
12:14–27	86	15:35–58	13, 32, 53, 54, 55, 57, 66, 70, 138
12:25	86, 88, 91, 101		
12:25–30	101	15:36	32, 52
12:27	86	15:36–38	15, 32, 33, 42, 53, 54, 56, 58, 59, 63, 65
12:28	81		
12:28–14:40	86	15:36–44	57
12:29–30	101	15:37	32, 61
14:2	79	15:38	55, 61, 62
14:4	79	15:39	61, 63, 65
14:5–6	79, 80, 101	15:39–41	42, 51, 54, 55, 58, 61, 62, 63, 65, 121
14:6	77		
14:9	79	15:39–44	56, 65
14:14	79	15:40	22, 33, 63
14:14–15	1, 77	15:41	63
14:15	80	15:42	33, 59, 61
14:18	80	15:42–43	22
14:18–19	80	15:42–44	11, 12, 16, 32, 33, 42, 51, 53, 54, 57, 63, 65, 66, 67, 105
14:23	79		
14:24–25	46		
14:26	77	15:44	57, 66, 67, 105
14:27–40	101	15:44–45	128
14:28–30	79, 80	15:44–49	42, 54, 57, 63, 66, 67, 105
14:32	80		
14:36–38	86	15:45	103
14:37–39	81	15:45–48	58
15	11, 12, 15, 16, 31, 41, 42, 126	15:46–49	69
		15:47	67
15:1–34	13, 53	15:47–49	22
15:3–4	66, 124	15:48–49	66
15:8	81	15:49–54	69
15:12–34	31	15:50	16, 42, 56, 57, 69, 121
15:18	31		
15:20	37, 66	15:50–51	66
15:20–22	67	15:50–54	57

15:51	67, 69	5:2–3	118
15:52	121	5:3–4	120
15:52–54	15, 38, 54	5:4	84, 121
15:53	121	5:5	120, 122
15:53–54	121	5:6	120
15:54	121	5:7	116, 120
15:54–57	69	5:8	84
15:55–58	54	5:10	84
		8:17	21
2 Corinthians		10–13	
1:8–10	84	11:5–6	85
1:23	117	12	84, 85
2:8–10	10	12:1–4	1, 77, 82, 85
2:12	10, 13, 140	12:5–9	85
3–5	13	12:9–10	113
3:14	107	12:10	85
3:14–18	107	12:12	78
3:16	107	12:15	117
3:17	103, 127		
3:17–18	76, 106	*Galatians*	
3:18	12, 13, 71, 72, 104, 107, 114, 117, 122, 127, 139	1:6	78
		1:12	77, 81
		1:16	78
4–5	84, 109, 124	2:17	21
4:6	112, 117, 135	2:19	128, 129, 130, 131
4:7	109, 112, 114	2:19–20	131, 132
4:7–9	112	3:1	131
4:7–11	110, 115, 116, 118	3:1–5	131
4:7–18	109	3:2	78
4:8–9	113	3:5	103
4:10	113, 114, 115, 118	3:6–4:7	131
4:10–11	118	3:16–18	131
4:11	109, 114, 115, 118	3:27	94, 96
4:12	104, 118	3:27–28	1, 94, 97, 98
4:13–14	116	4:6	103
4:14	114, 116	4:13–14	78
4:15	116	4:14	78
4:16	109, 116, 117, 120, 134	4:19	78
		6:4	128
4:16–18	116, 120, 122	6:14	128, 130, 131
4:17	117, 136		
5	85	*Ephesians*	
5:1	121	4:12	86
5:1–2	118	5:18	99
5:1–4	109, 118, 121		
5:1–5	114	*Philippians*	
5:1–7	109	3:20–21	12
5:1–8	21	3:21	9, 135
5:2	118, 120, 121		

Colossians	
1:24	86
2:12	132, 133
2:12–13	134
3:1	132, 135
3:5	135
3:9–10	135

1 Thessalonians	
1:6	29, 103
1:6–10	29
1:10	29, 30
2:2	29
2:16–19	30
3:3–4	29
4	11, 12, 13, 31
4:13	30
4:13–15	20
4:13–17	137, 138
4:13–18	4, 15, 66, 84
4:14	20, 26
4:15–17	108
4:16	20, 26, 29, 135
4:16–18	29
4:17	29
5:2–9	29
5:3	30
5:9	30

OLD TESTAMENT
PSEUDEPIGRAPHA

1 Enoch	
22:1–13	29
71:11	23, 24, 83
71:5	24
102–104	28–9
102:5	28
103:4–8	28
104:1–6	28

2 Enoch	
22:8	83

4 Ezra	
7:97	30
7:125	30

2 Bar	
49–51	26, 30
51:4–6	26

2 Maccabees	
7:10–11	26

Wisdom of Solomon	
29	50

Author Index

Achtemeier, P. J. 6
Ascough, R. S. 44, 45, 46
Asher, J. R. 7, 11, 12, 16, 22, 23, 31, 41, 50, 51, 53–5, 56–7, 62–3, 65, 67, 83, 142

Barclay, J. M. G. 46, 81
Bassler, J. M. 5
Bassler, J. M. 6
Batten, A. J. 121
Beker, J. C. 6
Boardman, J. 47
Bonneau, N. 41, 55, 57, 65
Bourguignon, E. 98
Bultmann, R. 113
Burchard, C. 62

Choi, A. 96
Chow, J. K. 51
Cross, A. R. 95
Cumont, F. V. M. 44, 47, 48, 50

d'Aquili, E. G. 82, 83
DeMaris, R. E. 43, 47, 49, 90, 97, 105
Dodd, C. H. 10, 71, 84, 108
Douglas, M. 74
Dunn, J. D. G. 93, 95, 96, 99, 133, 134

E Nickelsburg, G. W. 55
Eastman, S. G. 76, 77
Engberg-Pedersen, T. 78, 116, 117
Esler, P. F. 78, 79, 80
Evans V. 3, 3–4, 34, 75, 90

Fauconnier, G. 34, 35–7, 58, 65, 90, 91, 92, 112
Fee, G. D. 51, 55, 62, 80, 93, 95, 99, 101
Ferguson, E. 43, 47, 49, 51, 91
Fine, S. 48
Fraser, P. M. 46
Furnish, V. P. 114, 116, 116

Gillman, J. 120, 122
Glenberg, A. M. 3
Goodman, F. 79, 98
Gordon, R. L. 49
Green M. 3–4, 18, 34, 90
Grimes, R. L. 90

Harris, M. J. 113, 114, 117, 120
Hay, D. M. 6
Hertz, R. 48
Hodge, C. J. 131
Hunter, H. D. 93

Jeremias, J. 15–16
Jewett, R. 82, 84
Johnson, E. E. 6
Johnson, M. 3, 17, 18, 19, 20, 23, 24, 32

Kim, J. H. 121
Kurtz, D. C. 47

Lakoff, G. 3, 17, 19, 20, 21, 26, 32
Lampe, G. W. H. 94
Lattimore, R. 45–6
Leach, E. R. 43
Lee, M. V. 75
Lincoln, A. T. 82
Longenecker, R. N. 15, 16, 84, 107, 108
Luck, G. 50
Luck, G. 74

MacMullen, R. 45
Martin, D. B. 8, 49–50, 51, 71, 75, 76, 79, 84, 103, 105, 108, 110, 113, 116
McCane, B. R. 46, 48, 66
Mearns, C. L. 11
Meeks, W A. 94, 126
Metcalfe, J. 3
Meyers, E. M. 48
Mitchell, M. M. 72–3, 86, 87, 88, 103
Momigliano, A. 88

Mylonas, G. E. 47–8

Næss, Å. 100
Neufeld, D. 121
Newberg, A. B. 82, 83
Newman, J. 99, 100

Pfleiderer, O. 7–8
Plummer, A. 62

Rebillard, É. 45, 52
Robertson, A. 62
Rogers, E. R. 99

Sabatier, A. 7
Segal, A. 6–7, 83
Shantz, C. 2, 6–7, 77, 79, 80, 81, 82, 83, 85, 104
Smith, M. 91
Squire, M. 88

Stowers, S. 131
Sweetser, E. 90

Tappenden, F. S. 4, 8–9, 11, 15, 19, 20, 21, 28, 71–2, 73, 116, 117, 118, 126, 132, 133, 134
Teichmann, E. 8
Theissen, G. 51
Thrall, M. E. 109–10, 117, 120
Thrall, M. E. 84, 85
Toynbee, J. M. C. 47
Turner, M. 17, 34, 35–7, 58, 65, 90, 91, 112

van Nijif, O. M. 44

Wedderburn, A. J. M. 10, 127, 130, 131, 133, 134
Winkelman, M. 81
Witt, J. K. 3

Subject Index

Note: **bold** page numbers refer to section headings.

Adam 42, 57, 67–9, 110, 128, 131
aether 49–50
afterlife 41–2, 45, 47–52, 56, 66, 74, 83, 107–8, 115–16, 138
altered states of consciousness (ASC) 55, 77, 79–82, 137
ascent/heavenly ascent 16, 20, **23–31**, 42, 48–9, 50–2, 71, 74, 83–5, 107
  non-bodily ascent 42, 49, 52, 74, 83–5
  and resurrection 16, 20, 25–31, 71
  ritual assistance for 48–9
  and transformation 24, 26–7, 29–31, 85, 107
Augustus's statue from Prima Porta 88–9

baptism
  bodily experience of immersion 86–7, **92–8**, 101, 103, 127, 132
  co-burial with Christ 11n. 45, 38–9, 109, 124, 128, 130, 132
  for the dead 43–4, 49
  as initiation and boundary-crossing 87, 91, **92–8**, 99, 101, 105–6, 112n. 14, 123, 126–9, 130, 132, 136
  as metaphor for judgment 96, 98
  purification 91, 96–7, 141
  and reception of the Spirit 72, 81, 85, 87, **93–6**, 101–5, 107, 112n. 14, 139
  as resistance to the empire 72, 97
  as resurrection with Christ 109, **129–35**, 139, 141
  reversal pattern 13, 39, **126–9**, 132, 135–6, 137
  Spirit-baptism 93–6
  traditional formula of baptism in early Christianity 94n. 109, 97

body
  as container (in-out orientation) 21, 89, 99–105, 109, 113–15, 116, 118, 120–2, 127, 129, 131, 133–5
  and cosmos 22, 26, 38, 50–2, 56, 62–3, **72–6**, 87–8, 103, 129
  earthly body 21, 33, 42, 83, 121–2
  and flesh 24, 47–8, 50, 63n. 90, 83, 104, 115–17, 135
  heavenly body 21, 33, 121–2
  malleable body 71–2, **75–6**, 103
  porous body 75, 103, 107, 139
  resurrected body 8–9, 11–12, 15–16, 22–3, 26–7, 31–4, 41–2, **55–69**, 107, 118–23
  and society 73–6, 86–9, 103
  and self 2, 76–7, 83–4, 104
  σῶμα πνευματικόν 12, 65–9, 105, 128
  σῶμα ψυχικόν 12, 66, 67, 128
  transformation of the body 7, 9, 11–14, 15–17, **23–33**, 38, 41–2, 54–7, **61–70**, 71–2, 77, 82–7, 98, **100–6**, 108–9, 117–22
body metaphor 72–5, 85–9, 93, 97, 101, 103, 139
  Christ's body 21, 72, 75–6, **86–9**, 97, 100, 101–6, 116, 127, 129
  rhetoric of *homonoia* 87–88
  and social hierarchy 73–6, 86–9, 101, 103
boundary-crossing 43, 87, 91–2, 96, 98, 106, 123, 126–7, 129, 130–2
butcher metaphor for surgeon 34–6, 38

Christ
  Adam-Christ typology 42, 54, 57–8, 67–9, 128, 141

the body of Christ 21, 72, 75–6, **86–9**, 97, 100, 101–6, 116, 127, 129
  in Christ 5, 7–8, 21, 67–9, 95–7, 104, 107, 127, 129, 131
clothing metaphor 109, 118–23, 135
co-burial with Christ 11n. 45, 38–9, 109, 124, 128, 130, 132–3
  union with Christ (participation in Christ) 39, 90, 126–7, 129, 130
cognitive linguistics 3–5, 11–13, 16, 34–6, 39, 41, 69
conceptual blending theory 13, 17, **34–9**, 57–8, 69, 72, 86, 89–90, 122
  backward projection 36, 38–9, 97–8, 105, 123, 127
  clash of conceptual structures (*see also* double-scope blending) 38
  double-scope blending **38–9**, 65, 67
  elements and relations 20, **35**, 61–2
  emergent structure 36, 39, 65–6, 70, 115
  human scale 36–7, 39, 58, 123
  mental space 35, 61, 62–3, 98
  single-scope blending **36–8**, 59, 61, 93, 99
conceptual metaphor 3, 13, 17, 19, 21, 34–5, 39, 41
conceptual structure (*see also* image schema) 16–17, 23, 25–6, 29, 31, 34–5, 38, 90, 93, 99–101, 110, 117
consciousness (*see also* altered states of consciousness)
  and religious experience 55, 77, 79, 82, 137
  and transformation 77, 137
container metaphor 3, 18–19, **20–6**, 31–2, 49, 55, 67, 74, 78, 81, 85, 89, 99–105, 109–10, 114–15, 119–20
contextual reading of Paul 1–4, 5–14, 16, 40, 52–3, 70, 141–2
Corinthian community 41, 46, 51, 72, 79, 82, 89, 101
Corpus Imperii 72, 88, 97
cosmology
  cosmic polarity 20–3, 31, 42, 51–2, 56–7, 59–66, 83, 106, 138
  hierarchical cosmos 11, 22, 26, 47, **49–52**, 56, 62–3, 66, 69–70, 73, 106
  and human body 12–13, 16. 19, 41–2, **48–52**, 56, **72–7**, 83, 87, 103, 129

cross 78, 113, 131–2

death
  baptismal death 38–9, 123–4, 127, 130–5, 141
  Christ's death 39, 66, 98, 104, 109, 113, 124, 127, 130–5
  as cosmic power 21, 25–6, 37–8, 69, 121, 128
  metaphorical conceptualization of real death 19–20
  as metaphor for boundary-crossing 39, 129–30
  Paul's idea of death 5–6, 8–10, 33, 37–8, 108–9
death rites 2, 9, 12–13, 41–2, **43–8**, 107, 130, 137
  Christian practices 45–7
  and corpse (*see also* decomposition of the body)
  funerary practices 43–7
  inhumation and cremation 43, 52
  Mithras practices 49–50
  secondary burial 48
  social function 44–6
  transition and boundary-crossing 43, 47–8
  tomb and memorial meal 44, 46–7
  vicarious funeral 43, 46
decomposition of the body 51–2, 55–8, 61, 66, 69, 107, 124n. 53, 138
  and the transition of the deceased 47–8, 49–52
divine judgment 16, 23, 27–31, 49, 55, 91, 96, 98
  and exaltation 16, 26, 27–31
  and overturning 29–31, 55
  and resurrection 16, 23, 29–31
drinking metaphor 86–7, 94n. 108, **98–100**, 104, 112n. 14, 132
dwelling metaphor 109, 118–23

ecstatic experience
  escape of the body 83–5, 100, 104, 107
  somatic bewilderment 9, 82–5, 104, 137
embodied/embodiment **2–10, 15–17**, 35–6, 41–2, 71–2, 82, 88, 90, 95, 101, 129–32
eschatology
  and immortality 7, 19, 21, 28–29

and Paul's development 7–8, 67–69
and transformation 9, 13, 31, 105, 107,
    109, 121–4, 126, 135
eternity
  eternal life 27, 114, 117–18, 120, 128,
    136
  as spatially correlated 23, 83n. 65
bodily experience
  as basis for language/metaphor 3–4,
    17–27, 32, 34, 98–100
  as culturally interpreted 71–2, 79,
    82–5, 95
  as generative of ideas 1–2, 4, 6, 9,
    15–27, 137
  recurrent patterns/experiential patterns
    (*see also* image schema) 3–4, 13,
    15–16, 17–27, 29, 35, 39, 69, 90

glossolalia 77–81, 85–6, 98

image schema
  container schema **20–6**, 49, 67, 74, 78,
    81, 85, 100–1, 112–14, 118–20, 134
  metaphorical projection of image
    schema 4, 17, 19, 115
  path schema **23–7**, 30–2, 50, 55, 61,
    137, 141
  verticality schema 4, **17–20**, 22, 23, 25,
    42, 49, 51, 55, 69
in-out correlation 20, 74, 89, 100–1, 109,
  115, 118, 121–2

Jewish-Hellenistic dichotomy 7–11, 84
John the Baptist 91–2, 95–6, 98
journey metaphor (*see also* path schema)
  3, 32

life
  life in/through death 112–18, 130–5,
    139–40
  as metaphorically conceptualized
    17, 19–20
  resurrection life 8, 25–31, 39, 123

mental space
  blended space 35–9, 58–9, 61, 67, 97,
    101, 127
  framing input 36–7, 59, 61, 93
  focus input 36–7, 59, 61, 93

generic space 35, 61–2, 65, 110, 113–24,
  123, 127
input space 35–6, 38, 58–9
metaphor theory 3, 34–6, 95, 97
mind
  and body 2–3, 74, 101, 142
  and soul 74, 87, 116
mortality 1, 13, 19, 42, 84, 108–10, 113,
  115–18, 134–5, 139–40

neuroscience
  and ancient ideas of the body 71–2, 76–7
  and Paul's development 7, 76–7, 80, 87
  and religious experience/ecstatic
    experience 72, 77, 80, 82, 85, 87

Parousia 8–9, 29, 108, 135, 138
Paul's development
  versus contextual interpretation (*see also*
    contextual reading of Paul) 5–6, 9–11
  and Jewish-Hellenistic dichotomy
    7–11, 84
  the Pleiderer-Teichmann line 7–11, 84
  psychological approach 10, 72, 84,
    108–9
  timing of transformation 11–13, **15–17**,
    27–31, 33–4, 40, **62–6**, 138, 142
Plato 50, 74, 83
polarity
  in baptism/reversal schema 105,
    124, 126–9
  cosmic polarity 16, 20, 23, 31–3, 38, 42,
    49, 51–2, 56–7, 61–6, 83, 137–8
  eschatological polarity 126, 129
  temporal polarity 42, 57–8, 65–6,
    67–70, 105
purity and pollution 50, 91, 96, 105, 141

resurrection
  and Antiochus IV 27, 29–30, 55
  and baptism 11, 109, **129–35**, 139, 141
  and creation 56, 62–3, 65
  experienced resurrection 10–11, 13,
    137, 140
  and immortal soul 7–8, 27–9, 42, 116
  as precondition for divine judgment 23,
    26n. 42, 27, 29–31, 55, 141
  as restoration 25–7, 52, 55, 137

and transformation (*see also*
    transformation at resurrection) **15–17**, 27–31, 33–4, 40, **62–6**, 138, 142
  as vindication 27, 43
revelation (human aspect of) 14, 77, 140–1
reversal schema 12–13, **31–4**, 39–40, 41–2, **53–61**, 65, 69–70, 105, 107, 121, 124, **126–9**, 134–5, 138–42
ritual
  as bodily experience/performance 4, 10, 13, 36, 55, 59, 89–90, 95–8, 123, 126n. 54
  as boundary-crossing (*see also* baptism) 47–8, 91, 92–8, 105–6
  and conceptual blending/metaphor 89–92, 94n. 108, 97, 123
  and cultural context 91–2, 95
  as generative of ideas 11, 14, 36, 107–9, 129

seed-sowing metaphor 12, 15, 32–3, 42, 52, **53–62**, 65n. 91, 69–70, 105, 107
Seneca 75, 87–8
Sheol 20, 28–9
soul
  ascent 49–52, 56, 75, 84
  and body 47–9, 55, 73–6, 116
  descent 44, 49
  immortal soul 8, 12, 19, 27–9, 42, 50
  and mind 87–8
spirit
  ecstatic experience (*see also* spirit possession) 1–2, 7–9, 13, 72, **77–85**, 100, 103–4, 106

  and esoteric speech 77, 80–1, 85–6, 98
  indwelling Spirit 8–9, 79, 81, 85, 103–5, 116, 127, 130–1, 134
  as material 50, 131–2
  reception of the Spirit 8, 72, 79, 81, 85, 86–7, 93, 98–105, 110–12, 132
  and sexual intercourse 86, 104, 141
  as water 93, 98–100, 112n. 14
spirit possession 8, 13, 72, 76–80, 85–7, 97n. 121, 137
Stoicism 12, 50–51, 75
suffering 85, 88, 108–17, 122

transformation
  and angels 26–7, 30
  eschatological transformation 13, 41, 105–6, 107, 109, 121–2, 135
  experienced transformation 104–9, 116–18, 120–7, 130, 135
  and heavenly ascent 24, 26–7, 29–31, 85, 107
  at resurrection (*see also* timing of transformation) **15–17**, 27–31, 33–4, 40, **62–6**, 138, 142
  substantive transformation 12, 16, 23, 41, 49, 51
  two aspects of transformation in Paul 106–9, 122–4, 136
treasure in clay jars metaphor 83n. 65, 109–15, 117–18, 133, 135

www.ingramcontent.com/pod-product-compliance
Lightning Source LLC
Chambersburg PA
CBHW061839300426
44115CB00013B/2449